THE

MILLIONAIRE

REAL ESTATE LANDLORDS

THE
MILLIONAIRE
REAL ESTATE LANDLORDS

HOW ORDINARY PEOPLE ARE BECOMING EXTRAORDINARY REAL ESTATE INVESTORS & LANDLORDS

How to Manage Single-Family Homes, Duplexes, Triplexes, Quads and Larger Multi-Family Properties for MAXIMUM PROFITS!

M. MITCH FREELAND & JOHN FREELAND

LAS VEGAS BOOK COMPANY
Las Vegas, Nevada

SPECIAL SALES

Books published by Go-Getter Express and Las Vegas Book Company are available at special quantity discounts worldwide to be used for sales training or for use in corporate promotional programs. Quantity discounts are available to corporations, educational institutions and charitable organizations. Personalized front or back covers with corporate imprints can be produced in large numbers.

For information contact:
Email: MMitchFreeland@gmail.com
Website: www.MitchFreeland.com

1. Real Estate   2. Buying and Selling Homes 3. Landlording
4. Title: The Millionaire Real Estate Landlords 5. Property Management

First Paperback Edition: October 2, 2018

The Millionaire Real Estate Landllords

ISBN: 978-17241-9839-6

ABOUT THE AUTHORS

M. MITCH FREELAND

Mitch Freeland has bought and sold, fixed and flipped hundreds of single-family and multi-family properties and has managed over 100 units as a landlord. He had been called "a modern-day polymath" be-

cause of the diversity of subjects that appeal to him and for the subjects he writes about. He is a person of faith, a business person, and a writer. He writes both fiction and nonfiction.

Mitch studied Anthropology at UCLA and started writing at forty-four. Since then, he has authored over sixty books. Everything he writes about, he has experienced.

On the fiction side, he has produced six short story collections and a few novels.

He has been an active investor in numerous young companies and start-ups dealing in all classes of investments for over twenty-five years. He was President and founder of an online bookstore, and current President and founder of a publishing company (Las Vegas Book Company). He was also Managing Director of a private Investment Banking company, and a hands-on operator in his real estate investing and property management companies.

Regarding his nonfiction writing, his goal is to create intuitive, pertinent content that can be incorporated into your personal and work life to help you succeed faster and with less stress. His publishing company, Las Vegas Book Company, publishes over one hundred titles including books and courses on casino gaming, real estate investing, online bookselling and collecting, foreign language study books, business developent, personal achievement,family games and specialized fiction.

He has a new blog at www.MitchFreeland.com that focuses on strategies for personal transformation. He blogs on real estate investing, online bookselling and collecting, casino gaming, poker, and Christianity.

JOHN FREELAND

John Freeland has been a real estate investor for over 15 years and with his brother Mitch has bought and sold, fixed and flipped, and managed hundreds of single family and multifamily properties. Prior to his real estate career he was involved in Investment Banking, Mergers and Acquisitions and stock brokerage for over 14 years. He is currently authoring and co-authoring several books on real estate and other nonfiction with his brother Mitch.

Over the past 29 years he has served in leadership roles as Managing Director, Chairman of the Board, Chief Executive Officer and President of Investment Banking Firms, a Securities Brokerage Firm, a Private Equity Firm, a Real Estate Brokerage Firm, a Real Estate Investment Firm, Property Management Firm, Assisted Living Facilities and other companies and entrepreneurial ventures in various industries including furniture manufacturing and retail, sports manufacturing, circuit board technologies, semiconductor technologies, internet technologies, consumer internet, internet content publishing, online bookstore and recycling, and performance marketing and most recently; Author and Speaker.

He received a BA Degree in 1987 from the University of California Los Angeles in Political Science/International Relations/Business Administration and has obtained and received numerous certificates and awards relating to business, leadership and community involvement

Real Estate Books by
M. MITCH FREELAND and JOHN FREELAND

The Millionaire Real Estate Flippers

The Millionaire Real Estate Landlords

How to Make Real Estate More Valuable

How to Rent your House, Duplex, Triplex & Other Multi-Family Property Fast!

The Real Estate Hustle

5 Day Flip: How to Get Offers Accepted Fast on Fixer-Uppers

NEW RELEASES FOR 2019

The Airbnb Hustle: How Ordinary People and Enterprising Landlords are Cashing-in and How you can Too!

The Cash Flow Book: The 10 Most Important Calculations for Smart Real Estate Investors

Cash Flow & Co.: A Super System for Real Estate Investors
Discover 64 Proven Ways That Show you How to Substantially Improve Cash Flow from Your Rental Properties

How to Maximize Profits with Coin-Operated Laundry & Vending Machines for Rental Property

57 of the Best Real Estate Investors Forms & Agreements

51 of the Best Landlording Forms & Real Estate Agreements

CONTENTS

CHAPTER 2: Extra Expenses: Property Taxes, Insurance, and More—67

CHAPTER 3: Your Cash Flow—75

CHAPTER 7: Real Estate Clubs and Associations, Benefits of Membership and Why Should you Join—125

CHAPTER 8: Staying the Course—133

CHAPTER 9: Winning Principles of a Real Estate Investor—141

Action Highlights for Winning Principles of a Real Estate Investor—146

APPENDIXES—147

APPENDIX I: Applications, Agreements, Forms, Letters and Advertisements—148

APPENDIX II: Real Estate Investment and Landlording Terms—213

Introduction

The proactive real estate investor and the proactive landlord is highly engaged—that is, he is active in all facets of the investment process. Because he is highly engaged, the proactive investor transforms a good investment into a great investment. He does this by nurturing the investment along until such time that the investment is sold. By acting and not reacting, an investor can take control of his situations and take full responsibility for the outcome of every stage of the investment process: from utilizing contractors and sub-contractors, to fighting for lower property taxes, and managing tenants for maximum cash flow. The proactive, highly engaged, real estate investor produces higher than average income. He is not a passive investor.

In his 1946 book, *Man's Search for Meaning*, Viktor Frankl first coined the term "Proactive" to explain how a person is responsible for oneself and that outside circumstances are not the cause of a particular situation—and that others are also not the cause to one's successes, failures, crises or the unhappiness in one's life—everyone has the freedom of choice, even in dire situations. You must have faith in your abilities and faith that your future will be better and brighter all the days to follow.

> "Between stimulus and response, there is a space. In that space
> is our power to choose our response. In our response
> lies our growth and our freedom."
> —Victor Frankl

Frankl, a psychiatrist, first designed his concept of proactivity as a prisoner in German concentration camps during the Second World War. His parents and wife died in the camps. Being proactive was a way of thinking—a way of surviving—and a way of being free. Although, still behind fences and physically controlled by guards, his captors could not control his thoughts—those were his to control. The prisoners whose thoughts were optimistic for better days, while being held captive, survived better from the day-to-day horrors of camp life, and did not suffer as much; mentally they were in control. The ones that gave up had a tendency to suffer more and died. The power is in controlling your thoughts.

Frankl eventually wrote over 30 books on psychology and psychoanalysis and his ideas on proactivity were even discussed in Stephen R. Covey's best seller, *The 7 Habits of Highly Effective People*. Covey dedicated "Habit 1" to being "Proactive."

There is a way of thinking, a way of doing things better, and doing things the proactive way. Proactive investors are in control.

It is said, that real estate is the best investment in the world. We *disagree* with this statement, and I'm sure anyone who has lost money in real estate would disagree with the statement as well. An investment in any real estate is only as good as the investor behind it. It takes time and a lot of hard work to locate, analyze, buy, manage, and sell real estate. The best investors, as we have mentioned many times in other books, make money in good times and in bad times. A professional investor can also make money in any market, in any city, and in any area—this is a proven fact. There is a systematic approach to success in real estate investing—a process.

A professional real estate investor doesn't wait for property to perform; he buys it *correctly* in the beginning and manages it proactively to perform in ways beyond average appreciation and the inflation rate.

As in any investment or business, real estate investing can produce outstanding returns for the investor, especially when the investor begins to think creatively, imaginatively and is able to communicate effectively with others. Working in harmony with others is also necessary for success.

Having an optimistic outlook and positive expectations for the future and enforcing a proactive management style is a prerequisite to your overall success. When challenging situations arise, the proactive investor understands that nothing is as bad as it seems, and there is a solution within reach. Taking time to think, and to think with full concentration, is the right beginning to every critical decision, and the proactive investor understands this activity all too well. A clear thought will more often than not, produce a clear decision.

Why this Book?

There are thousands of landlords out there making millions of dollars a year renting property. Landlording has been around for thousands of years. How would you feel about receiving a couple of checks in the mail, on the first of every month for $2,500, and the work you did to receive it took two hours a month out of your time? Sounds pretty good doesn't it?

Landlording can be fun and extremely profitable with little overall labor expended when executed correctly. This book is about executing the activity of landlording correctly. Becoming a landlord is not difficult and the activity of landlording should not be something you cringe at. Landlording is easy when you know how to manage people (your tenants). When you have great tenants there is little for you to manage. The idea for this book is based largely on getting good, solid, respectful tenants. The rest is just managing the little problems that pop-up occasionally as in all business related activity.

Why We Are Uniquely Qualified to Write this Book?

We have managed over 100 units at a time, ranging from single-family homes, small multi-family properties (duplexes, triplexes, quads, eight unit buildings), and larger multi-family apartments and assisted living facilities. We have always been hands-on landlords since starting fifteen years ago. We believe good landlording has two characteristics: (1) clear communication with tenants; and (2) serving your customer (tenants) with integrity and fairness. Not all tenants will be good tenants—you make the choice. Good landlording is specializing in good customer relations—it's all about managing people.

Now that we've gotten all this out of the way, it is now our hope that you have a general idea of the workings of a proactive investor/landlord and what will be expected of you to succeed.

In fact, this book is a companion to our first book, *The Millionaire Real Estate Flippers.* Both The *Million-*

aire Real Estate Flippers and *The Millionaire Real Estate Landlords* can be used together; they complement one another and include enough information to launch you on your way to successful real estate investing (flipping) and landlording. Both books also cover a hands-on approach to investing by *forcing appreciation* and thinking and acting proactively about managing people (tenants), and managing construction crews for rehabs and renovations.

As always, GOD BLESS AND GOOD LUCK TO GREAT INVESTING AND LANDLORDING!

M. Mitch Freeland
John Freeland
Las Vegas, Nevada

1

Becoming a Landlord
&
Property Manager

*The most important single ingredient in the formula of success is knowing how
to get along with people.*
—Theodore Roosevelt

"Is your name really Mr. Landlord?" said the young boy.

"It is now," replied the man. "Is your Mother or Father home?"

"You're not Mr. Landlord," cried out a taller boy. "You're Mr. Rentman; that's what my mamma calls you."

The man looked squarely at the boys and said, "Yes, I'm Mr. Landlord and I'm Mr. Rentman and people call me other names too."

Becoming a landlord is one of the oldest and most profitable professions in the world. Most landlords on average are millionaires and many multi-millionaires. There are large multi-national corporations who are landlords and there are single mothers who own one rental house or rents a room or a basement in her house—she is a landlord too!

To fully be exposed to all the information you should know about landlording and property management would take about one thousand pages, but that would present another book—a book which might be produced in a couple of years—but for now, the following pages of this chapter will cover all you will need to know about getting tenants and managing them.

In this chapter we will expose you to the wonderful world of landlording and property management. Becoming a proactive landlord and property manager is all about dealing with people. That is rule number one; if you can not deal with people, then you will not be an effective landlord—no matter how efficient you are.

Becoming an effective landlord is not complicated. As long as you are reasonably logical and are able to deal proactively with tenants and the processes involved, you will be okay—no, you will *do better* than okay, you'll be in the top 10 percent of all professional real estate investors.

Becoming a landlord can be part of your long-term objective; landlords are always in demand. Here are a few reasons why:

- Renters consume 33% of all U.S. households
- 80% of households aged 25 and under are renters
- 66% of households aged between 25 and 29 are renters
- The number of Hispanic renters will double by 2020

There is no science to landlording; it is a business of managing people: tenants, prospective tenants, handymen and contractors are among the people you'll be managing. The only science to landlording is to try to make it as easy and stress-free as possible for yourself and at the same time, collect as much rental income, and ancillary income as possible. This, of course, works well when you maintain operating expenses at a mere minimum while collecting from satisfied tenants the higher rents. Producing high cash flow is why you are in the business of landlording. Long-term appreciation is the second reason you are in this business or should want to be in this business. The value of your rental property is based on the income it produces—the greater the income, the more valuable the property.

Duties of a Highly Engaged Landlord

What are the duties of a highly engaged landlord? Here is the rundown:

Office (Home) Duties

- Run comparable rent rate statistics in your target area weekly
- Study occupancy rates in area (increasing or declining)
- Print property fact sheets and information for rental package for new tenants
- Print applications, leases, supplemental information for future tenants
- Constantly study rent rolls for increasing income opportunities
- Investigate ancillary income opportunities to boost cash flow
- Pay all bills for property including taxes, license fees, etc.
- Review and pay contractor (plumbing, electrical, etc.) invoices for repairs and maintenance
- Deposit tenant checks in bank
- Record rents collected
- Record each unit and tenant complaints
- Send out letters to tenants who are in breach of their lease and other correspondence
- Phone tenants when letters are not answered and problems persist
- Inform tenants of late rent and late rent charges
- Prepare and issue in person to delinquent tenant "Pay or Quit" notice
- Prepare and file evictions

Advertising and Marketing Vacant Units

- Place "For Rent" signs in front of property
- Place ads in papers and online (Craig's Lists, etc.)
- Print flyers

- Post ads on bulletin boards at laundries, schools, and markets

Vacant Unit(s)

- Take calls on vacancies
- Interview prospective tenant(s) over the phone
- Show prospective tenants vacancies
- Select new tenants
- Explain property advantages
- Accept funds for rent and deposits
- Review *Rental Package* (this is the *High Engagement Rental Package*) with new tenant(s) (The Rental Package is introduced later in the chapter)

With Current Tenants

- Collect rents (when not sent in by tenants)
- Collect late rents and late fees
- Issue receipts for cash payments
- Inform tenants of changes in policies and procedures
- Inform tenants (in writing) any city or state regulations that could affect their lodging

Common Maintenance

Much of the maintenance that hands-on landlords have is cleaning units and the surrounding rental property and common areas if it is a multi-family property. Other duties require minor repairs and maintenance due to wear and tear.

- Cleaning vacant units after tenant moves out: bathrooms (toilets, sinks, tubs, floors, etc.); kitchen (insid and outside stove, refrigerator, microwave, sinks, floors, ceiling fans, etc.); walls, floors, doors, windows, blinds, drapes, carpets.
- Paint both interior and exterior
- Clean the grounds free of litter
- Clean/replace filters in A/C units
- Vacuum rugs
- Sweep and clean common area hallways, entryways and walkways
- Clean oil marks on driveways and in garages
- Mow lawns and keep hedges trimmed
- Remove snow from parking areas, driveways, walkways and sidewalks

Making Repairs or Replacing Items

- Change out or replace light bulbs in units and common areas
- Repair and/or replace damaged or inoperable applicances (stove, cooktop, refrigerator, A/C units, dishwasher, microwave, dishwasher, etc.)
- Replacing stain ridden carpets
- Water heater
- Broken and cracked windows

- Replace stove knobs
- Leaking faucets
- Replace broken ceiling fans
- Mini-blinds
- Damaged doors
- Entry door locks and keys
- Light switches, cracked receptacles and covers
- Toilet tanks, seats and handles
- Garbage disposal
- Plumbing clogs

When House or Apartment Unit(s) is Vacant

- Inspection checklist after tenant has moved
- Billing former tenant for damages (holding security deposit)
- Inspection checklist prior to new tenant moving in: Appliances and A/C units cleaned and in good operating condition, walls electrical fixtures, plumbing fixtures, blinds, windows, carpets and floors, handles, knobs, and other items.
- Paint interior

When you have finally made the repairs to the property and it is ready to be rented, there are a few things you ought to pay close attention to—they include:

1) Receiving the highest possible rents
2) Handling property maintenance and repairs quickly
3) Getting and retaining good tenants
4) Knowing how to deal with bad tenants
5) Collecting rents without hassle
6) Collecting more than 100 percent rent—through anncilary means
7) Obtaining a rental license
8) Creating your home office

How to Get the Greatest Possible Rent for Your Rental

Your rental property is a business, do not forget this. Passive investors have a tough time remembering this fact. Don't be a passive investor. You should strive to maintain your rents at the greatest possible price that keeps the property rented and the tenants content. When your rental property is a single-family home, check prices of homes for rent rates online and in your neighborhood papers. When you have rental units (duplex, triplex or other multi-family property), compare your property (size, amenities, location) with others in your area, then decide on a fair rental price. Check online at Rent.com and Realtor.com for comps. Notice the differences in the property and prices other landlords are asking. Your property should be the most attractive one available for rent in your area (this means it is fresh, groomed and clean). You should first ask a little higher price for your rent; $20 or $60 more than what the going rate is in your area. When showing your property to prospective tenants, explain all the extra amenities your property has:

- New refrigerator and stove, microwave and dishwasher included

- New tile or carpet

- New air conditioner

- New paint in every room

- Updated kitchens and bathrooms

- Schools, parks and shopping are all near by

- A quiet, neighborly street

Any unique or special characteristics about the house or neighborhood should be brought up and explained in detail to the prospective tenant. Show the prospective tenant that you are proud of the property and the neighborhood as if the property was a person. You could say: The apartment has 2 bedrooms and 2 baths and is in excellent condition and ready for a family like yours." If the bedrooms are large, say the bedrooms are spacious. If the bedrooms are small, say the bedrooms are cozy and comfortable. Or, "The house has 3 bedrooms and 2 baths and is in excellent condition and ready for a family like yours." You could also as the prospective tenant direct questions: "Do you feel you can be comfortable here?" Or "The school for the kids is nearby, there is low traffic on the street, so it is quite and safe and the supermarket is only two blocks away...Does this work well for you and your family?" When the tenant says "Yes," you simply state: "I have the application here—why don't we get started?"

Before you acquire any property as an investment, you should know what the rental rates are in your target area. Compare the units with others in the area and determine whether the units are offered at fair rental rate, higher than comparable rates, or lower than the comparable rates. If lower, immediately notify each of the tenants with a rent increase letter. If you have also owned property for a while without paying much attention to your rental rates, it's probably time for a rent increase. In reality, the average inflation rate over the last one hundred years has been around 3.5 percent annually. By raising rents about 3 percent to 4 percent per year, it's safe to say most of your tenants will stay with you. Remember, people, in general, do not like to move.

When rents are way below average for your area, you may adjust rents much higher than the 3 percent or 4 percent. Sometimes you need to raise the rent 10 percent, 20 percent, or even 25 percent higher if the rental house was managed poorly. Of course, if tenants have current leases at the lower rates you would have to wait until the leases expire. But more often than not, poorly managed rentals typically have tenants on a month-to-month lease or the previous owner neglected to update the lease when the old one expired.

When You Become the New Landlord

When you take possession of your new property you should already have an idea of what you will rent the house or unit(s) for. Compare the units with others in the area (go to www.Rent.com or www.Realty.com to compare your rents), and determine whether the units are at fair rental rate, higher than comparable rates, or lower than the comparable rates. If rents are low, immediately notify each of the tenants with a rent increase letter. If you have also owned property for a while without paying much attention to your rental rates, it's probably time for a rent increase.

When rents are way below average for your area, you may adjust your rents much higher than the 3 percent or

4 percent as we mentioned earlier. Also, you may have tenants on a month-to-month lease. It is easier to raise the rents when tentants are month-to-month, but you may have to wait if the tenant is on an annual lease. Figure 1.1 and Figure 1.3 are sample rent increase letters you can use. And since many of our tenants have been Hispanic, we have also included the Spanish version of these letters in Figure 1.2 and 1.4.

Figure 1.1: **Sample Increase Rent Letter #1**

NOTICE OF RENT INCREASE

_____, 20___

Mr. Mary Smith
123 Main St. #3
Anytown, CA 30000

Dear Ms Smith:

Due to the increased costs for maintenance, taxes, repairs and, of course, inflation, the time has come where we must raise rents.

Effective _____, 20__, the new rent will be **$925 per month**. Please find enclosed a new lease. Please execute and return the new lease to our office. You are also required to increase your security deposit to **$925** and your last month's rent, which in total is **$60**.

If you wish not to renew the lease, you must give us written notice on or before _____, 20__ in order to get your security deposit returned. If you should have any questions, please call our office at 555-555-5555 or mail a note stating your intentions.

Thank you for your cooperation and understanding and for being one of our most valued tenants.

Very truly yours,
Worth Property Management

Mitch Freeland
Property Manager

Enclosure: Lease

Figure 1.2: **Sample Increase Rent Letter #1 Spanish**

AVISO DE AUMENTO DE ALQUILER

_____, 20__

Sr. Jose Rivera
123 Main St., #3
Anytown, CA 90777

Estimado Sr. Rivera:

Debido a los crecientes costos de mantenimiento, impuestos, reparaciones, y por supuesto la inflacion, ha llegado el tiempo de aumentar el costo de alquiler.

A partir de _____, 20___, el Nuevo costo de alquiler sera **$925 por mes**. Le incluimos un Nuevo contrato de arrendamiento. Por favor firme y devuelva este contrato a nuestra officinal. Tambien se require aumentar su deposito de seguridad a $925 y el pago de alquiler del ultimo mes.

Si usted no desea renovar el contrato de arrendamiento, debe darnos un aviso por escrito en o antes de _____, 20___ para que su deposito sea devuelto. Si tiene alguna pregunta, llame por favor a nuestra officinal al 555-555-5555 o envie una nota con dejandonos saber sus intenciones.

Gracias por su cooperation y compression y por ser uno de nuestros mas valorados arrendatarios.

Sinceramente suyo,
Worth Property Management

Big John
Presidente

Recintos: Nuevo contracto de arrendamiento

Figure 1.3 Sample Increase Rent Letter #2. When you have just purchased a rental property and the tenant has no lease, and the tenant is on a month-to-month or the lease will expire within two months you can use this form letter. (Note: you do not want tenants on a month-to-month lease. In many states, if the lease is under seven months you may be liable for sales taxes because your property will be classified as short-term lodging like a motel or hotel.)

Figure 1.3: **Sample Increase Rent Letter #2**

NOTICE OF RENT INCREASE

_____, 20____

Ms. Maria Villa
123 Spruce, #2
Anytown, Fl 33400

Dear Ms. Villa:

As you may now know, the building where you live is now managed by _Worth Properties_. We have been instructed by the owner of the property that there will be many repairs completed in the coming months. Of course, with higher taxes, maintenance and inflation, costs of maintaining the property where you live has increased substantially. Therefore, we are forced to increase the rents to match the going market rate.

Effective on _____, 20___, the new rent will be **$925 per month**. Please find enclosed your new lease. Please initial each page where highlighted and sign the last page. You are also required to increase your security deposit to **$925**.

If you wish not to renew a lease, you must give us written notice on or before _____, 20___ in order to get your security deposit returned. If you should have any questions, please call our office at 555-555-5555 or mail us a note stating your intentions.

Thank you for your cooperation and understanding and for being one of our most valued tenants.

Very truly yours,
Worth Property Management

Big John
Property Manager

Enclosure: Lease

Figure 1.4:

Sample Rent Increase Letter, Spanish Version #2

AVISO DE AUMENTO DE ALQUILER

_____, 20___

Srta. Maria Villa
123 Spruce Street, #2
Anytown, FL 33400

Estimada Srta. Villa:

Como usted debe saber el edificio donde ahora vive es manejado por Worth Properties. El dueno de la propiedad ha determinado que muchas reparaciones seran terminates en los proximos meses. Por supuesto con el incremento de impuestos, mantenimiento, inflacion, los costos para mantener la propiedad han subido substancialmente. Por lo tanto hemos sido forzados a aumentar el costo de alquiler para emparejar la tarifa del Mercado.

A partir de _____, 20__, el Nuevo costo de alquiler sera de **$925 por mes**. Le incluimos un Nuevo contrato de arrendamiento. Por favor ponga sus iniciales en todas las paginas y firme la ultima pagina. Tambien se requiere incrementar su deposito de seguridad a **$925**.

Si no desea renovar el contracto de arrendamiento, debe darnos un aviso por escrito en o antes de _____, 20___ para que su deposito de seguridad sea devuelto. Si tiene alguna pregunta llamenos a la officinal al 555-555-5555 o mandenos una nota por correo.

Gracias por su cooperation y compression y por ser uno de nuestros mas valorados arrndatarios.

Sinceramente suyo,
Worth Property Management

Big John
Presidente

Recintos: Nuevo contrato de arrendamiento

Purchasing Tenants

We use the term "Purchasing Tenants" because when you have purchased rental property with existing tenants you have in essence purchased them too. An example of this can be when you decide to purchase a fourplex that is fully occupied with tenants in good standing, meaning their rents are paid up and there is no money owed.

Before you close on the property and even before you make an offer, you should talk to the tenants. Tell them you might be the new property manager and ask about any grievances they have with the current owner or problems with their unit. Most times the current owner with say "Do not disturb the tenants." Pay little attention to this. If you are interested in the property, then by all means talk to as many tenants as you can. They are the ones that will be paying your monthly bills. You need to know about them firsthand. Believe it or not, some landlords are not exactly upfront regarding their current tenant's behaviors. Ask tenants about their security deposits, last month's rent, and the last time they had a rent increase or decrease. Again, some landlords won't be exactly honest about the deposits they have received from tenants. You want to get all of this out into the open before you close on the property. Prior to closing we recommend you get an estoppel letter or certificate for each tenant.

What is an Estoppel Certificate?

By definition, an estoppel certificate is a "signed statement by a party certifying for another's benefit that certain facts are correct, as that a lease exists, that there are no defaults, and that rent is paid to a certain date. A party's delivery of this statement stops that party from later claiming a different state of facts." (Black's Law Dictionary, 572 (7th Ed., 1999).

In other words, a **tenant estoppel** is a certified statement by a tenant that verifies the terms and conditions and current status of their lease. The tenant estoppel provides proof of cash flow, which as an investor you are concerned with.

A typical tenant estoppel certificate will have the common points:

- The start date of the lease.
- The date rent has been paid.
- That there are no defaults by either the landlord or the tenant.
- If there are defaults by either party, then a specification of these defaults will be required.
- Verification that the lease is unmodified and in full force and effect.
- If the lease has been modified, then the estoppel certificate will include a statement verifying what modifications have been made.

The tenant estoppel certificate is a common item that comes up during the due diligence phase of an acquisition. As the purchaser you should have examined the estoppel certificates prior to closing.

Before you close on the property, you want to know as much as possible about your tenants, current problems and possibly potential problems that might hit you immediately when you take over.

All the problems or potential problems will help with your negotiation in getting the price of the property lower. Now you can bring to light this new information and work the asking price down. The more you know about the property, the tenant base, and the cash flow, the better situation you have to not only lowering the purchase price but this will also give you an opportunity to start possible evictions immediately, if necessary, with problem tenants.

Who to Contact

On day one as the new landlord you will contact:

- Utilities. Change into your name (business name preferred) any communal services, which could include, water, gas, electric, garbage and sewage.
- File a rental permit with the city
- Business license
- Setting up banking if not already completed

Many of the "to do" things will be expanded later in this chapter.

Updating Tenant Files

With rental houses or small multi-family properties you will want to meet each tenant and update your leases and present your own rental package. The *High Engagement Rental Package* that is presented later in the chapter is a full package with documents that explain the tenant's obligations. The package sets the tone of your management style. The *Package* also represents your professionalism as a serious landlord—who cares deeply about the property and the people who live there.

The best time to reach tenants in on a Saturday. Plan to inspect each unit for maintenance issues and at the same time present the package with a thorough explanation. If leases are to expire soon, fill out new leases (increase rents if under market). Have all tenants files completed with all additional or missing information added. Much of the forms can be fill out on site.

One thing to lookout for is that as the new landlord, or property manager, the tenants will want to share with you all the little problems they have with the unit. Many of the problems will be minuscule. If the problems are easy to fix—fix them immediately. This could be as simple as a cover for an outlet or a running toilet (this you want to fix immediately—because you are usually paying for the water). A running toilet can be fixed with adjusting the apparatus in the toilet tank or replacing the rubber stopper—a simple fix. Parts are available at any hardware store.

You also want to test all of your keys to the units and ensure that they are working properly . Every time you get a new tenant you want to replace the door locks. If you have lots of units or houses you can exchange the locks between the units to save money. But, don't be carless about this. If you have a duplex, by no means exchange these locks—get new locks.

What Do You Do With an Onsite Manager?

We were in the process of purchasing a 20 unit building which had an onsite manager living in one of the units rent free for seven years. For seven years that's $37,800 the landlord could have pocketed. What a waste. The unit could have been rented for $450 a month, an automatic increase of 5.3 percent to the bottom line. What do you do with the onsite manager? Get rid of him or have him start paying full rent. Why would you throw away $450 a month? You do not need an onsite manager for a twenty unit building.

If you live far from your building and do not plan to make regular visits, you can ask one of the tenants if he or she would like to take a few of the duties of a manager without managing for a little bit off the rent. Break their duties down hourly. Most of what they do it clean-up. Clean parking area once per week. Make sure there are no disturbing elements at the property, etc. If you have decent tenants who are quiet, respectful, and pay on time, you will not need a full-time onsite manager. From our experiences, there will be one or two tenants who will be willing to notify you of any problems or potential problems at your property. Do not be a stranger to your tenants. Remember this is proactive landlording—highly engaged property management. To get high returns, you have to pay attention to the people who pay you—your tenants pay you and they will pay more and be more conscienceous about their rental when they know you care.

What about Professional Property Management Companies?

This book is not about hiring out, but rather, doing it yourself and saving a lot of money. As you grow, you may not have the time to oversee all of your properties. Your priorities may change and you might what to spend your free time with your family, rather with your tenants. When your priorities change and your time becomes more valuable, it might be the right time to hire a professional property management company. But before you do this, starting out, you should spend at least a year being a hands-on landlord. How else will you be able to tell if you are getting a raw deal from the property manager when he bills you for replacing light bulbs. You must be very careful with expenditures when dealing with an outside manager. The typical property manager will charge 8-10% of collected monthly rents. They will also have an itemized list of duties and their charges.

Property Maintenance and Repairs for Single-Family Rentals

Unlike apartments or other multi-family properties, when you rent a house, the tenant is responsible for the general maintenance of that house, including the lawn and landscaping—this should be a condition in the lease. Other maintenance and repairs such as leaking faucets, leaking roof, and electrical shortages would be your responsibility unless it is specifically noted in the lease that those repairs are the obligation of the tenant. Do not do any repairs until you get a call or a written letter. Once you receive a letter regarding maintenance, investigate the problem within 24 hours. If it is a problem the tenant has caused, explain it, fix it, and bill them, or ask for the money upfront to repair the problem. Charge for your time and anyone else you called to handle the situation (plumbers, electricians and so on). Don't forget to bill for any materials you paid for.

What do you charge for your time? Try $50 per hour. This is a reasonable price for your time. Tenants have to be accountable for their negligence; by remedying the situation quickly and billing the tenant quickly, you show your professionalism and hopefully the tenant will get the message—the message, you are serious and the tenant must take responsibility.

Maintenance and Repairs for Multi-Family Properties

With multi-family properties you will have to take charge of the exterior and interior maintenance issues; this also means maintaining the common areas, parking lots, and lawns and gardening. A list of "duties" of a highly engaged landlord was noted earlier. A lot depends on your particular property. We have had garden apartments which needed weekly attention and other multi-family properties that did not have lawns or gardens or parking areas. Here is how to handle the recurring maintenance issues:

- *Gardening and lawn care.* You could take care of this yourself or hire a gardener. It depends on how much there is and how big your lawn is. Always consider the time involved with recurring maintenance tasks. If you can be doing something that makes you more money—then hire it out. If you enjoy gardening the lawn maintenance, then do it.

- *Parking area.* Picking up trash in the parking area can be taken care of once or twice a week.

- *Interior common areas.* The common areas are halls, grilling area, pool areas or green areas. Once a week when you visit your property you could make your tour of the property. This would include changing out light bulbs (energy efficient florescent) in all common areas and fire extinguishers. Regarding swimming pools, you could hire a pool cleaner or do it yourself. It is not difficult work, and you could save yourself a lot of money. If you have questions about pool cleaning, visit a pool supply store or research online.

- *Laundry area.* If you have a laundry make sure you have posted signs about clean-up and a trash can or two in the room or area. You could clean this area once per week. If you have a laundry or want to make more money with your rental properties, I suggest you get the book ***How to Maximize Profits with Coin-Operated Laundry & Vending Machines for Rental Property*** (Release date in 2019) (M. Mitch Freeland, Las Vegas Book Company). If operated correctly, you could substantially improve your cash flow from your rental units with a simple coin-opt washer and dryer and other vending machines. This book will give you many ideas, tips and strategies on how to maximize cash flow with minimal investment. Laundry machines are a passive income investment and if you have multi-family property, it would be wise to investigate all possible ideas to increase cash flow with minimal effort.

- *Interior units.* The most common problems you will face will be problems with applicances and plumbing. Calling a refrigerator repairman is expensive, so is buying a new refrigerator. So here you will have to assess the problem quickly. Your best bet can be to form a good relationship with a used appliance dealer who makes timely deliveries and offers credit for your broken down frig and halls it away.

  Plumbing problems are typically due to clogged toilets or kitchen sinks. This is usually caused by the tenant and can be resolved by the tenant by either using a plunger or pouring acid (all home improvement stores carry Cloric acid or other useful drain decloggers) down the drain or toilet. The tenant should take care of this themselves. Any work you do or cost of a plumber will have to be billed to the tenant—state this upfront to the tenant. With older properties that still use fuses for electricity, you will need to have a supply of the correct fuse when the lights go out.

- *Exterior.* Painting the exterior is an infrequent maintenance issue unless you run into harsh weather. In this case you might have chipping of older stucco buildings that will now need touchup. You do not want to repaint the entire house or building unless it absolutely needs it. Make touch-ups here and there. Windows are another issue. Broken windows caused by tenants will have to be replaced. You can do this yourself fairly quickly. And naturally, you will present the tenant with a bill. You could also call a handyman and have the handyman bill the tenant.

Getting and Retaining Good Tenants

A good tenant is really worth his or her weight in gold. That might seem like a common compliment, however, it is very true—ask any landlord. Better yet, ask any landlord who has had bad tenants. Here is a quick list to check and find good and qualified tenants:

1) A tenant should make 3 to 3.5 times the rent in monthly income. If the rent is $1,000 per month, the tenant should have a monthly income of $3,000 to $3,500. Income of $3,500 per month would certainly be better.

2) A tenant should have a good and long job history, and preferably with the same company. If a tenant has been with the same company for many years, it shows a pattern of responsibility and consistency.

3) The tenant is family orientated.

4) The tenant preferably has a checking account and credit cards, and a clean and newer model car.

5) A tenant should have reasonably good credit.

6) Good references, especially from past landlords.

Applications and Forms

All prospective tenants are required to fill-out a rental application. A rental application will have a fee of $25 or $50 upon submission, perhaps more. The fee you charge depends on what you are renting and for how much. Some large apartment complexes have an application fee upwards of $150. When you are dealing with very high-end properties, an application fee of $150 would certainly separate your class of tenants. We have found that a $50 application fee is good for apartments or houses were rent is $900 and above. We also charge $25 on top of that for each adult who will be living in the house or apartment. For properties in lower rent areas we have charged $25 to $35 for application fees and $10 for additional adults.

The application fee you charge should be non-refundable, whether the applicant qualifies for the unit or not. Running a credit check on each adult can run you under $10 per applicant. If you want to run a criminal check, it costs about $30. You can check online for the cheapest credit check service. Make sure all adults interested in the rental unit fill out and submit an application with the fee. All adults will also be required to sign on the lease, including the names of all children and pets (a pet agreement is in the back of the book, attached to the lease. There is also an alternative pet agreement, which is more detailed in the Appendix.

You must use good old common sense and your good judgment when evaluating prospective tenants. If they seem a little too slick, weird, or trashy, forget them. You want tenants for the long-term—5 years and up. This should be your mission. Don't be in a big hurry to rent out your unit. Taking a little more due diligence time is better than getting stuck with a bad tenant, that will end up costing you a lot in the long run.

SAMPLE RENTAL APPLICATION

Rental Application Form

PLEASE PRINT

Dr., Mr., Mrs., Ms, Mdm.: _____ _____ Date: _____
                                    First Middle Last

SECTION 1: Rental Property For Which You Are Applying

Property address: _____ Apartment number if Applicable: _____
Rent per month: _____ Security: _____
Names of others to occupy unit:

_____

each Applicant must fill out a separate Application From and provide all required info

Dates of Occupancy: From: _____ To: _____

How did you find us? (circle and/ or fill in as applicable)

⏱ Internet Search Engine(s) Used

_____

⏱ Real Estate Broker _____ Agency _____ Which listing did you use?_____

⏱ Print Advertisement: NY Times / Village Voice / Other (name)
_____

⏱ Did you see a sign on one of our buildings? Which building?
_____

⏱ Referral: Friend / Relative / Current or former tenant
_____

⏱ School Housing Office: NYU / Parson's / FIT / New School / Other

(name)_____

SECTION 2: Applicant Information

Date of Birth: _____/_____/_____ Social Security Number: _____-_____-_____
Driver's license number: _____ State: _____
Passport number (if not a U.S. Citizen): _____ Issuing Country: _____Type: _____
Present home address: _____ City_____
State_____ Zip_____
Home phone: ( ) _____ Work phone: ( ) _____ Cell phone: ( ) _____
Email _____
How long at present address? _____ Leaseholder: _____ (If different from applicant)
Landlord or Property Manager: _____ Phone: ( ) _____

Landlord address: _____ City_____
State_____ Zip_____
Applicant Previous Home address: _____ City_____
State_____ Zip_____
How long at previous address? _____ Leaseholder: _____ (If different from applicant)
Do you have any pets? _____ How many? _____ What kind?
_____ .

SECTION 3: Applicant Financial Information

Employer: _____ Address: _____

City_____ State_____ Zip_____
Position/title: _____ Supervisor: _____
Phone: _____ Annual income: _____ How long with present employer? _____
OR if currently enrolled:
Name of School: _____ Year: _____ Expected Graduation: _____
Program: _____
Address: _____ City_____ State_____ Zip_____
Bank Information:
Name of Bank: _____
Address: _____ City_____ State_____ Zip_____
Checking Account Number: _____ Savings Account Number: _____
Other Accounts:
Name of Institution: _____ Account Number _____ Type of Account _____
Name of Institution: _____ Account Number _____ Type of Account _____

SECTION 4: Guarantor Information
Guarantor Name: Dr., Mr., Mrs., Ms, Mdm.: _____
                                          First Middle Last
Social Security Number: _____ - _____ - _____ Date of Birth: _____ / _____ / _____
Month Day Year
Relationship to applicant: _____ Years known: _____
Address: _____ City_____ State_____
Zip_____
Home Phone: ( ) _____ Cell phone: ( ) _____ Work phone: ( ) _____
Fax: ( ) _____ Email: _____
Employer: _____ Address: _____

City_____ State_____ Zip_____
Position/title: _____ Supervisor: _____
Phone: _____ Annual income: _____ How long with present employer? _____ 3

SECTION 5: Personal References
(Applicant must provide at least 3 verifiable references, not relatives)
Ref. #1 Name: _____ Time known: _____
Address: _____ Phone: ( ) _____
Ref. #2 Name: _____ Time known: _____

Address: _____ Phone: ( ) _____
Ref. #3 Name: _____ Time known: _____
Address: _____ Phone: ( ) _____

I hereby certify to the best of my knowledge that the above information (from page 1 to page 3) is true and correct and I hereby authorize Worth Avenue Property Management, Inc. to obtain any credit, criminal check, job, and school, past rental history or references at its discretion.

Applicant's Signature_____ **Date**_____

STEPS FOR SUBMITTING APPLICATION:

Each Applicant for the Apartment must bring a completed application directly to our office along with the following:

1. Photo ID (Driver's license or passport or other U.S. Government issued ID)

2. FOR STUDENTS: Enrollment certification is required. FOR OTHERS: Employment letter and the 1st page of the latest 1040 tax return is required.

3. A Guarantor is required for EACH applicant (The 1st page of the latest 1040 tax return is required)

4. $50.00 processing application charge per applicant. (Note: All human occupants over 18 must be named on the lease.)

5. $500.00 Deposit to hold property during application process. Additional deposit may be required for rentals greater than $3,000 per month.

♦ If applicant is accepted, deposit is applied to balance of rent and security due at signing

♦ If applicant is rejected by Worth Avenue Properties any deposits will be refunded.

♦ Deposit is NOT refundable for ANY other reason.

♦ MOST applicants are notified within 24 hours.

♦ Application processing charges are non-refundable.

♦ All funds are payable in the form of **CASH, CERTIFIED CHECK**, or **MONEY ORDER**

♦ No **PERSONAL CHECKS** or **CREDIT CARDS** are accepted

One deposit is required per unit regardless of how many other prospective occupants are applying. If Applicant is accepted, this deposit is applied to balance. If Applicant is rejected for any reason, any deposit will be refunded immediately. All fees are due in cash, certified check, money order or cashier's check. No personal checks or credit cards are accepted. Most Applicants are notified within 48 hours. Application processing fees are non-refundable.

What to do with Bad Tenants

Get bad tenants out fast. A bad tenant is said to be worse than having a vacant unit; this is true. What constitutes a bad tenant?

1) A bad tenant is always late with rents or stops paying all together.

2) A bad tenant deals drugs, is a drunk, a slob, a pig and transforms your once clean rental into filth.

3) A bad tenant disturbs neighbors, is rude, vulgar, disrespectful to you and his or her neighbors.

4) A bad tenant is engaged in criminal activity on your property, typically drugs.

5) A bad tenant breaches the lease agreement over and over again.

6) A bad tenant will not vacate the premises when asked.

7) A bad tenant usually must be forcibly removed by the sheriff after an eviction has been processed.

8) A bad tenant wastes a lot of your time and money.

Screen your tenants very carefully. But remember, you are an equal—opportunity landlord. When you can, pay a bad tenant to leave, this is cheaper than filing an eviction, which can sometimes take a longer time and possibly time and money spent in court. This is a waste of your time and energy. Most times you will spend more money, and your chance of actually collecting any money from a deadbeat tenant is usually slim.

It is very important to meet all the adult and teen age tenants that will be occupying your property. Many times you will lease to a respectable tenant and one month later their boyfriend or girlfriend is living in the space with them. The boyfriend or girlfriend ends up to be bad news. You can evict them immediately since they are not on the lease. But, it may be to your advantage to pay them to leave, if they do not leave cordially when asked in person and in writting.

Some bad tenants are up-to-date on tenant rights and the lengthy process of being evicted. And sometimes a smart deadbeat can stay for months, depending on what your state laws dictate. Even deadbeats are protected by ridiculous tenant laws. Some savvy deadbeats know this, and they will use it against you. When the situation looks dire, forget your pride and pay them to leave. As a landlord you will have to think reasonably and logically when making this type of decision. Here is an example when we had to pay a tenant to leave.

Even make mistakes. We rented an efficiency apartment to an individual, who soon became one month past due on rent. A notice of "Pay or Quit" was posted. He did not pay and said he knew his rights and would wait for a lawsuit and then answer it (of course, he would go to free legal aid to help respond to it). The deadbeat figured he could stay for another month or two for free.

The deadbeat was a drug addict and we offered him $20 to leave. After negotiating for about five minutes we gave him $50 to pack up and be out of the unit and off the premises in an hour. We then had our handyman change the locks and even move some of the deadbeat's belongings out the door. This was the cheapest and easiest way to remedy the problem. Paying $50 to remove a problem tenant was well worth it. This guy just wanted enough money to go buy his crack for the day. Remember, landlording is about managing people—all types of people with all types of problems, addictions and afflictions.

Rental License

In most cities you will need a rental license to rent a house or any other rental unit. The license costs typically $15 to $20 or less. It is no big deal to a lot of landlords who rent rooms in their house or small guest houses for extra income. I do not feel that people who post listings on Airbnd, Home Away or other short-term rentals, have bothered with their city in obtaining a rental license. But, to prevent any municipal problems, obtain a rental license for your rentals as soon as possible. If code enforcement or the city housing inspector finds out that you do not have a license, you will usually have a few weeks to obtain a license without penalties. You will then have to file an application and send in a check. The inspector will then make an appointment to inspect your property to make sure your rental is compliant with the city's uniform housing code. This is one reason why many small timers will not file—they feel it is a hassle and well worth taking the risk to dodge the code enforcement officer. We believe you should always do the right thing, don't play games, get your rental license when the unit is ready to rent.

Many landlords who rent houses go years without ever filing an application. It all depends on your area. Recently, in one area, city inspectors were going house to house, knocking on doors, and asking whoever answered the door, whether they were the home owner or renting the house. Since property values have dropped in the past few year, during the Great Recession, collection of property taxes had naturally been lower—revenues down. Some city governments even raise occupancy license fees, building permit fees and other construction related impact fees to make up the revenue short fall. Of course, these new fees (taxes) will never be reduced during good economic times. Instead of eliminating unnecessary city jobs in deflating real estate markets, some liberal, even fearful city bureaucrats afraid of job cuts will go to great lengths to raise revenues by gauging landlords and other real estate investors who are believed to have more than their fair share of the upper one percent.

Rent Collection

Tenants should mail checks or money orders to you on the first day of the month, but no later than the fifth of the month. You should make it clear; a late fee will be imposed after the fifth day of the month. If you are in the neighborhood, you can stop in and ask for the rent, but when they are good tenants, don't bother popping in on them.

Depending on the lease term, we give every tenant enough self-addressed envelopes with monthly vouchers. Tenants use the vouchers and the envelope to mail in their monthly payments. This builds professionalism and makes it easier for the tenant each month (sample vouchers are in the Appendix). This is like paying a car payment or other recurring monthly payment.

When it is the seventh day of the month and you have not received the rent check, make a call and remind the tenant. If you do not receive the check by the ninth day of the month, post or hand deliver "Pay or Quit "notice for 3 or 5 days—the exact days would depend based on your particular state code. If you still do not get the payment, talk to the tenant and resolve some form of payment before you start the eviction process. It is better to try and get some money out of the tenant than nothing. If it goes to eviction, you probably won't get anything. Even when you are awarded a judgment, the chances of collecting money from an eviction, as mentioned earlier, is slim to none. You have better things to do with your time than hunt down deadbeats—forget it, and move on. There is more money to be made in finding good tenants than chasing down deadbeats. Proactive tenant management is creating cash—not chasing it down. Unless the deadbeat tenant has a very steady job and has been there for a while, don't spend too much time with it. We once had to evict a lady who was a police officer and had been one for several years. It would be easy to garnish her wages and collect the money owed as long as she was employed. She made promise after promise, but never paid. After she was evicted, we filed a lawsuit and we were awarded a judgment for over $6,000.

Letter to Delinquent Tenant in English / Spanish

Date: _____

Property Address:
Dear Tenant:

This is a notice regarding the monthly payment (March) amount that you must pay immediately to Rental Brothers Properties, Inc (check or money order), and you will need to add 10% of your monthly payment (late fee) before we apply an eviction. You can drop your payment at the office located at 12928 N County Rd., Suite 18A, Palm Beach, Fl 33480 between 8:30a.m. to 4:30 p.m. today. Any questions, feel free to call us at 555.555.5555.

_____

Querido Inquilino:

Esta noticia es para recordarle que usted tiene que pagar su pago mensual (Marzo) a Casa Partners (cheque o money order solamente) immediatamente, y necesita agregar un 10% de su pago mensual a la renta (cargo por pago tarde) antes de que apliquemos una eviccion a su apartamento. Usted puede dejar su pago en nuestra oficina localizada en 139 N County Rd., Suite 18A, Palm Beach, Fl 33480 de 8:30 a.m. a 4:30p.m. hoy. Cualquier pregunta puede llamar al 561-255-3683. Disculpe la incoveniencia.

Thank you,
Yours truly,

Office Manager, Rental Brothers Properties

Collecting More Than 100 Percent Rent

In the real estate business, it's called ancillary income—income derived from other sources outside of rent. Ancillary income can be many things: coin-op laundries, soda or vending machines, cleaning services, pet fees, and almost anything you have the imagination to charge a fee for.

A common add-on fee is caused by late payment of rent. You can charge 10 percent after the fifth day. You can also collect the interest from deposits, and of course you charge an application fee. All states are not the same, so check with your state regarding how much you can charge for late fees and whether tenants are required to receive interest on their deposits.

We had a tenant who did not get her pay check until the 15th of each month. Since rent was due on the first of the month and late after the 5th, this tenant could never save enough money to pay by the 5th of the month. She always paid her rent every month on the 16th. The tenant's rent was $750 per month and with a 10 percent late fee of $75 was routinely charged each month. She paid the late charge every single month. Like clock work, it was paid each month for over a year this way. She was so consistent about paying on the 16th of the month we stopped notifying her of her late rent, it always came in at the same time each month with an extra $75. That is an extra $900 at the end of the year. She was a good tenant who paid regularly, albeit late each month. At the end of her lease term we entered into a new lease and allowed her to pay on the 16th with no late rent penalty. This was done because she was a good tenant and well worth keeping.

Increasing cash flow is one of the most important concepts to the proactive investor. We will discuss cash flow later in the text.

Do Tenants Understand Their Obligations?

Some tenants move around a lot and some feel little obligation toward maintaining the property they lease. In fact, a study had shown that the turnover rate is roughly 45 percent per year. In most cases, and in our experiences, tenants in houses stay much longer (many years) than in apartments. Home renters have families and most feel they understand their obligations toward you and your property, but mostly their obligation is to give their family a safe and comfortable place to live and grow.

Studies have also shown that there is 30 percent more use of electricity when tenants do not pay for it. The same is true for water usage. It is also a fact that clothes washers and dryers in units are used about 30 percent more than community coin-op laundry rooms in apartment buildings. This causes a large amount of water and electricity waste. Tenants waste water, electricity and abuse appliances more when they do not have to pay for them, this is a statistical fact. Therefore, we have put together a presentation package for the new renter that explains the new tenant's obligations and to make sure the tenant understands the rule of law when renting from us.

You may copy the following presentation pages—punch holes in them, and place them in a three ring presentation binder. Flip through each page and explain these terms to your new tenant. This presentation is what we call the "Lockdown." After the presentation, we have the new tenant initial each page. This confirms their understanding of what was presented to them. Make a copy and enclose it in their rental package.

What is "The Highly Engaged Rental Package?"

AKA "The Tenant's Rental Package" is a folder or binder with all important documents regarding the tennant"s lease. The "Package" includes the following:

1) A copy of the signed lease and all attachments
2) Pet Agreement
3) Emergency Contact phone numbers
4) Payment Vouchers
5) Business envelopes to mail in monthly payments (with Vouchers)
6) A copy of their "Obligation Agreement" with their initials
7) All other agreements (satellite fee, self-storage rental and others)

The presentation begins on the next page. You can substitute your name in the place of Worth Avenue Property Management. The following pages consist of a presentation of the tenant's "Obligation Agreement."

WORTH PROPERTY MANAGEMENT

Presents

The Rental Program

What's it all about?

WELCOME ABOARD

- **Congratulations, you have been accepted into the Worth Avenue Rental Program.**

- **Our Program is designed for conscientious people like you.**

- **We are proud to have you a part of our family. Thank you for choosing us.**

How Long do Things Last?

- We believe in building relationships that last a long time. We also believe your new home and the appliances and fixtures in it will last many years when cared for.

- You are obligated to replace damage to carpets if the carpet is less than 10 years old.

- Smoking ruins interior paint. Most interior paint will last 10 years. If the room was painted within 10 years and needs repainting—you are responsible.

Most fixtures inside and outside of the unit/house last over 20 years—this includes:

- Lighting fixtures

- Doors (interior and exterior)

- Door knobs and hinges

- Windows and screens

- Plumbing fixtures (faucets)

- Electrical switches and covers

Standard Wear and Tear

Nearly everything lasts over 10 years.

- When you move into a home or apartment and everything in it is functional and in good working condition, it is expected to be in good working condition when you move out.

- You are responsible for cleaning and making repairs when uncommonly high wear and tear has occurred.

- Air conditioning filters should be replaced every three months and Central AC units serviced once each year by a qualified air conditioning rep. Tenant understands and will bear the costs associated with this service.

———————

Initial

What Does it Mean To Rent from Us?

- Worth Avenue Property Management is a professional company dedicated to working with qualified tenants—providing clean, comfortable home and an enjoyable living experience in the properties we manage. We'll provide this experience throughout the term of the rental lease.
- We will always provide you with:

  ✓ Prompt and courteous service by all those associated with Worth Avenue Property Management.

  ✓ A great place to live and raise a family

  ✓ Professional and time conscientious service

  ✓ Fair and reasonable rates

  ✓ An option to move into a larger unit

  ✓ Help and assist with homeownership—if this is your dream

This is our promise to you. In trade for what we offer:

We expect you, the tenant, to care for the property throughout the lease period and pay the rent on time. This is your obligation, as part of the term of your lease.

_____

Initial

YOUR HOME

A rental house is your home and you have certain responsibilities for maintaining your home, as outlined in your lease. These would include:

1) Front yard and backyard maintenance: cutting the lawn, pruning trees and making sure all plant life has adequate water for healthy growth

2) Roof gutters must be free of leaves and dirt

3) Changing batteries in smoke alarms and making sure the fire extinguisher is full and works properly

4) Changing out filters in the air conditioner and having it serviced once per year

5) Making small repairs: faucet leaks, interior door knobs, and replacing cabinet knobs and handles

_____
Initial

Repairs for House and Apartment

There are certain repairs that you are responsible for and you will be charged for. Damage caused by you and/or your family members and friends include:

1) Broken window frames, glass and screens

2) Broken doorknobs, locks and ceiling fans

3) Damaged doors and hinges

4) Faucets and faucet handles

5) Clogged toilets and sinks

6) AC that you did not maintain or change filters

_____
Initial

Scheduling a Maintenance Call

1) You may place a maintenance request by mail or calling our office. A representative will contact you to schedule a convenient time to investigate the situation or make repairs.

2) All maintenance requests must be authorized by the property manager. After work orders are approved, a service representative will be contacted and a scheduled time will be made.

3) We respond to all maintenance calls within 24 hours. This is our policy. This does not mean the problem will be repaired in this time frame.

4) A service representative will not enter your home unless you are present.

5) If the repairs were caused by your negligence, a labor charge of *$45 per hour* will be incurred during normal working hours between 9 am and 5 pm. Before 9 am and after 5 pm a labor charge of *$55 per hour* will be incurred to you. Any outside professional work by plumbers, electricians, etc., will be billed to you directly. Pay close attention to your pets and make sure they are not causing mischief and potentially expensive repairs.

6) Excessive repair requests can lead to your eviction and/or an increase in your monthly rent.

7) Always let us know when there is a water leak. If we receive an unusually high water bill, you will be charged the excess amount.

8) Your rent and/or security deposit are not used to pay for maintenance expenses caused by you.

_____

Initial

Where Does Your Rent Money Go?

Your rent pays for:

1) The Mortgage

2) Property Insurance (Liability, Fire and Natural Disasters)

3) Property Taxes (Schools, parks and other public places)

4) Property Maintenance

5) Utilities (Water and garbage and/or Electricity)

_____
Initial

Payment of Rent

It is important that rent is paid on time. We incur many expenses—and to provide you with your apartment or home, we need your rent paid on time. Our mortgage lenders, insurance agents and of course the taxing authority do not wait for payment. They have what is known as a

ZERO TOLERENCE POLICY

for nonpayment and so do we. Let's make it easy for everyone—pay on time.

_____
Initial

What Happens When You Do Not Pay On Time?

1) You will be responsible for paying a late fee of an additional 10% of the amount owed.

2) You will be evicted.

3) You will incur attorney fees and court costs.

4) Your credit will be ruined.

5) A judgment will be attached to every asset you have.

6) A judgment will stay on your credit report until satisfied.

7) Your wages will be garnished.

8) You will end up paying more than you ever dreamt possible.

_____

Initial

Learn to Save

It is important to have money set aside in case of an emergency. We recommend the following:

1) Set aside as much savings as possible. It is better to not succumb to instant gratification. Do not buy something you really don't need immediately. Saving money takes discipline.

2) You should try to save at least enough money to cover 6 months of expenses.

3) It's never too late to start—it simply takes discipline. Invest your money and watch it grow. After a year or two, you will be surprised at how fast it has grown.

4) If you haven't already begun, take 10% of your monthly income, or more if you can, and simply set it aside in a savings account or money market fund. Do this each and every month. This takes discipline.

5) Be in the top 10% of the population. Set aside your money and invest it. When an emergency appears you'll be ready for it.

6) If you are interested in owning your own home, let us know. We can help you get started.

7) We can also help you design a program for saving. Just let us know—it is as simple as that.

Initial

We are glad to have you with us!

Enjoy the benefits of living a lifestyle you deserve.
Discover how

INSERT YOUR NAME

can help you with your residential needs

Attracting Good Tenants

As discussed earlier, good tenants are certainly worth their weight in gold. But to attract good tenants you must market to all prospective tenants—good and bad. You won't know what kind of a tenant you'll get until you meet everyone, that is, every adult on the lease who is planning to live in your rental unit. Much of the time, a bad tenant will be filtered out during the application process—either during the time the application is completed (in front of you), or after you have checked the appropriate details on the application, such as, job verification and income history, past landlord opinion, credit check and so on.

A proactive landlord knows that good tenants can typically come from your current good tenants as referrals. But there are many ways to attract a steady stream of qualified tenants; and here are the most effective ways:

1. *The lawn sign.* This is the easiest and most common way to attract tenants—the ever popular "For Rent" sign. A rent sign placed in the yard targets tenants who are already interested in living in your area. And if they are calling off your rent sign, they are more than likely already interested in the unit or rental house.

We have used four different types of signs over the years; each with a different strategy in mind: (a) the simple red and white "For Rent" signs; (b) the red and white "For Rent" signs written in Spanish; (c) the professional custom made steel sign; and (d) the custom made professional steel sign that reads: "For Rent—1, 2, 3 and 4 bedroom units available." This sign advertises every possible unit, whether you have them available or not. Now let's explore the strategy behind each sign and why they all work well for different situations.

a) "For Rent" sign. This is your common sign available at most hardware or do-it-yourself stores. Do not get the small version of this sign. Always have the large one—it needs to be seen (18" x 24" or 24" x 36"). This type of sign tells the prospective tenant that you are a small time operator. And sometimes you will find prospective tenants less intimidated by calling on a rental, knowing they are not dealing with a large company. You will also get people who may not qualify for class A or B rental property, typically handled by large companies. You will attract average working folks—folks your property may be suitable for. This type of sign can be posted on a steel frame and anchored into the ground or you could use a wood stake. The steel frame is much sturdier and recommended.

b) *"For Rent" in Spanish.* This is the same sign as (*a*) above, however, you write the property information in Spanish. This works very well when your property is in a predominantly Hispanic area. Sometimes, individuals who are not fluent in English will not call the number on a sign, because they feel they will not be able to communicate with the rental agent (you). By writing your message in Spanish, you open the door to more prospective tenants—tenants who may feel more at ease calling you, than calling a competitor with a sign written in English. It's to your benefit to learn a little Spanish if you own rental property in Hispanic areas.

c) *Professional steel or aluminum sign.* This is the same type of sign most real estate agents use (18" x 24" or 24" x 36"). This type of sign costs about $40 each and can be custom made at sign companies who specialize in real estate signs. We use a local sign company and you can get information online by using your favorite search engine. Fast Signs (www.fastsigns.com) is a national company with many locations across the U.S., they might be a good place to start. Since it is steel, it is durable and should last for the several years. In stead of placing your phone number and a personal name on the sign, you should buy riders with your name and number. *Riders* are typically 6" x 18" or 6" x 24" in size and are attached to the top or bottom of your main sign. You could have *riders* that say anything from *Price Reduced* to *Se Habla Espanol,* or even *Lease Option.* By providing the phone numbers on *riders*, it will allow prospective tenants to call your assistant, should you decide to get away from the day to day rental leasing part of the business. Also, you will not need to trash the sign if you change your phone number.

d) *Multiple unit sign.* This is the sign everyone will call. You are inadvertently advertising: efficiency, 1, 2, 3 and 4 bedroom units from one sign. The great thing about this type of sign is that, it allows you to see what type and size of property is most in demand in the target area. We have found that in our target market 2 bedroom units are popular. Another advantage to this type of sign is that, it allows you to show people interested in a three bedroom—where a two bedroom at around the same price might be suitable.

If someone calls and is interested in a two bedroom and you have none available, you can refer them to another landlord who has one available. You can also act as a leasing agent for other landlords in your area and collect a customary fee on one month's rent if you should lease the unit. There are, as you can see, a lot of advantages to using this type of sign.

Bandit signs may also be used when your rentals are in a heavily Hispanic area. Signs could be written in Spanish and English. Again, knowing a few words of Spanish can work to your advantage. Bandit signs are typically white, corrigated cardboard with attached wires as a stand. The wired ends are they inserted into the earth. You can purchase white signs and write in black marker "For Rent," unit features, price and phone. This works well attracting lower income tenants in mixed areas. The sign is less intimidating than a custom made steel "corporate looking" sign. The frequency of calls will increase with this type of sign. Bandit signs costs $1 to $2 each. You can buy them at 100 at a time and place two at each property and all around your area. Make sure to place them at busy corners where cars have to come to a stop.

If you have multi-family property or several rental properties, it is a good idea to leave your rental signs up indefinitely. Even when your houses or apartments are fully rented, you should leave signs up to advertise other rentals you have available. This is hassle free advertising and it works well. The more people call inquiring about your vacancy, the odds are you will find the right tenant for your rental. Numbers, numbers, numbers, everything in sales works out to be numbers games. You are selling a lease!

2. *Craigslist*. Believe it or not, the web posting site www.craigslist.org is a very popular and extremely effective site to post your rental property listings. We have had great success with this site and believe you will too. Another great thing about Craigslist is that it is free of charge. You pay nothing to post your rental properties. You should spend a few minutes each morning and update the listing to the top of the page until you find the right tenant.

Newspapers are a lousy way to attract tenants anymore. Advertising costs are simply too expensive and the frequency of tenants calling from newspaper ads have, over the past few years declined significantly. Save your money and don't bother with newspaper advertising to attract tenants.

3. *Tenant or neighbor referrals*. You should always let your good tenants and neighbors know when you have or will have a vacancy. If you are fair and reasonable with your tenants and nice to your neighbors, they will gladly refer friends, family or co-workers your way. Proactively maintaining an open pipeline to all your tenants and neighbors is good business.

4. *Fliers*. Spend a few minutes with neighborhood kids and hire one or two of them to distribute a flier advertising your rental property. If you have the time, you may want to walk your target neighborhood and distribute the fliers yourself. You will get some exercise and you might meet people ready to rent from you that day. You may also get plenty of referrals from neighbors knowing people interested in relocating to the area.

In an hour, two kids can deliver several hundred fliers in your target market. And the costs will be about $20 for printing and $10 for delivery.

5. *Free papers and Hispanic papers*. There is absolutely no need to pay for advertising in your local paper unless it is extremely affordable. However, the chances of that are slim. Most city newspapers are not making enough money due to the fact that not only small operators discovered online billboard site, but large companies have discovered them as well. And many of those sites charge little or nothing to post rental property advertising.

There are, however, two paper types you should advertise in that payoff: free papers and free Hispanic papers. Community free papers are filled with thousands of items the lower to middle income renting class use. And advertising in Hispanic papers make perfect sense when your properties are located in Hispanic or culturally diverse areas. We have had good success with local Hispanic papers. If you cannot read or write Spanish, the advertising executive can translate your advertisement to Spanish.

With a fast growing Hispanic population, it may be time for you to learn a few words so you could communicate effectively with prospective tenants when they call. Most of your Spanish speaking tenants will know a few words in English, so why don't you learn a few words in Spanish. It will certainly help you and it is a proactive approach to growing your rental business. You could obtain a simple Spanish phrase book or listen to a language course in your car.

The Lease

Included in the Appendix is a sample lease that we use. Also included is the same lease in Spanish. Go through the lease and make sure you understand each of the provisions. We won't go through and dissect the entire lease here; however, you should read it through thoroughly and make certain your tenant initials each page, signifying that they understand it thoroughly.

The term of a lease should always be as long as possible. Do not let a tenant convince you on to a month-to-month lease or even a six month lease. Always go after a 12 month lease or longer—the longer the better Frequent tenant turnover costs a great deal of time and money—money to clean and make repairs and money lost from the vacancy time. Some states may have residential lease limits—that is, as a landlord, you may not legally force a tenant to perform under a lease that is over 12 months. A new lease would be required. If you can lock a tenant in on a three year lease, by all means do it, if you believe the tenant will be a good tenant for the entire duration of the lease, go for it. If the tenant leaves before the three year term comes to fruition, then you probably won't have a strong case of collecting the remaining rent due. This is of course, when your state law places a limit of 12 months on residential leases. Then, all you would need to do is renew the lease for another 12 months.

In many areas, if your lease is less than 7 months, your local municipality or state may consider you to be conducting business similar to that of a hotel or other short-term lodging establishment. They might then bill you for local sales taxes. To prevent this from becoming a financially damaging situation, make all leases longer than 6 months. In tough markets, some landlords sign 7 month leases instead of 12 month leases. Keep this in mind when you can not persuade a tenant to sign a 12 month lease and vacancies in the area are climbing.

Section 8

Section 8 housing is undoubtedly the most visible of governmental agencies subsidizing and sponsoring private housing for disadvantaged families on a low-income. Almost every city has a Section 8 office (Housing Authority). You could go online to the government website, (www.hud.gov) or call information for the phone number in your area to locate an office near you or in your target area.

During the Great Deprecession, the U.S. government formed the U.S. Housing Act of 1937 that would assist families with their rent. The Housing and Community Development Act of 1974, creating the Section 8 Program. In the program, government pays about 80 percent of the rent for the tenant and the tenant is responsible for paying the remaining 20 percent of the rent. In simple terms, a landlord with a house for rent at $1,000 per month would receive $800 each month from the Section 8 (Housing Authority) and $200 would be the tenant's responsibility. Sometimes your tenant will be on other welfare type programs, such as local child services groups, smaller city and state sponsored programs or private non-profit organizations that help low-income families pay rent. Sometimes, you will be getting two or more checks from government agencies for the payment of the tenant's rent. We had a tenant whose actual contribution to her rent was zero. She received about $825 from Section 8, $220 from Children

Services, $200 from a private church group, and $120 from a City run organization each month. This did not include the food stamps she received which was believed to be about $180 per month. She did not work. Her rent and food were completely paid for. With her new, unauthorized, live-in boyfriend, they were living the *New American Dream* at the expense of the American tax payer. We reminded her of her responsibilities and that she would lose all of her financial benefits, including Section 8 rent if she did not evict the boyfriend. She evicted the boyfriend and got her responsibilities straight.

How to Get Registered with Section 8 and Other Requirements

1. Stop in at the local office and fill-out an application. List a full description of each property you have available that you would like a Section 8 tenant in. A good idea is to have a photo or two of the houses or apartments attached to the description page and place it on the bulletin board in the reception area of the Housing Authority office.

2. The house or apartment must be clean and ready for a tenant to move in. All repairs should have been completed before you submit the application or you will be wasting time when the housing inspector comes for the inspection.

3. A prospective tenant will have a "voucher" form Section 8 that exhibit's the amount Section 8 will pay for him or her. If a prospective tenant calls to look at the property, ask for the amount on the voucher. If the amount is sufficient, show the unit. Your rent can be adjusted on the way up. It depends what the voucher is good for.

4. If the prospective tenant likes the property and wants to move in, they should have an application from Section 8 for you to sign. The tenant must turn the application in at the Section 8 office immediately. Collect a holding fee of $200 from the tenant. Within about two weeks a Section 8 inspector will call to set a time for inspecting the property. They have very specific housing regulations. The property must be in very good condition--everything must be in good operating order.

5. Typically the tenant would have to come up with the money for the security deposit and remainder of the rent (20% of the total rent about). The Section 8 lease is for twelve months and it is guaranteed by the Housing Authority. You will receive a check directly from Section 8 at the beginning of each month.

6. When the inspector is ready to view the property, meet him at the property. Remember, everything in the house or apartment unit must work perfectly: screens on windows; no cracked or broken windows; all appliances must work; doors and door knobs must work perfectly; faucets cannot leak; light bulbs must work and electrical covers cannot be cracked or broken; GFI (ground-fault interrupter) plugs must be in kitchen and bathrooms; and the unit must be clean. The water and power must be on. If the house fails the inspection, the inspector will give you a list of the items that failed the inspection. You will tell the inspector that the problems will be repaired immediately and set another appointment with him to inspect the property as soon as possible. This may take another week or maybe two. You can avoid this by having everything in topnotch shape at the first inspection.

7. There is a time delay in the process of getting a Section 8 tenant, but we believe if you get

the right tenant, it is well worth it. We have know some Section 8 tenants to live in the same house for over fifteen years and were very clean and quiet--the perfect tenant.

8. At the end of the twelve months, if the tenant wishes to stay, raise the rent to the maximum Section 8 will pay for the property. Section 8 has rent sheets that seem to be increased each year as the cost of living increases – typically, 3 to 4 percent. Another inspection will be set, so make certain the property is in excellent shape.

This was a clean 4 bedroom, 2 bathroom rental house we had rented to the same family for many years. We purchased it directly from the owner, a long-time investor. There was only minor interior cleaning to be completed. The South Florida rain always kept the grass green. We had leased the home to a special nonprofit agency that assisted low income families. The tenants worked out great. The house was just a few bloks from block from our office. It is nice to have your investments nearby. When you can, try to invest in your own neighborhood; the advantages are enourmous.

Some Things you should Lookout For

Simply because an individual was accepted into the Section 8 program does not mean they are of an outstanding moral character. Those that want to be in the Section 8 program need to file an application and prove they are poor. That is more or less all there is to it. Here are a few things you might want to lookout for:

1. *Kickbacks*. When a Section 8 tenant has a voucher good for $980 and you have an apart-

61

ment set at $850 per month, the prospective tenant may ask you to raise the rent to $980 and kickback $130 (the difference between the prices) in cash, each month. You should stay clear of this type of person, period. You might even inform the Section 8 office of this person and his/her dishonest behavior. Something like this could get them kicked out of the program altogether—and should.

2. *Relatives move in.* Mother, brother and boyfrriend all move in. Again, this is a lease violation and is prohibited by Section 8 rules. Inform tenant that everyone except those individuals on the lease must move out immediately or you will be forced to notify the Section 8 office. Also, explain to the tenant that she will lose her free Section 8 money and possibly other social welfare funding she may be receiving.

3. *Boyfriend moves in.* After the Section 8 tenant moves in, you realize there are more people living in the house/apartment. And there is someone not on the lease. Apparently, the boyfriend who is the father of the tenant's children has moved in. There are benefits to not being married, unfortunately. The government is kind enough to give money to unmarried woman with children—so why get married. In some social circles this is completely acceptable and not only tolerated but encouraged. You should inform Section 8 of the problem. This is a breach of the lease agreement with you and the rules of the Section 8 program as well.

4. *Don't pay their share.* Section 8 typically pays about 80 percent of the lease amount; the tenant pays the rest. Some tenants stop paying there portion of the rent thinking they will not get evicted while Section 8 remains paying. If the tenant is evicted, Section 8 will continue paying rent for the duration of the lease. You could warn the tenant (in writing) that unless the full rent is paid, plus late fees and charges, you will contact Section 8 and recommend that they be withdrawn from the program. Hopefully, that will motivate the tenant to pay and get current.

HUD and the Section 8 program have specific rules and requirements on the size of bedrooms and ceiling heights of dwellings. You should check with the Section 8 office for an updated list of requirements. In the past, a bedroom had to be 70 square feet and have at least one window of a specified size. The window does not have to lead to the outside—it could lead to another bedroom or hallway that has an exit to the outside. A closet is not required and sometimes a room could qualify as a bedroom if it has a partition or even a drape separating it.

Fair Housing

All landlords should be aware of the Fair Housing Act—it is actually part of the Civil Rights Act of 1968. From the hud.gov website it states:

> "prohibits discrimination in sale, rental, and financing of dwellings, and in other housing related transactions, based on race, color, national origin, religion, sex, familial status (including children under the age of 18 living with parents of legal custodians, pregnant women, and people securing custody of children under the age of 18), and handicap (disability)."

Everyone is a potential tenant—that is, everyone who can pay the rent and pay it on time. Whether your tenant is black, yellow, green, white, 80 years old, 18 years old, in a wheelchair or has three legs and one thumb, gay, straight, bent or curved, makes absolutely no difference. You are in business to collect the highest rent possible with the least amount of hassle. A proactive landlord is an equal opportunity landlord. Equal opportunity landlording is good business and it is a good policy for your growing business.

Antidiscrimination laws regarding housing are important to know and they protect you as well as tenants. That's it—period. By the way, are Siamese twins considered as one tenant or two? And would it be discrimination if you filed an eviction suit against one and not the other? If one get evicted what happens? The answer is….

Federal Law Disclosures on Lead-Based Paint

A proactive real estate investor and landlord is up to date on government laws regarding disclosure rules on lead-based paint. The proper disclosure document should be read and signed by all tenants before moving into your unit. In 1992 Congress enacted the Residential Lead-Based Paint Hazard Reduction Act. This Act was to "protect families from exposure to lead from paint, dust, and soil." And according to "Section 1018 of this law directed HUD and EPA to require the disclosure of known information of lead-based paint hazards before the sale or lease of most housing built before 1978." The disclosure handbook can be found at www.HUD.org

What are you Required to Disclose on Lead-Based Paint?

There is a one page form which we have included in the Appendix, and it is attached to the sample lease agreement. This is a form required by federal law which the landlord or sales agent discloses to the buyer or lessee. The disclosure statement is titled: "DISCLOSURE OF INFORMATION ON LEAD-BASED PAINT AND/OR LEAD-BASED PAINT HAZARDS." This statement is attached to the tenants lease and signed by both you (landlord) and tenant. A booklet explaining the hazards of lead-based paint produced by HUD should also be presented to the tenant.

If your rental was built after 1978, you are not required to present the disclosure statement. Prior to 1978, paints included lead. Therefore, tenants must be presented with a disclosure statement and a booklet introducing them to the potentially harmful effects of lead-based paints in buildings built before 1978.

As a landlord, you are only required to disclose if you have knowledge of lead-based paint in your rental property. You are not required to do an inspection to locate lead-based paint. You are also not required to remove lead-based paint if found.

If you know there is lead-based paint on your property—disclose it. And if you know where it is—do not try to remove it. You will need professionals to do the work and it could be very costly. The law states, you are not required to remove it, but to simply disclose you are aware of it on the property. There are probably millions of homes in the U.S. that have lead-based paint. As long as the property is maintained and freshly painted periodically, you will have no problems. Removing all lead-based paint from doors and walls adds no value to your property—it only produces a large expense. For more information on this subject you can go to the U.S. Department of Housing and Urban Development website: www.hud.gov/offices/lead/enforcement/disclosure.cfm.

Asbestos, Mold and Radon Gas Disclosure

Most state laws regarding asbestos, mold and radon gas disclosure are similar and if you have purchased or sold a property in the last few years you would have come across disclosure documents acknowledging the potential harm asbestos, mold and radon gas could cause. Since disclosure forms vary from state to state, go online and check what form is right for you. We've enclosed a sample asbestos, mold and radon gas disclosure forms in the Appendix for your convenience.

One last word about disclosures—to protect yourself—disclose it. Attach all disclosures to your lease. When it is time for the tenant to sign the lease, review the disclosures and have the tenant sign them. It is as easy at that. If a tenant asks questions about the disclosures, simply state: "I am required by law to disclose this information."

HQ and the Home Office

Eventually, you will need a few things to manage your properties. "Will I need a home office?" You may have asked yourself. With a few properties, such as one to three single family homes, you will not need a so called *home office*. However, you will need a few basic things to make your business a little easier—and I'll discuss this further in this section. When you grow larger with many investment properties, then you will need to set-up or designate an area in your home which you can organize your business and allow you to work without much distractions. It could be a separate room or a designated area in your home where you can keep all of your real estate investment paperwork and other office equipment.

We will discuss the Home Office in the chapter titled "The Business Side."

Are you Really a Landlord?

Yes, you are a landlord. And you are a property manager. But more than this, you are an investor. You think like an investor and run your real estate holdings like that of an investor—always— thinking of ways to increase value, to increase cash flow and keep your property(s) fully rented with good, respectful, law abiding tenants,

Are all Landlords Rich?

Most people think all landlords are rich; however, that isn't necessarily the case. Many new investors and landlords, who have been investing for a few years, are not rich. They have more than most people, but they also have large mortgages on properties and little positive cash flow if any. Many are working hard to build a real estate portfolio one property at a time. They are focused on the long-term, and the benefits of cashing-out with a large retirement nestegg. They are not yet millionaires, but many landlords are on their way, and they will be millionaires in the near future, should they remain consistent with their real estate investing.

Most real estate investors, who have been investing consistently for a period of seven or more years are millionaires; they have a net worth over a million dollars. And some are doing well with over 10 million in net worth. These are average people who stayed the course through thick and thin and worked hard at their real estate investing. Persistence, diligence, tenacity, discipline and a positive attitude are common attributes of many millionaire real estate investors.

There are more millionaires created from real estate than any other investment class. This is because, over time, inflation works its magic in most locations. And many who have purchased the home they live in and hold onto that home for decades can simply build a large long-term equity position in their property(s).

The Benefits of Becoming a Long-term Landlord

The greatest benefit of becoming a long-term landlord is creating wealth with positive monthly income and benefiting from long-term appreciation. However, not everyone is cutout to be a landlord. Some try it for a short time and simply cannot deal with tenants and the problems bad tenants create. After a while, those investors who develop a certain proactive, business based mind-frame will do well. This type of mind-frame has a lot to do with understanding and dealing effectively with people—tenants and prospective tenants.

We know of many investors who have tried landlording and have left it in search of other types of real estate investing. To be a successful landlord, you have to have a certain mindset. As we discussed earlier, landlording is an experience—an experience of dealing with people. If you haven't the patience or you simply do not want to deal with tenants, you could hire a property management company. Most property management company's charge about 8 percent to 10 percent of gross income collected. We know several successful long-term investors who are not hands-on landlords or property managers. These investors do very well in real estate, but they leave the daily management to a professional company. One such investor we know owns over 18 townhomes, and has an outside management company handling his properties and tenants, while he does what he really enjoys—he plays poker everyday and takes grand vacations whenever he feels like it. He partakes in activities he enjoys and landlording is not one of them. He makes more money playing poker than he pays the management company to handle all his properties.

With an appreciation rate of around 5 percent compounded, your property will double in about 10 years. At the same time, hopefully, you will be receiving enough monthly cash flow to cover all of your expenses and provide a lifestyle you have planned for.

While being a landlord is not for everyone, it is, and has been, a great way to build equity and increase monthly income over the long-term for many part-time investors.

In this chapter, we have just touched the surface regarding the activities for you to begin your landlording venture. In the future, if time permits, we hope to produce a more comprehensive book on landlording—something that could be referred to as "The Bible of Landlording."

ACTION HIGHLIGHTS FOR LANDLORDING
& PROPERTY MANAGMENT

---

1) Know your rental rates and receive the highest possible rents.

2) Handle all property maintenance and repairs quickly.

3) Attracting and retaining good long-term tenants is one of your major objectives.

4) Deal effectively with bad tenants by being firm.

5) Collecting rents without hassle.

6) Collecting more than 100 percent rent.

7) Create your home office.

8) Explaining tenant responsibilities and obligations.

9) Attracting tenants by simple, yet effective ways of advertising.

10) Shoot for a long lease with your tenants.

11) Understanding the Section 8 tenant.

12) Understanding Fair Housing Laws.

13) Understanding federal and/or state laws regarding disclosure of lead-based paint, asbestos, mold and radon gas.

"Successful landlording and property management can be attributed to one thing: dealing effectively with people."

2

Extra Expenses, Property Taxes, Insurance and More

"Nothing is so permanent as a temporary government program."
—Milton Friedman

When you invest in real estate you must know the expenses that will eat up your cash flow. Property taxes, insurance, and utility bills are expected. You will also have general operating or maintenance expenses, such as gardening and air conditioning service, to name a few. Then you will have the unexpected expenses; these could be anything from roof repair, electrical upgrading, plumbing, or replacing an exterior doorknob or broken window. For a single-family rental house, your annual expenses will run about 20 percent to 25 percent of your gross income on the property; this would include vacancies, but not include mortgage payments. On commercial buildings, such as large apartments, the expense can typically run between 45 percent to 50 percent. As you can see, expenses are usually lower for a single-family rental home than for larger multi-family properties. If you have just finished renovating your property, your possible deferred expenses on repairs could be quite low. This is the good news, low possible maintenance expenses moving forward.

As you read on, you'll find an overview of what you could expect as additional expenses and ways in which to deal with them. We will start with property taxes; it is typically the largest recurring expense you will have.

Property Taxes

Once each year you will have to pay your property taxes. Generally, the tax is based at about 1 percent to 1.25 percent in most states, like California and Nevada, respectively, and about 2 percent to 2.5 percent, in states like Florida (selected areas) or New Jersey on the estimated market value of your property.

Highest Property Taxed States

State	Tax Rate
New Jersey	2.38%
Illinois	2.32%
New Hampshire	2.15%
Connecticut	1.98%
Wisconsin	1.96%
Texas	1.90%
Nebraska	1.84%
Michigan	1.78%
Vermont	1.71%
Rhode Island	1.67%

(Tax Foundation)

You can file a petition with the county assessors' office to reduce your property taxes. It will take a little time and you or your representative will need to attend a hearing to state your case, but it is a fact that nearly 70 percent of people who petition for an adjustment to their property tax have had the assessed value lowered.

To reduce the assessment on your property, you should take photos and write out what is wrong with the property. If the property is uninhabitable because of uncompleted repairs, this can be part of your argument to lower the tax. Compare your property to others in the neighborhood and create a "hit list" of why your property is a dump and why it is only worth a fraction of the assessed value. Also, note the deflation in the area and the downward trend of the real estate market in your city. You can get information on your general area regarding real estate inflation or deflation from a simple search on your favorite search engine. Download articles and statistics on your area.

You should make plans every year to petition your property taxes. It takes a simple form and a filing fee, but it is worth the hassle if you are able to save a few hundred or a few thousand dollars by having the property reassessed at a lower valuation.

In Los Angeles County, California the petition form is just one page as it is in Palm Beach County, Florida. This is a simple form to complete and it is probably the same in your county. When you receive your property tax bill in the mail, just read the fine print and follow the instructions. It's really easy and it is worth spending a few minutes per year to complete.

Property Insurance

Carrying property insurance on your rental property or property you plan to flip is required if you have a mortgage. If you do not have a mortgage it is still a good thing to have to protect your investment from damage caused by fire, vandalism and personal injury that might occur on your property. If you live in Florida or other states in the Gulf Coast or some of the Atlantic states where tropical storms or hurricanes occasionally appear, you may be required by your mortgage company to carry windstorm insurance. Windstorm insurance is expensive and if you do not carry a mortgage or your mortgage company does not require you to have it, then it would be your option. We personally would not recommend it. The chances of a hurricane destroying your property are slim. Although it seems more frequent, Florida is hit with a hurricane about every 10 years.

If you have less than 20 percent equity in your home, you will also be required to pay mortgage insurance (PMI). The PMI is paid once per month and the payment is made with your mortgage payment. Sometimes you can pay the premium for the entire year and receive a discount. Check with your insurance company regarding a discount. Many lenders will escrow your insurance and PMI eliminating the risk that you are late or miss a payment.

Accounting

Accounting fees, including bookkeepers and tax preparers can run you several hundred dollars to a few thousand annually. This all depends on the size of your operation. With one or two single family rentals, you could keep the expense under $1,000 per year. With many properties you could have a bookkeeper one day per week crunch the numbers or once per month. Depending on the hours spend, your annual bill could range from $1,200 to $5,000 per year or more.

General Maintenance

With all property there is wear and tear, and especially with older properties over 30 years old. General maintenance could include the following:

- Gardening and landscaping.
- Painting and cleaning when tenants move out.
- Air conditioning and heating repair and cleaning and replacing filters.
- Repairing and/or replacing old appliances.
- Replacing broken doorknobs.
- Repairing handle, knobs and hinges on cabinets and doors.

Most replacement of items and repairs will be made after a tenant has moved out. And a great deal of the maintenance that is required will be based on the quality of the tenant. Although, it is very difficult to always get tenants who are respectful of property and believe in cleanliness, do your best during the interview process and screen your prospective tenants carefully. In the long run, good tenants save you a lot of money on maintenance issues.

Roofing, Electrical and Plumbing

You will need professionals most of the time when you are in need of a roofer, electrician, or plumber.

- *Roofing.* Depending on a roof and the materials used, most roofs will last at least 20 years. Sometimes it is very hard to locate the precise spot where a leak is coming from. Therefore, a roofing professional is needed to locate the leak and then make the repair. If the roof is very old or it has been battered through many hurricanes, it may be time to replace the whole thing. If the sub-roof is in good shape it will cost roughly $5,000 for a new shingle roof on a typical house of 1,000 to 1,500 square feet. If there is a lot of wood to be replaced, costs will be a lot more.

- *Electrical.* Installing a light fixture, replacing outlets and covers, and of course, changing light bulbs are all simple tasks you or a handyman can accomplish. But when you need to change or update the electrical system from fuses to breakers, you should contract a licensed electrician. When there are shorts and not enough power to supply the house, you should also call an electrician to investigate.

- *Plumbing.* Most plumbing problems are caused by tenants clogging drains and toilets. Always have a plunger in the rental and make sure the tenant knows how to use it. This may seem obvious, but some tenants are exceptionally lazy. You should also warn the tenant about what should not go down the drains.

- Leaks from the shower and other faucets can be fixed by tightening the connection or by usually replacing a washer. This is something a good tenant will fix themselves. But more often if you pay the water bill, you will not hear about this problem until after the tenant has moved out or you do an inspection. You can fix the leak yourself or have a handyman do it. If a pipe bursts or there is a serious leak, by all means, call a plumber as soon as possible.

When you need to replace the toilet or sink, it is sometimes best to do it yourself or have the help of a handyman or friend who has installed a toilet before—this is not a difficult task, just time consuming. A good handyman is worth his weight in gold, so find a good one and make sure to treat him right if you are completely adverse to manual labor or haven't the time.

Are There Other Operating Expenses?

Of course there are; everything in the course of spending money to operate your rentals is an expense.

- **Utilities: Electric, Water, Gas and Garbage.** You will be paying these expenses from the time you buy the property, and up until you rent it or sell it. If the rental is a house, the tenant will pay the bills and all utilities. It you have a multi-unit apartment, you will typically be responsible for water, garbage and the common area electric bills.

- **Advertising.** This could be a recurring expense depending on the frequency of vacancies you have. Advertising in your local newspaper does get expensive, so, stay with free online site advertising like Craigslist.com and specialized smaller publications such as ethnic or Hispanic papers if your rentals are in predominantly mixed areas.

- **Auto.** Fuel will be the greatest expense when you are driving around looking at properties or making several daily trips to the hardware store or meeting with prospective tenants. Some investors invest in a small economical car when their days are filled with a lot of driving. After a few deals, this may be a good option and it will be well worth it over the long-term. However, you will still have extra insurance and registration fees, so keep this in mind. Calculate what your expenses will be before you buy a new vehicle.

- **Office and Corporate Expenses.** Recurring office expenses would include: copy and printer toner, paper and so on. Larger expenses occur with computers and other office equipment which could costs about $2,000 to $4,000 every few years. Incorporation fees to the state and annual costs for business and rental licenses could run several hundred dollars annually. Keep track of these expenses for tax deductions.

Unexpected and Catastrophic Expenses

There are some unexpected expenses that may occur on occasion. These would include expenses related to:

- Storms
- Earthquake
- Mold and/or Asbestos eradication
- Lawsuits

In 2004 a hurricane swept through Florida. The day before it blew through our area, we had our work crews visit all our properties and fasten-down the storm awnings and secure plywood over windows where there where no shutters. The costs came to about $5,000 for labor and materials. When the storm passed, the clean-up work was mostly comprised of collecting fallen tree branches, and some old wooded fences had fallen by their rotted posts being snapped. Much of the damage occurred at our 15 unit apartment building. The workers lowered the storm awnings, but did not fasten them to the building. The hurricane forced winds mangled many of the awnings and with the awnings crashing into the windows, many windows and window frames were broken and needed to be replaced. The replacement costs of the awnings and the broken windows costs roughly $7,500. The sad thing about this, is that, this was not caused by the hurricane. It was caused by human negligence—the workers did not complete the job assigned to them and they were outright careless. The two handymen in charge of this debacle ultimately skipped town with our company van and a $500 generator. We filed a police report soon thereafter. Two years later the van was recovered in a different city, 50 miles away. It was junked up and we told the police to keep it.

All the rental houses we owned were not damaged by the hurricane. We also noticed that some of the large investors in the area hadn't bothered to prepare their properties for the coming storm; they didn't spend any time or money preparing. Our preparation costs and damages after the hurricane were estimated at roughly $20,000. We included the nonpayment of rents from tenants who were put out of work for one or two weeks, they simply decided to cry poor (a typical response). We included this loss of income to our hurricane expense list.

The following year another hurricane came in mid-October. This time we secured the homes and buildings that had storm awnings and shutters and had crews double check them. We did not use plywood over windows on the majority of the properties. After the storm, we found one broken window and a tree had fallen from a neighbor's yard on to one of our houses and caused a small leak at the corner of the roof. Total repairs after the storm were under $1,000. That's not bad for having over 70 units at the time. Most of the damage from the hurricanes was from snapped tree branches.

You will never be able to predict when you'll run into *unforeseen* expenses—for this reason; you should always keep cash aside in case such emergencies should occur. Keeping about 10 percent of your assets in cash or cash equivalents will make is easier in times of emergencies.

Recurring Expense Checklist

Before purchasing any property, you should know what the common recurring expenses will be as we discussed earlier in the chapter. Figure 2.1 is a sample checklist of common recurring expenses. The Recurring Expense Checklist is in the Appendix.

Figure 2.1

SAMPLE COMMON RECURRING EXPENSE CHECKLIST
BEFORE PURCHASE OF PROPERTY

Property Address: Santa Rosa Apartments, #1-6
123 W. Main St.
Anytown, CA 99334

Expenses	Monthly	Annually
Property Taxes	$416	$4,992
Insurance	$150	$1,800
Vacancies (3%)	$62.5	$750
Utilities:		
Water	70	840
Electric	35	420
Gas	0	0
Landscaping and Gardening	$50	$600
General Maintenance	$20	$240
Mortgage estimate:	$1,330	$15,960
$200,000 at 30 years fixed at 7%		
Projected Expenses	$2.133.5	$25,602

Sample Income Statement

Average Annual Income Statement. Review the revenues and then all the expenses. This is a very common statement you should prepare every year on your investment properties. Not only will you need the information for your tax's, but it lets you know exactly where you stand and it should open your eyes to over spending and income deficiencies. Make changes to your expenses immediately when you are spending too much and increase rents and add more ancillary income generators when income is not sufficient to your expectations.

Sample Income Statement
Big John's Six Unit Apartment
For the year ending December 31, 2016

Revenues		
Rents Collected	54,000	
Laundry	1,440	
Application fees	600	
GROSS PROFIT	56,040	
Expenses:		
Utilities	$720	1.30%
Licenses and permits	290	0.50
Garbage	600	1.20
Yard maintenance	840	1.50
Maintenance and repairs	3,600	6.40
Insurance	1,900	3.40
Property taxes	8,000	14.30
Legal services	740	1.30
Accounting	1,500	2.70
Advertising	760	1.40
Bank fees	140	0.20
Misc. (auto/travel, etc.)	980	1.70
Mortgage interest paid	15,700	28.00
TOTAL EXPENSES	(35,770)	64.0%

NET OPERATING INCOME	$20,070	36.0%
	======	

ACTION HIGHLIGHTS FOR
EXTRA EXPENSES, PROPERTY TAXES, INSUR-
ANCE AND MORE

1) Know your expenses before you invest.

2) Petition your property taxes every year, and especially when prices have fallen in your area due to economic downturns.

3) Check your property insurance rates frequently. Don't over insure and cut your rates when values fall. Check your rates with other property owners to make sure you are not over-paying.

4) Work with a knowledgably accountant and learn as much as possible for yourself regarding proper accounting.

5) Know all about general maintenance costs and pay close attention to recurring expenses.

6) Set aside some cash for unexpected emergencies. 10 percent in cash or cash equivalents should be enough to cover unforeseen emergencies.

"Cutting expenses is the same as making money—but with less hassle and usually with one phone call or letter."

3

Your Cash Flow

"Even if you're on the right track, you'll get run over if you just sit there."
—Will Rogers

Cash flow is referred as the cash left over after all the operating expenses are paid. This would include cash spent on repairs, insurance, taxes, and mortgages. If the operating expenses exceed the income, then you will have negative cash flow; and that is the dread of every real estate investor, especially if you decide to rent your property and plan to hold it for the long-term. So, how do you know what your current cash flow is and how can you accurately project what it will be in the future? After you have reviewed this chapter you should have a working understanding of cash flow and the ways of improving your income.

What is Your Cash Flow?

The goal of every investor should include receiving maximum cash flow from their rental property. Unfortunatly, most investors typically believe the only real income received from their rental property is the monthly rent. This is anything but accurate. Any aggressive investor should be making upwards of an additional 15% on top of the normal monthly rental rate. We will discuss this further and in more detail under the section *Increasing Cash Flow.*

Now, how do you determine your cash flow? Do the following:

List your current income. This is all the income including rents collected, late charges collected, application fees, interest paid on deposit accounts, and any other income collected related to your property. Do each property separately and start with the monthly income. Later you can do it quarterly and annually and combine all of your properties to discover your true cash flow.

List your current expenses. Start with all your monthly expenses such as your mortgage, insurance, utility bills, gardening, taxes (if paid monthly), and money spent on repairs (painting, broken windows, cleaning, etc.). Categorize and calculate together.

Now deduct your income from your expenses. Have your expenses exceeded your income? If you said yes, then it is time to get to work—fast. The first thing to do is to figure out why your cash flow is negative and then design a plan to stop the cash drain and return to positive cash flow.

After accumulating your income and expenses for about six months, you will have a pretty good idea as to what your cash flow is, and whether you are making money (positive cash flow), or losing money (negative cash flow). And of course, in the end, even if you are showing a negative monthly cash flow, you could still have a positive year with tax deductions and depreciation factored in. Consult with your accountant about all the deductions and depreciation you can take with your property.

Sample Cash Flow Balance Sheet

Sample Cash Flow Balance Sheet

Income

Rent Collected $_____

Other Income

Application Fees   _____
Pet Fees   _____
Laundry Machines   _____
Vending Machines   _____

List all other income (interest earned)   _____

Gross Operating Income   _____

Operating Expenses

Monthly Mortgage Payment[*]   _____
Insurance   _____
Vacancies (3%)   _____
Property Taxes   _____
Utilities   _____
Repairs and Maintenance   _____

List all other expenses (permit fees, ect.)   _____
Total Operating Expenses   _____

Net Operating Monthly Income   _____

---

[*] We include the entire mortgage as an expense rather than the interest only expense. We are trying to secure actual cash flow—the cash coming in versus the cash going out.

The Negative Cash Flow Problem

Many investors have now been deluged with an ever increasing problem of negative cash flow. And it is based entirely, 100% of the time on a false contrived plan of investment. Most investors who have negative cash flow problems can contribute it to one of four reasons: (1) Buying property at too high a price; (2) the down payment is too small; (3) the property is in bad shape; and (4) the investor lacks imagination and desire to create more income.

1. *Buying a property for too high a price.* Many areas where properties are selling for 10, 12 and even 15 times gross, (the Gross Rent Multiplier, GRM, or the annual gross income of the property) makes it very difficult to obtain positive cash flow, even with a sizable down payment. Since your monthly mortgage payment will be the largest cash outlay, the best strategy would be to make sure it is very low. Here is an example of a single family rental house in a suburb of Los Angeles.

The house is a three bedroom, one bath, built over fifty years ago and has 1,050 square feet of living space. An investor purchased the house with the intent to rent it. The house is purchased for $500,000 and the investor puts a down payment of $100,000. The investor believes he got a great deal on the house because all comparable houses were selling for $550,000 and higher. The mortgage loan is $400,000 at 6.5% amortized for 30 years. The monthly mortgage payment is $2,528.

The house is located in a home owners (owner-occupant), neighborhood, not a rental neighborhood. Within two weeks after closing, the house is rented for $2,000 per month. That is the maximum amount that renters in this neighborhood can afford and would pay for a house of that size. Already you can see that there is a negative cash flow problem of $528 just from the monthly mortgage. Property taxes will run about $5,500 annually or about $458 per month and insurance will be another $120 per month. Already, our investor is losing over $1,100 per month...cash. The investor believes the appreciation of the property will far exceed the negative cash flow. This is faulty thinking and it can lead to a large loss over time if the current market stagnates over a few years or even heads down. If the tenants move out after a few months, there is a good chance the property will be vacant for at least a month and the investor will most certainly need to spend money on cleaning and making certain repairs. How much money is lost now? How can the bleeding stop? This is a tough one. The house, because of its high valuation and low rental projection makes it a bad investment for trying to make monthly income. The owner should sell the house and take the funds and invest it in an area where rents are high and property values lower.

You have to run your numbers carefully and know your market. A good rule of thumb to follow when investing in houses is what we will call the 1 percent rule. The monthly rent you collect should equal about 1 percent of the purchase price of the property. This should be your minimum standard. For instance; if you buy a house for $100,000, can you collect $1,000 per month rent from it; if you can collect more than that—great? If you are only able to collect $900 then that may be all right too, provided you are planning to raise rents in the next twelve months.

In good rental houses you will be able to fetch much better than 1% per month—1.3% to 2% and more can be collected from some good buys, especially with duplexes and triplexes and other larger unit buildings. In many parts of the United States, you can collect about 1.5 percent monthly rent of the price of the house; for example, a house that costs $60,000 could be rented for $900 per month. This is 1.5 percent of $60,000. This is a great rental return for a single family house.

The following is an example of a good investment.

Example: Rental House where Positive Cash Flow Works

West Palm Beach, Florida: An investor buys a four bedroom, one bath house for $160,000. It is currently rented for $1,200. After researching current market rental comparables in the area for four bedroom homes, it is realized the house is under rented and the rent should be increased to market rent of $1,460 a month. After the closing the rent is increased to the higher number. The investor puts up a down payment of $30,000 and has a $130,000 mortgage at 6.5% amortized over 30 years. His monthly mortgage payment is $821. Taxes and insurance come to $390 per month. Total monthly cash outlay is $1,211. And total monthly positive cash flow is $149 per month. Maintenance and repairs are not included. Now, this isn't a great monthly cash flow; but it is better that running negative cash flow per month.

---

2. *The down payment is small.* Typically, when a down payment is under 20%, monthly cash flow is usually nonexistent for rental houses unless the investor has secured an interest only payment schedule with a balloon payment typically due sometime in one to seven years. The plan in this situation would be to sell the house quickly and secure a high capital return.

3. *The property is in bad shape.* When a property is in bad shape and needs a lot of repairs before it can be rented or sold, generally the short-term cash flow will be nil. If an investor has purchased a fixer-upper for $100,000 and invests another $20,000 for the fix-up, which takes two months (slow contractor), a positive cash flow could be attained once the fix-up is completed and the house is rented within the third month. By using the same four bedrooms, one bath house in West Palm Beach, Florida that we used above, we could show a nice profit each month colleting $1,400 each month. Let's see how it works out:

You buy a fixer-upper for $100,000. You put down $20,000 and have a mortgage of $80,000 at 6.5%, amortized over 30 years. Your monthly mortgage payment is $505 and taxes and insurance another $290 per month, for a total monthly outlay of $795. You collect $1,300 rent, showing a $505 positive cash flow.

There is another way of figuring out what the expenses will be. By using a straight 25 percent deduction from the monthly gross for repairs, maintenance, taxes, and insurance, the total would come to $325. After deducting the $325 and the mortgage payment of $505, you are left with a positive cash flow of $470. Since unexpected expenses and certain repairs are hard to predict, it is wise to use 25 percent of the gross income to be allotted for these expenditures when you are determining a figure for expenses.

Remember, in general, a house will eat-up about 20 percent to 25 percent of the gross income that will go to expenses. This number would also allow a vacancy rate for the entire year. And typically multi-unit buildings and apartments eat-up about 45 percent to 50 percent of your gross. Of course, these percentages are not fixed, and your expenses could be much lower or even greater if you are lacking in some basic managerial skills or choose a very poor location; but in general, this is a good rule of thumb to follow.

Because the house was vacant for two months for fix-up, you had negative cash flow of $1,660 and another $20,000 was invested for the fix up. With the down payment of $20,000, you are out of pocket a total of $41,660.

This time, using the same house, you've decided to fix and flip the property—you have no interest in renting it. You list the house for sale for $179,500, about $15,000 lower than comparables. It stays on the market for three months and you finally sell it for $168,000. With two months taken for repairs and another three months to sell, you lose another $830 per month on mortgage payments and other expenses totaling $4,150. You paid a $5,040 (3%) to the buyers agent (you did not use a sellers agent). Title insurance and other miscellaneous insurance have come to $1,500. Your grand profit in five months is:

Purchase Price	$100,000
Repairs	20,000
Carrying Costs	4,150
Sales Commission Paid	5,040
Closing cost from sale	1,500
Total Costs of Property	$130,690
Sales Price	$168,000
Profit	37,310
Total Cash Outlay	44,150

($20,000 down; $20,000 repairs; $4,150 carrying costs)

Total return on invested cash: 84.5% for six months.

---

4. *Investor lacks imagination and desire to create more income.* Sometimes this has to do with prioritizing. Landlords are busy. They are sometimes working full-time jobs or have careers outside of investing in real estate. Other times, managing property is not very interesting; it's more exciting to find the right property at the right price, and then do the deal. Many investors fall into this paradox; it is fun to find the property and acquiring it at your price and your terms, this part makes real estate interesting; however, the day-to-day management of property is a bore for many investors. And many investors find it difficult to escape this attitude toward managing property. If we put the duties of managing property (tenants) into prospective, it is one of the highest paying jobs in the world, given the amount of

hours expended and the income that one receives. Where else can you get a check in the mail for $1,700 every month and spend two hours a month working for it? Most times you won't even spend one hour a month managing a tenant in a rental house.

Other landlords feel that an addition $20 or $30 per month is not a big deal and don't really bother with raising rents or investigating other means to increase income. It's true, $30 per month will not make you rich with one property—that is only an extra $360 per year. However, $360 over a five or ten year period really begins to add-up. And the effort it takes to initiate a rent raise, is certainly worth it. But what if you own fifty rental homes or even a hundred. With fifty homes, that $30 per month, just became worth $1,500 per month and $18,000 per year. And with a hundred homes, $3,000 per month and $36,000 per year, extra. You can see that a little change can create a big change under different circumstances.

A few years ago there was a landlord in Los Angeles who owned over 2,000 units. He decided to raise all the rents at one time. He sent rent increase letters to all his tenants. We believe he increased the average rent by $100 or thereabout. With this rent increase, he increased his monthly income by $200,000. Wasn't that a nice increase to his cash flow? You should do the same.

How Do You Project Your Future Cash Flow?

This isn't as difficult as you might think. When your objective is to hold a rental house for the long-term and have it rented, your cash flow projection can be compiled easily. Simply take your estimated expenses and deduct them from the total income you will receive. Your income will include all rents and all other ancillary income.

Cash Flow on Rental House

Example: House purchased vacant and need of repairs before rentable

	The Day You Purchased the Property	Two Months After Purchase
Monthly rental income	$0	$1,200
Total monthly income	0	1,200
Total annual income	0	$14,400
Purchase price:	$47,000	
Down payment	47,000	
Mortgage:	0	
Annual Expenses		
Mortgage payment	$0	
Property taxes		940
Insurance		980
Water/Electric		300

80

Maintenance/Repairs		22,000
Vacancies	3,600 (12 months from day of purchase)	
Total cash out	$27,820	
Total annual income	14,400	
Total first 12 months cash flow	<13,420>	
Total second year cash flow	$12,480	
Total third year cash flow	$15,120 (5% rent increase)	

This house was purchased at a HUD auction for cash for $47,000. It was uninhabitable and repairs came to $22,000. After completing the repairs, the house, a 4 bedroom, 2 bath Spanish eclectic style home was rented for three years and sold for $195,000 to another investor. A real estate agent was not used in the transaction and no sales commissions were paid. With a cost of $47,000 and another $22,000 invested on repairs, the house returned a $126,000 profit or 183% from the sale and another $14,180, the total positive cash flow over the past three years. Total return of $140,180 over the three year period with a cash outlay of $69,000 shows a 203% return or roughly a 27% annual compounded return. When the property was repaired after the second month, it should have been put up for sale at a below market price of $160,000. If it had sold within the first twelve months, it would have returned a profit of $91,000 or 132% profit. That would have been the best strategy, especially in a sellers market. If you are not familiar with the term *sellers market*, it is simply a market that has appreciated rapidly and sellers are receiving nice prices based on appreciation.

Increasing Cash Flow

Increasing cash flow should be a recurring thought on the mind of every investor. There are numerous ways to increase cash flow and depending on the size and type of property you have, can determine the cash flow methods you can employ. Placing a coin-operated laundry facility in a rental house does not make much sense. This, most of us understand. However, placing a coin-operated laundry in your 20 unit building does make sense and could increase your monthly cash flow by $200 to $300 or more, depending on the size of the units.

Creating ancillary income can play a big part to increasing your cash flow. A lot has to do with the extra time and energy you put into creating new revenue generation from your captive audience—your tenants.

Top 10 Ways to Increase Monthly Cash Flow with Little Hassle

1. *Application Fee.* We discussed earlier in the book on charging an application fee. This is a fee that should be charged to everyone who wants to rent from you. A $50 minimum fee with an additional fee of $25 per adult (18 years of age) living in the unit. This fee is nonrefundable and part of it

will be used for credit checks and your time to call on references and employers and to verify other information on the application.

2. *Late rent fee.* Typically, you should charge a late rent fee of 10 percent of the total monthy rent amount. Hopefully, you will never need to collect a late rent fee--but this would be highly unlikely. Late rent fees do add up, so don't neglect to collect them and make it a business practice that your tenants know they have to pay-up when they are late with the rent.

3. *Pet fee.* Nearly 60 percent of all households have pets. If you decide to not allow pets, you will alienate a large possible tenant population. You will also eliminate the possibility of receiving a monthly pet fee. Pet fees can range from $10 to $50 per month or more, depending on the pet and the number of pets.

Pets can cause damage—so we tack-on an additional security deposit of $250—with large dogs you can charge $250 per dog. Dogs are the big culprit when it comes to damage. They scratch doors, ruin carpets and dig holes in yards. To compensate for these things, you charge a reasonable monthly pet rent and an adequate extra security deposit—it's that simple. The extra income you make by accepting pets is well worth the damage they may potentially cause. The nice thing about charging pet rent, is that, it costs you nothing to implement. We have enclosed a comprehensive pet agreement in the Appendix and there is a simpler pet agreement attached to the tenants lease.

4. *Laundry facility.* Having a laundry facility on the premise is a great convenience to your tenants. This is why you should charge more for the service than a Laundromat or other coin-operated store charges. If you have four or more units and they do not have a clothes washer or dryer hookup inside the units, it could make sense to install a coin-operated washer and dryer on the premises. Here are a few things you'll need to do:

(1) Find a location on the property
(2) You'll need water and electrical connection.
(3) Connection to a sewer line.
(4) Lower end machines will costs $1,400 for pair.
(5) Installation and build-out could cost $500-$2,000.

We have available at www.MitchFreeland.com (available late 2018) book that covers nearly everything you need to know about installing and operating a coin-op washers and dryers. The book is: ***How to Maximize Profits with Coin-Operated Laundry & Vending Machines for Rental Property.*** Also, explained are the types of machines to use and breakdown of profit margins, in detail, depending on the size of your building and units. You could increase your cash flow by $100 to several thousand dollars per month with a laundry room. This can become a very lucrative business in and of itself, with very little work involved. The time you spend on your coin-op laundry could be less than 15 minutes per month. And you do not need a room to house your washer and dryer. Just find available space in a convenient area that has some shelter from rain and with nearby water hookup. Get the book—you won't regret it—it is worth investigating.

5. *Soda Machine.* With apartments of 15 or more units, a soda machine can gross between $150-$200 per month. You can purchase soda from 23-28 cents each and charge 75 cents or $1 per soda. Electricity to run the machine will cost $30 to $50 per month depending on your location. Soda

machines are free from Coke or Pepsi as long as you buy your sodas from a distributor. A distributor will also deliver to your location. Operating a machine, however, does require some work and may not be worth the hassle for a monthly net profit of $100. If you have a larger apartment of 40 or 50 units, then you could show a monthly profit of $300 to $500 per month. You will need to stock the machine about once per week. This will take you or your helper about 15 minutes.

You also need a place to store the sodas. You can find a location next to or near your laundry room. This is also a good location for other vending machines if you decide to go this route. If you have larger apartment buildings, you could try a machine or two and see how you like it.

With soda and laundry machines you must think long-term. The money you make on a monthly basis may not seem like much, but over the course of a year or two or three, the money starts to look like something worthwhile.

6. *Increase the number of bedrooms*. When you have a rental home with an extra large family room or bedroom, you can erect a wall or two and install a door and create another bedroom. A 3 bedroom home will rent for $100 to $200 more per month than a 2 bedroom home. Always lookout for extra large rooms that can be divided into two rooms. You also increase the value of the property by adding more rooms even when you are not adding more square footage. Building a wall or two and insulting a door can cost anywhere from $300 to $2500. You will also be required to install a window if there isn't one situated in the right place (a window need not lead to the outside—check with local building codes on this requirement). The price of installing a wall or two and a door would depend on who does the work and the configuration of the build-out. On the low-side, your payback would take about 3 months. On the high-side your payback would take 10 to 25 months. In the long run, you will make out well.

7. *Unit upgrades*. Make sure you are charging the right rent for the amenities you are offering; for example, if you have a scenic balcony in one of your units, don't rent it for the same price as a unit without a balcony. You could probably get an extra $15 to $25 more per month for the balcony. Also, a larger one bedroom unit should typically rent for more than a smaller one bedroom unit. Even if the extra large unit rents for $10 or $20 more—it all goes to the bottom line.

A dishwasher is an upgraded amenity in older buildings, therefore, you should charge an extra $10 to $15 per month for it.

8. *Reducing or eliminating expenses*. This can be completed by monitoring all of your expenses and determining if the check you are writing each month to pay for those expenses is necessary.

9. *Lower rents*. Sometimes in deflating markets, you will need to reduce rents to fill your units. Don't let pride get in the way to you lowing rents. Filled units with paying tenants is better than having vacant units. You could always raise rents when the market firms-up.

10. *Raise rents*. Check the rental rates in your area—and if your units are under rent, raise rents across the board when leases expire. Raising rents is typically the first method you should employ to increase cash flow. An increase of $30 per unit in a four unit building will add $120 per month to your cash flow. With 20 units, that is an addition $600 per month and $7,200 per year. Learn to manage your rents closely. The extra cash generated from simply increasing rental rates can add-up significantly over the long-term and at the same time boost the value of the property.

What Expenses Can you Reduce or Eliminate Permanently

Nothing is ever permanent, but you could eliminate some expenses for several years when you have the right tenant—tenant selection is critical. When you rent your investment house to a good tenant, many expenses can be eliminated. These expenses will include:

1. *Water and Garbage bills.* From a rental house standpoint, tenants pay the water and garbage bills. Most multi-unit buildings have one water meter along with one garbage bill. You can divide the bill and separately charge tenants individually. This will become a problem if the rent is too high. Most owners of multi-family buildings pay for the water and garbage; this has become standard in the industry, but it doesn't mean you have to go along with it. You can always bill it out and see what kind of a response you get from your tenants. Some of your tenants may pay it without making a fuss and other tenants may start looking for somewhere to move to if your rentals are already priced at or above their comfort level.

2. *Electrical bill.* Tenant pays this bill in a house also. In separately metered apartments, tenants pay their own electric bill. In a master metered (one electric meter for all units) building the landlord can separate the bill and have each tenant pay their share depending on the square footage of each unit.

3. *Gardening and landscaping.* Tenant is responsible for all lawn and garden care when renting a house.

4. *General maintenance.* If you have good tenants, they will make small repairs without bothering you and they are more respectful of private property. This could eliminate the costs of many small repairs that may occur over the years.

5. *Private Mortgage Insurance* (PMI). Get the equity of the home back over twenty percent and get rid of the mortgage insurance.

6. *Windstorm, earthquake and flood insurance.* These are endorsements or add-ons to your insurance policy you may not need; usually they are all a waste of money, unless you are in a very low lying area where flooding is frequent; then you might feel more comfortable with flood insurance; but still, it is insurance that you could eliminate. Other endorsements might include riot insurance, loss of rent and inflation guard. Check your policy and cancel these endorsements, they are generally a waste of money and you could bring your insurance premium down significantly.

7. *Self insure.* If you own the property free and clear, you won't be forced by a mortgage company to carry a home owner's policy. Stop paying the insurance company and take whatever your premiums were and put it in a separate account. You could even call it house insurance; for example, if your premiums were $2,000 per year, you could put aside $166 per month in an interest bearing account. Only use the money for emergency repairs; don't touch it if you do not need it.

Typically, a major disaster that cause great damage to your property is rare It may be a good idea to carry liability insurance, personal injury, since you will have people living in your rental property.

8. *Late payment penalties and fines.* You can eliminate these completely if you pay your bills on time.

Example: House purchased with tenant.

	The Day You Purchased the Property		Two Months After Purchase
Monthly rental income		$1,000	$1,300
Satellite Fee	0	15	
Total monthly income	$1,000	$1,315	
Total annual income	$12,000	$15,780	

Purchase price: $85,000
Down payment: 17,000 (20%)
Mortgage: 68,000 amortized for 30 years at 7%

Annual Expenses (First 12 months)		Annual Expenses (Second 12 months)
Mortgage payment	$ 566	$ 566
Property taxes	1,700	1,700
Insurance	2,000	2,000
Water/Electric	200 (2 months)	0
Maintenance/Repairs	7,000 (fix-up costs)	0
Total cash out	11,466	4,266

After the first 12 months you show a positive cash flow of $1,684. This takes into account of 2 months vacancy for fix-up and fix-up costs and utilities of $7,200.

With income of $15,780 and expenses of $4,266 in the second 12 month period you show a positive annual cash flow of $11,514.

After 24 months your out of pocket cash on cash investment of $24,200 has returned $13,198 or 55 percent return on rental and ancillary income only. The appreciation on fix-up and buying at the right price would give you another 40 to 50 percent return. The property would be valued at $125,000 to $150,000. This is the right return you would have on your property.

Operating Statement From a Single-Family Home Rental

Operating Statement From A Single-Family Home Rental

	Monthly	Annually
Gross Scheduled Income (3 bed/2 bath)	$1,250	$15,000
Less vacancy factor of 5%	63	756
Gross Operating Income	$1,187	$14,244
Expenses		
Property Taxes	$150	$1,800
Insurance	100	1,200
Utilities	10	120
Management	0	0
A. Lawn care	5	60
B. Maintenance/Repairs	10	120
C. Supplies	2	24
D. Legal	0	0
E. Accounting	30	360
Total Expenses	$307	$3,684
Net Income	$880	$10,560
Less Debt Service ($60,000 @ 7%, 30 years)	500	6,000
Cash Flow	$ 380	$4,560

Operating Statement From A 16 Unit Apartment

Operating Statement From A 16 Unit Apartment

	Monthly	Annually
Gross Scheduled Income	$11,200	$134,400
Other Income		
Laundry	220	2,640
Vending (Soda)	200	2,400
Less Vacancy Factor of 5%	560	6,720
Gross Operating Income	$11,060	$132,720
Expenses:		
Property Taxes	$1,725	$20,700
Insurance	542	6,500
Utilities/Garbage	360	4,320
Management	400	4,800
A. Lawn/Grounds Keeping	60	720
B. Maintenance/Repairs	120	1,440
C. Supplies	40	480
D. Legal	67	804
E. Accounting	60	720
F. Laundry/Vending	70	840
Total Expenses	3,444	41,328
Net Income	$7,616	$91,392
Less Debt Service ($550,000 @ 7% for 30 years	$3,680	$44,160
Cash Flow	$3,936	$47,232

One of our 16 unit buildings that was purchased as a fixer-upper. Each unit was rehabed and rents were increased. For several years it was fully leased-up.

Cash Flow & Co.: A Super-System For Real Estate Investors

Because cash flow is so important to a real estate investor, we've have designed a book devoted to increasing cash flow and reducing expenses. We strongly recommend as a companion to this book, ***Cash Flow & Co.: A Super-System For Real Estate Investors***. (Release date Summer 2019)

There are over fifty ways described in *Cash Flow & Co.* on how to increase income substantially from your real estate holdings. The techniques used in the book are proven and have been applied by us and other successful investors. The strategies and methods used in the book will make or save you thousands and even tens of thousands of dollars each year. The book is designed for increasing cash flow for investors with one rental house, multiple rental houses, apartments and even commercial space. Everyone with rental property should add this book to their real estate investment library. This is an excellent reference guide and should be read and reviewed frequently. The book is jammed packed with straight forward and reliable information to help make you money and increase your monthly cash flow and build equity. The methods in the book are used for both active and passive investors with a passion for learning and a desire to increase income through many ancillary and methods.

You can go directly to **Amazon, eBay** or www.MitchFreeland.com to get your copy. It will be one of the best investments you make—we guaranteed it. By implementing just one strategy you will be in a position to make thousands perhaps millions.

This apartment contained 16 units. It was acquired with 15 vacant units. Each unit was rehabed and fully leased-up within sixty days. We bought the property for $450,000 with rehab costs of $60,000. The property was appraised for $1,550,000 six years later. We managed the property for several years securing solid cash flow.

INTRODUCTORY DISCUSSION ON CASH FLOW AND CASH FLOW ANALYSIS ON REAL ESTATE INVESTING

When you're projecting your cash flow goals for the short-term (one year) or for the long-term (over one year), you might want to include the following financial objective:

1) Establish a minimum of cash on cash return for the first year of 8% and higher in the longer term.

2) Establish a minimum Internal Rate of Return (IRR: Your projected holding period over your overall return, including income and appreciation) for your holding period; for example, if you plan to hold the property for exactly one year and with value added fix-up, appreciation, and positive rental income, you could expect an IRR of 50% for the first year.

3) Establish an occupancy level of over 97% in your rental units.

Every real estate investor's goal should be to buy property for less than its intrinsic value. In the real estate investment world, a true investor should buy property that has a present value, after repairs and fix-up, of a minimum 30% from actual costs of the property. This is after the "fix-up." 30% is a minimum figure and a more realistic percentage would be about 50% for both houses and apartments. Our average gain above 55% of purchase price and fix-up costs. For example, if we buy a house for $100,000 and put another $40,000 in fix up, we generally will expect the house to be worth $217,000. We have created $77,000 in equity or 55% over all gain. In a market where there are many foreclosure bargains, you will come across properties that will give you over 100% profit over your purchase and fix-up costs.

Models

There are typically two decision based models: (1) a single period model (one year); and (2) a multi-period model (multiple years).

Single period models include:

- *Cash on Cash return (CC).* Cash flow before taxes over your cash equity.

- *Gross Rent Multiplier (GRM).* Purchase price of the property divided by its annual gross income (rents, laundry and all other income collected from the property. The lower the GRM, the greater the possibility for a positive investment.

- *Capitalization Rate (CAP Rate).* All the income of the property, subtracting all expenses, except debt service; then, divided by the purchase price.

Your *multi-period model* would include your Internal Rate of Return (IRR).

Financial Feasibility

When determining the feasibility of an investment property, there are a number of financial ratios you should use. Some are *Leverage Ratios* and others *Operating Ratios.* A Leverage Ratio is simply the debt to equity or borrowed funds to ones own funds.

The Operating Ratio shows the efficiency of the operation. This ratio is also the Operating Expense Ratio (OER) and it is a ratio that determines the cost and maintenance of income properties. It is the ratio of operating expenses and the effective gross income.

- Gross Rent Multiplier
- Loan to Value (LTV) Ratio (Leverage Ratio)
- Debt Coverage Ratio (Leverage Ratio)
- Breakeven point or payback timeframe (Operating Ratio)
- Expense Ratio (Leverage Ratio)
- Cash on Cash

- Return on Assets
- Internal Rate of Return
- After Tax Return on Equity
- Resale Price

Key Ratios and Calculations You Need to Know to Value Your Investment

The following will give you a better understanding of the ratios involved for deciphering the feasibility of choosing winning strategies for cash flow investments.

Gross Rent Multiplier (GRM): Purchase price over gross rent.

- *Loan to Value Ratio (LTV):* This measures your financial risk on your real estate. Your LTV is the mortgage loan balance over the purchase price. As the LTV rises, the default risk rises. A LTV of 75% is typical in real estate investment to maintain adequate cash flow.

- *Debt Coverage Ratio:* The Debt Coverage Ratio is your Net Operating Income over your Debt Service. To make your mortgage payment, your debt coverage ratio must be over 1.0. Lenders will typically require a debt coverage ration of 1.1 to 1.3.

- *Breakeven Point:* The Breakeven Point is your operating expenses and mortgage payments over your gross rent. The percentage of occupancy that a building must achieve to pay all of it's expenses and pay for it's financing; this is typically in the 65% to 95% range.

- *Expense Ratio:* The Expense Ratio is the operating expenses over the effective gross income. This should be high. It is typically high, about 45% to 50% for apartments and about 20% for smaller income properties, such as duplex or a rental house. The expense ratio can be much lower for a rental house that has recently been rehabbed, probably in the 10% to 15% range with good tenants.

- *Cash on Cash:* As mentioned earlier, this is your before tax cash flow over your cash equity. Cash on cash will measure your initial profitability; and the higher the better. In most Real Estate Investment Trust's (REITs), or large real estate investment companies, the typical cash on cash for the first year is between 4% and 10%. A small company or an individual investor can capture a cash on cash return over 12% by eliminating extraneous expenses and becoming more active in the management of the investment.

- *Return on Asset (Capitalization Rate):* This is your net operating income over your purchase price, typically called the "CAP Rate". CAP rates in expensive areas or the country typically range from 4% to 7%; and in better cash flow areas about 12%. An investor should be looking at investments that have a CAP Rate of 8% and higher. The higher the CAP Rate, the more debt you will be able to support. The CAP Rate is the overall return you receive on your investment.

- *Internal Rate of Return (IRR):* This includes the projected holding period over your overall return, including the rental growth rate and property value appreciation. The average IRR is 12% to 15% for large apartments and other real estate investments. The IRR can be well over 25% on more speculative investments including properties that need fix-up or on foreclosures.

- *After Tax Return on Equity:* Simply, after tax cash flow over cash equity. This is very similar to cash on cash; it takes into account tax incentives an depreciation. And it is typically 5% to 12% in the first year.

- *Resale Price:* This is of course, the Gross Rent Multiplier for your property, multiplied by the gross income of the property. Remember to deduct selling costs and commissions.

ACTION HIGHLIGHTS FOR YOUR CASH FLOW

1) Know how to define your cash flow.

2) Learn how to cure your negative cash flow situation.

3) Know how to project your future cash flow.

4) Learn and execute the proven ways to increase your cash flow.

5) Know what expenses to reduce or eliminate completely to increase your cash flow.

6) Obtain a copy of the five book set: ***Cash Flow & Co.: A Super-System for Real Estate Investors***. (www.FlippingBrothers.com) (Release winter 2016)

> *"Few things are seldom more important than positive cash flow for the long-term investor."*

4

Contractors and Labor

"Man is a reasoning, rather than a reasonable, animal."
—Alexander Hamilton

Note: This Chapter is also found in our book *The Millionaire Real Estate Flippers*. It is included here because as a landlord you will be in need of fixing up your rentals from time-to-time, making repairs, over-due updating and other renovations.

Before you decide to hire a contractor to make the repairs on a flip or any rental property, you should go through the property thoroughly and write down all the repairs, changes and clean-up that must be completed to get the property in rentable or saleable condition. Everything in the house should be functional and very clean. But if you want to sell right away, you will need to get the property in near perfect condition for a quick sale. This means investing a little more money.

After you have decided what to do with the property, your next step would be to interview contractors, subcontractors, handymen, and general laborers for hire. This group of individuals has not been categorized as the most reliable or business-like. A good example of this comes from the California Contractors State License Board which has over 230,000 licensed contractors. In fact, over 80 percent of the contractors who fail do so because of bad business skills—skill insufficiencies such as poor money management and the inability to bid correctly on projects is the number one reason most contractors fail in their chosen profession.

Nationally, because of poor skills, over 95 percent of contractors go out of business in the first five years. The reasons for this are numerous, and can be attributed from very poor business skills, dependence on alcohol and drugs and eventually theft and fraud. So, be prepared and work with people that you feel 100 percent comfortable with.

General Contractor (GC)

If you do not want to be involved managing the project, subcontractors or other general labor, you could hire a General Contractor. Your expense for the General Contractor will typically be 10 percent to 20 percent of the overall cost of the project—lean more toward the 20 percent.

Most General Contractors are rip-offs. They will mark-up everything: materials, labor, and of course, their time to manage the project. Most GCs will tell you they make 10 percent profit. It is more like 35 percent and higher because they take a piece of everything. GCs like to charge for *overhead*. Overhead is what a GC spends—his tax deductibles.

If all possible, I would not hire a general contractor. It is a waste of money. On a project expecting to cost $35,000, a GC will cost you $7,000 (20% low side), to manage your project. Remember, your average fix up will generally take 3 to 4 weeks. You could hire the subs (electrician, plumber, drywaller, etc.) yourself, and purchase all the materials and fixtures yourself as well. If you knowledgeable and handy with general fix up such as painting, replacing door knobs and faucets then you could do much of the work yourself. If you have the time, you can be your own GC, you will save 20 percent to 40 percent on the project.

One thing you should do when first starting out and you are unsure about the fix up cost is to get at least three bids from different GCs. These bids could vary drastically in price for the whole project. A 10 percent or 15 percent difference or greater would not be uncommon. On one project we was quoted by three different GCs: $25,000, $15,000 and $10,000. I went with the $10,000 bidder. He completed the project ahead of schedule, passed all inspections without hassle and I was extremely happy with his work. So, the lesson here is to check around if you feel you must hire a GC.

Subcontractors

Yours subcontractors include: roofers, plumbers, electricians, A/C installation, carpet and other flooring installers; and landscapers. If you hire a general contractor, he will be in charge of locating and contracting with qualified subcontractors. However, if you decide to act as the general contractor yourself, you will be responsible to locate, hire and sometimes fire these individuals. I highly recommend that you be your own GC.

Handyman

When you have a small project, such as painting, landscaping, and some small repairs (replacing door knobs), you may not need a general contractor or subcontractors, but you could use the service of a handyman. Some handymen are very good and some very bad, so get as many referrals as you can from friends, family, neighbors, or other investors. Check out HomeAdvisor.com for the skilled labor you need. A handyman will generally be cheaper than a contractor, but may not possess the necessary skills to complete all the tasks required. Make sure the handyman knows how to complete all the tasks involved before you sign a contract with him. Make sure they are fully insured and licensed.

Labor

Day laborers have very limited skills--remember this. Many do not have their own tools or transportation. These are things you would typically furnish. If you need very minor work completed, one or two laborers could do basic clean-up, painting and some landscaping--that is about it. The costs are minimal, usually about minimum wage. And you typically get what you pay for.

Doing it Yourself

When you have made your mind up to act as your own general contractor, you will be in charge of hiring subcontractors, handymen and laborers. You will also need to be flexible with your time. Here are a few things to consider when you are thinking about acting as your own general contractor:

1) You will need to spend the time to interview all subcontractors.

2) You will need to negotiate, hire, and fire contractors when needed.

3) You will need to make more time in your schedule to: (1) inspect the work being done; (2) estimate the time taken to complete each task; (3) run out and collect information on products; (4) purchase necessary items and materials; and (5) fill-out and file permits (if needed).

4) You will need to make a lot more decisions on materials to be used.

5) You will need to schedule around subcontractors and make sure the work environment between working groups is cooperative.

6) You will be dealing with inspectors and city stooges. Some are very fair and reasonable, and others appear to have woken-up on the wrong side of the bed every day of their lives; and some are just arrogant idiots.

Negotiating with Contractors

After you have gotten a quote from at least three contractors you should do the following:

1. Breakdown the cost per hour and gather a list of names and phone numbers of people who will be working on the project.

2. Estimate the cost of building materials with the contractor. Visit your local Home Depot or Lowe's or check online for prices. Make sure the prices you are quoted are similar or cheaper to the prices the contractor has quoted.

Check your item prices, such as specific hardware, faucets, sinks, tiles or interior doors, and get an estimated price. Sometimes the contractor will be able to beat the prices at the retail stores, and he should be buying items wholesale. Ask the contractor for pricing on your specific items you want, such as faucets, sinks, toilets and so on.

Sample Bid

The following is an example of a fix-up bid on a rehab:

To get a 3 bedroom, 1 bath house in near perfect condition inside and out, with updated kitchen and bath, paint and landscaping, and refinishing hardwood floors, a contractor has given you a quote of $18,000 which doesn't include specific items or material costs.

You should ask the contractor the following questions after you have chosen the specific items you what to use, such as tile design and size, faucet styles and so on.

1) What is the material cost for the kitchen?
2) What is the material cost for the bathroom?

3) How much paint will you be using inside and out?
4) How many people will be working on the project?
5) What is your hourly rate? What is the hourly rate for your employees and subcontractors?

Compare material costs with prices from your local Home Depot or Lowe's. Subtract all the costs of materials and supplies. And what is left—the labor costs. Divide the labor costs over the timeframe expected for completion of the project and narrow the dollar amount per hour, per worker. If the per hour rate comes to over $35 per worker, you are paying too much to the general contractor. At $35 per hour, you are paying labor $280 per day each. That is absurd. Skilled labor should be between $120 and $175 per day or about $15 to $22 per hour. Typically, the general contractor will charge between 10% to 20% of the total costs of the project.

Always explain to the contractor, you are getting other bids. Ask: "What is your best price?" After he gives you a number, which can take him a while to figure out, ask: "I have other bids, can you do better?" After his response, ask, "Do you think that is fair?" Always be shocked at the first price. Contractors always think you have plenty of money at your disposal. Explain, you are on a very tight budget and you cannot afford time delays and redo work. Explain to the contractor you are looking for a long-term relationship with a serious, skilled and professional contractor, then break his price down at least 10%.

Your contractor or handyman should be insured, licensed and bonded.

If you feel uneasy about any contractor, do not hire him. Professionalism is paramount. There are a lot of fly-by-night individuals in the construction trade—it's just part of the fix-up business.

When you find a contractor or handyman who is knowledgeable, fair, honest and punctual, keep his name and number handy for future work.

Who Not to Hire

Someone once said, "Never hirer anyone you wouldn't invite home to have dinner with you or your family." There are certainly many people you wouldn't think of inviting home for dining, since most people these days simply do not have formal diners. However, who would you invite over for a barbeque? Would you invite the people you hire into your home? You have to feel very comfortable with the people you hire; not only must they be competent in there job, but they must also be extraordinarily trustworthy.

The list compiled below of, "Who not to hire" is not in a hierarchal order—so, the first one listed is in no way more important than the last; each is extremely important in its own right. Furthermore, this list is based on our experiences dealing with these types of characters over the years.

1. *Obese people.* Obese contractors, handymen and laborers have a predisposition to working slow. Time is money, remember. Obese workers move slow, work slower and have problems completing tasks in small places. They take more breaks that cost you more money. And they simply have low stamina.

There are underlying psychological problems that all obese people posses; and you do not want these problems consuming your project. By obese, we don't mean people 20 or 50 pounds overweight, we mean those individuals probably 80 pounds and greater over recommended normal weight.

2. *Without transportation or tools.* Anyone who says he is a carpenter or contractor and does not

have his own tools or transportation is simply not believable. Be leery of contractors and handymen without a truck. And those who do not own any transportation have usually lost their drivers license, either from a DUI or from a consistent pattern of reckless driving. Handymen and contractors without tools may have temporarily loaned them to a pawn shop. Forget about them.

3. *People without personal character references.* Ask for personal references. You should visit properties that the contractor has worked on and talk to the homeowner or investor: Were they satisfied with the quality of the work? Was it completed on schedule? If character references cannot be produced, then move on to the next contractor or handyman.

4. *People fresh out of prison.* It's nice to give people a second, third or fourth chance and we have done our share of it; however, in the long-run it has never worked out. Many times people fresh out of jail or prison start off alright, especially if they have learned a trade; but the vast majority are not skilled enough and there are underlying psychological problems with a large majority of ex-cons. Many had and still may have, drug and alcohol related problems which eventually becomes exposed after a few weeks of being on the job. Remember, every new worker puts on an act the first couple of weeks; they know they are on a probationary period so they behave themselves--that is, most of them. But sooner or later, many fall back into the character they are most comfortable with. Do you know the story of the turtle and the scorpion? If not, here is a story that may explain a simple truth:

A flood was coming and a turtle was on the riverbank ready to cross the river to safety, when a scorpion approached him: "Hello turtle," said the scorpion. "If you are going across the river could I travel on your back? I do not know how to swim and I am afraid I will die from the flood."

"But you are a scorpion and you will sting me and kill me," said the turtle.

"Oh no I won't, I promise I will not sting you. You will save my life: Why would I sting you? Please take me across the river; I promise I will not sting you, please help me now, the water is rising.

The turtle had a good heart and believed the scorpion would not hurt him. "Okay scorpion, crawl onto my back and I will take you across the river."

When they finally reached the other side of the river, the scorpion crawled off the turtle, said thank you, and then stung him.

"Scorpion!" the turtle snapped. "Why did you sting me? You promised you wouldn't, and I saved your life from the flood."

The scorpion replied: "I am a scorpion, that is my character, and that is what I do.

Writing letters to the court and their P.O. (Parole Officer) takes time; and you have better things to do. So, the lesson of the story is to be very leery of hiring workers fresh out of jai—you just might get stung.

5. *Out of state license plates.* Be cautious of contractors with out of state license plates, they are usually not licensed. During times of disasters, such as hurricanes, many fly-by-night handymen and contractors come from out of state to take advantage of homeowners and investors with damaged properties. Many do not complete the job, take the money, and split town.

6. *Unlicensed contractors*. If you are doing minor work, it isn't always necessary to hire a licensed contractor when a handyman or even an individual who is competent in moderate tasks can do the job.

Unlicensed contractors are generally not as proficient in following code requirements as a licensed contractor. Do not hire an unlicensed contractor for major plumbing, electrical or major construction unless you know the individual very, very well and you are familiar with his work and the level of his competency. Moreover, his work must be up to par with the local code or the Uniform Building Code.

7. *Unqualified contractors*. An unqualified contractor is an individual who does not know how to do the work required, he simply acts as a middleman when hired an contractor; he doesn't know code and does not know how to judge other workers competency. He is also unlicensed or uses a license of another contractor for a fee.

8. *Vulgar language and racial remarks*. When you are interviewing contractors, you may, from time to time, come in contact with contractors and handymen who displace a plethora of vulgar language, or during the interview make racial remarks and innuendos. Do not hire these types of people no matter how competent they appear in rehabbing properties. These people do not make good managers and they already have a negative attitude.

9. *Talks to much as an authority*. Again, during the interview process, when the interviewee will not shut his mouth about everything he knows about rehab, it is best to cut the interview short and let him go. You can't make time for a boaster or a blowhard. And typically, most bigmouths do not know or know how to execute everything they believe they are an authority on.

10. *Negative attitude*. During the interview, you will be exposed to a person's energy level and whether he has a general positive or negative attitude about his work and life in general. If his energy level is low and he posses a negative attitude, or one not in sync with yours…next please.

11. *Physically unfit*. No need to hire a contactor, handyman or laborer who is physically unfit and complains about pain or fatigue.

12. *Who talks of filing discrimination suits*. After asking an interviewee what were the circumstances behind her leaving her previous employer, she replied, "they were racist and I filed a discrimination suit against them." This is someone you do not want to hire. Unfortunately, such things happen. You want people that can get along with others and have an easy going past history. Attitude plays a big role and you want workers with a good and pleasant attitude. One bad apple can spoil the bunch. You are not looking to hire potential trouble.

13. *Lots of legal action pending*. Some people with prior legal problems seem to never escape legal actions. This can range from almost anything from DUI problems, drug problems, dealing or possession, battery, expired car registrations and insurance and even domestic issues like child or wife beating and a host of other problems. People that are involved with a lot of legal actions are always taking time off, and for most, time on the job is not productive time. Emotional issues frequently appear at the job site. You should always use your judgment and if the worker becomes unproductive—let him go.

14. *Alcoholics and drug users*. Only problems are created with these individuals. You should terminate anyone who drinks on the job or you suspect is drugged-up.

15. *Contractor who can't speak or understand English or your native language*. Well, it happens—we had an interviewee who brought an interpreter with him to the interview. The contractor could not speak English and we did not speak fluent Spanish. Misunderstood communication is the number one problem between contractors and investors. It is hard enough when everyone speaks the same language but when the project manager or general contractor does not understand you…you have a problem. Therefore, you should not hire anyone you cannot understand. This might appear to be common sense, but when you are in a bind and need to complete your project more people seem to fit your qualifications. However, a general contractor or subcontractor that you cannot communicate with would seem like a nightmare waiting to happen. As long as the project manager or contractor understands English or your native tongue, that's fine. There are many Hispanic workers who are limited in the English language. With a bilingual English/Spanish speaking manager or contractor, many projects can move along quickly.

When to Fire

You will need to use a great deal of personal judgment when you decide to fire the contractor, handyman or laborer.

Drinking and drugs: Anytime there is alcohol consumed on the job or a worker shows-ups for work and there is evidence of drinking, it is grounds for termination; and ditto regarding drug use. You should have a "zero tolerance" attitude towards this type of behavior. Too many accidents and sloppy workmanship are its result. It is also a fact that most drug addicts will eventual steal from you to support their habit.

After about a year into doing rehab investing, we hired a part-time handyman to do some simple maintenance. Part of his responsibilities included keeping-up the landscaping and mowing lawns of some of the properties we owned. It was much cheaper to have him do the work than hire a regular gardener to service the yards twice per month. He used our mower and other tools necessary to do the job. After making a drive by several properties, it was obvious the lawns were not mowed. Strike one. And after talking to the handyman, he apologized and said he would get to it right away and that the mower was at his brother's house. After questioning why it was there. He said his brother needed to borrow it. Strike two.

A day or two passed and the lawns were still not cut and the yards had become unkempt. After questioning him again, he explained again that the mower was at his brothers. The situation didn't smell right and after requesting the phone number of his brother, he finally broke down and began to sob like a little girl searching for a lost doll. All of a sudden, his emotions took complete control over him. Surprising as it was, he confessed that the mower and other tools totaling about $700 were at a pawn shop. He had hawked our property to raise enough money to purchase crack. The pawn tickets totaled $170. I went to the pawn shop, paid for the items and had him work off the $170 and then some more for troubling us before we fired him.

A very common situation that occurs with drug attics is theft—so be very careful of whom you hire, and keep track of your tools.

Excessive tardiness: Contractors and other workers who have a pattern of excessive tardiness should be dealt with in one of three ways: (1) after the second time, talk to them about the time and money wasted by their tardiness; (2) if the tardiness is not cured, deduct money from the time missed, in 15 minute increments; and (3) tell the consistently tardy to hit the road--he isn't serious about his job, and his excessive tardiness shows his lack of respect for you and the men that work with him.

Poor workmanship: Poor workmanship should never be tolerated. And an individual, who consistently, after being informed of his poor workmanship, persists on doing sloppy and unprofessional work, should be let go. Some workers have a completely different idea as to what is acceptable; they come from third-world nations or very poor or blighted areas where mediocre workmanship is acceptable.

Redo work: Constant redo work costs money and time. And typically this is a result due to: (1) workers unable to follow instructions; (2) poor skill level; (3) poor attitude and understanding of professionalism and acceptable workmanship; and (4) lack of communication skills and instruction from project manager, general contractor or you.

If workmanship is sloppy and items and materials are ruined, have the worker or the contractor pay for the materials wasted and time spend for redoing it. If the redo work is completely overwhelming and the project manager or contractor is not doing the job to your specification, then you may be forced to replace the culprits.

When a contractor or laborer begins to make mistakes by not following instructions and the mistakes are continually costing you money, be quick to fire after the second mistake. Typically, people in the construction trade should know their business. If the individual in question does not improve quickly, fire him. You want to be quick to fire and take your time to hire.

Lying: Lies typically beget more lies. If you catch someone lying, terminate immediately; the person can not be trusted and the lying will more than likely happen again and again until he is caught and finally dealt with. Liars will always get fired because there are usually other character flaws that they possess that will expedite there termination.

Stealing: Anyone caught stealing should be terminated and perhaps even prosecuted; prosecution would be a judgment call—a call which you would pursue given the seriousness and value of the crime. If you suspect a worker in stealing, confront him and others to expose the truth.

Here is an incident that happened to us a few years back:

We had purchased four brand new window box air conditioners to be installed in two apartment units we were rehabbing. We stored them in a vacant apartment; they were to be installed the next day. They stayed in the vacant apartment for two nights. When we instructed the foreman to install them, he told us they were not in the room. After questioning everyone about the missing air conditioners, we came to the realization that they had been stolen. Our first suspicions fell on the people working for us. We questioned them, but we could not prove anything. There was no break-in, so the thief had a key to the apartment or one of the workers left a window or the door unlocked.

The case was never really solved until a month later. We were rehabbing another project and had purchased a ceiling fan to be installed. The fan was given directly to the foreman—the same man in charge when the four air conditioners were stolen. He was given instructions to install the fan the same day he received it. The following day the fan was still not installed. When asked why the fan hadn't been installed, he replied he did not have a fan to install. This was crazy—he was given the fan the previous day. I had handed the fan directly to him.

Later that afternoon we told the foreman to meet us at one of the vacant apartment units. We had a short conversation with him and accused him of stealing the fan and stealing the air conditioners. He didn't defend himself and he did not deny it. He broke out in a rage, pounded the table several times with his fists, and then began laughing loudly. He then said something to the effect of: "If I'm fired, I want my money for this weeks pay." We told him he was not getting a penny and to get lost and to never show his face around our properties again. We never saw him again. We found out later he, his wife and son all had a drug problem.

Over billing: Anytime you feel you are being over billed, you should discuss it with the contractor or handyman and have it resolved immediately. If there is evidence of purposely flagrant or reckless over billing, do not pay it. Question every receipt, and if you are still suspicious, you want to see where every fixture, item or materials were used and who did the work. Refer to *Poor judgment and buying skills*, for ways to resolve the issue.

Unorganized: Some contractors take on more than they can handle; they try to work on several projects at the same time trying to manage labor and sub-contractors at different locations. One must be extremely organized to manage workers at different locations. When mistakes are repeated and time schedules are broken and extended, it is time to have a discussion with the contractor and his over burdened undertakings. You should be talking to your contractor daily regarding timeframes on completing individual tasks, and if still on schedule of completing the project on time regardless of setbacks.

Poor judgment and buying skills: Over the course of a renovation, poor judgment and buying skills of your contractor could cost you plenty. Review receipts at least once per week and count the heads working on your unannounced visits to the property. If you do find that the contractor or handyman does not have the basic cost efficient buying skills that he should posses, have a serious talk with him and come to a resolution as to his particular shortcomings. There are four ways to resolve this issue: (1) Do not pay for the items at all; the contractor will have to eat the price; (2) have the contractor pay the difference from the more suitable and less expensive item; (3) you have to start doing all the material buying, whereby exuding a great deal of your time; (4) if items have not been yet used or installed, have the contractor return them and exchange for the more suitable less expensive item. You should then deduct money from his pay for time wasted. If there are several incidences of poor judgment and recurring problems regarding buying materials, you may need to terminate the contractor for simple lack of experience and knowledge and for being led to believe in his competence as a professional.

Uncooperative complainer: Any contractor or worker who is consistently uncooperative in following through with instructions and/or is a habitual complainer should be let go immediately. Complainers have a way of ruining the attitude of all workers and resentment from all the other workers quickly forms against him.

Characteristics of a Professional Contractor and Handyman

Here are a few character qualities you should look for in a contractor or handyman. All the qualities are extremely important.

- Positive Attitude
- Professionalism
- Reliable
- Dependable
- Accountable
- Trustworthy
- Time and money conscious (knows how to save time and money on your project, and presents you with lots of ideas)
- Knowledgeable
- Excellent communication skills
- Excellent references
- Respected by workers (If a contractor or handyman has all the aforementioned qualities, then this is a given).

Locating Reliable Contractors

- Church. If you attend church, this is the perfect place to start
- Club Affiliations – Real Estate Clubs and Meetup Groups
- Recommendation from a solid neighbor
- Recommendation from other subcontractors
- HomeAdvisor.com
- Angieslist.com

Workers Unite

Dissension among workers is still alive. When you have a lot of independent contractors, subcontractors and other workers doing your rehabs, sooner or later everyone knows what everyone else is getting paid. Sometimes a worker may feel his pay is not equal to another worker and will eventually bring it to your attention. Even though his skill level may or may not be the equivalent of the other workers, he has, in no doubt, agreed to the terms set forth commencing his employment. The way you deal with this worker can unfold three ways: (1) Tell him you understand and if he is a good worker (skilled and efficient), you can tell him you will raise his pay on the next job and that the budget is already set on this one; (2) if you believe he will walk off the job, and it might be hard to replace him (you will need to use a great deal of judgment here), give him the raise and tell him you expect his performance to improve; and (3) if unskilled and unreasonable, tell him to hit the road, but tell him first to finish the job he was hired to do.

Other times, one worker may take the part of a foreman and may organize others to demand higher pay after terms and pay schedules have been agreed to and the job is halfway finished. When this happens, it is best to hear-out the concerns and then fall back on the original agreement. You could even say: "I am a man of my word, I stand by our agreement. Are you a man of your word?" Remind them they have already agreed to the terms and that you will consider a wage increase on the next job. If the organizer makes threats and tells you, "everyone will walk off the job if they do not get a pay raise," then you should fire the organizer immediately in front of the others. This will set several examples: (1) You will stick to your agreements; (2) you will not be trifled with; (3) trouble makers will be dealt with; (4) each person is expendable and each can be replaced.

If you have enough money set for the rehab, it might be in your best interest to give a little raise when you are near completion of the project. This may help motivate everyone to complete their work faster and make it possible for you to list the property sooner.

Loyalty among Labor

Yes, there are those who are loyal and grateful for the opportunities that you have given them. Not everyone is after the fast buck and ready to split on a dime. When you do realize a grateful and loyal worker who truly appreciates his job, he/she is definitely worth your attention. Give praise to those who deserve it and give it often. Let it be known you are aware of the extra effort put forth by diligent workers.

After you do a few fix and flips you will know how to put a crew together, including your tradesmen and labors. If you run into any snags you can fall back on HomeAdvisors.com or AngiesList.com for tradesmen.

ACTION HIGHLIGHTS FOR CONTRACTORS AND LABOR

1) Know the type of labor you'll need.

2) Do you have the time and energy to be your own general contractor? Decide how you want to operate your projects.

3) Learn how to negotiate properly with contractors and labor.

4) Know when not to hire.

5) Know when to fire and when.

6) Know the characteristics of professional contractors and handymen.

7) Deal with workers concerns on a one-on-one basis. Measure compensation with skill level.

8) Be aware of possible "clicks" that form within labor.

> *"Contractors and labor come and go with the wind. When you come across a reliable contractor who does meticulous work—keep his number close at hand. He's worth gold."*

5

The Business Side

"Business is always good when you have good tenants who pay their rent on time."

Note: Because real estate investing, including landlording, is a business, many of the same concepts, ideas and methods in this chapter are also included in our book, *The Millionaire Real Estate Flippers (New Edition).*

Landlording is a business. You are engaged in it to make money. You lose money when you neglect any business, and this is true with landlording as well. Much of your profit in landlording boils down to the quality of tenant(s) you have. Good tenants are quiet, respectful, pay their rent on time and stay for many years. Naturally it is your goal to attract good tenants. There are many ways to attract good tenants and keep them. A lot of what you will learn about landlording is geared around customer service—tenant service. Remember, as noted earlier, successful landlording is all about managing people and managing tenants correctly. Everything about landlording boils down to managing effectively and much of managing is also managing and organizing your time effectively with your rental properties and understanding the needs of your tenants. Always put yourself in their position. What would you want from a rental? What would you want from a landlord?

Landlording is a business and needs to be set up as a business.

Choosing your Name

Keep you name simple and easy to remember. Most people will not care what your name is; however, if your company business name is Punky Pothead Rentals, you will not attract the tenants you desire. Don't try to be cute or funny. Remember, this is still a business and you are trying to get respectable people to rent from you. Be conservative with the name you choose.

Here are some ideas for names:

- Cozy Property Rentals
- Pleasant Planet Apartments
- Whispering Oaks Rentals
- Green Pine Properties

- Green Meadow Properties
- Happy Home Properties
- Welcome Home Properties
- Clean Street Rentals

You could also use the words "Property Management" in your name. For example: Welcome Home Property Management. If your property(s) have a pronounced or distinctive character in landscaping or architecture, you could identify your rentals by naming your property(s) after the specific character. For instance, if you own an apartment building with a lot of yellow roses planted in the flower beds, you could call your enterprise, Yellow Rose Properties. If a number of rental houses you have are mid-century modern, you could use Mid-Century Properties or Modern Home Properties. And if you have a Spanish eclectic apartment building, and if you are in a heavily Hispanic area with a Hispanic tenant base, you could call your enterprise Hacienda Properties or Casa Rentals. Again, choose a simple name that sets a style or atmosphere for your future tenants, and a name that may represent your style.

Address and Mail Box

I wouldn't use your home address. You want to be more professional. UPS stores or the U.S. Postal Service box are your best bets and a less expensive option than an office lease or corporate suite. There are other mail box retail services where you can use a real street address with suite number. Some of these places cost $10 to $18 per month for a small box. You may be able to get a mail address for less—check around. If you only have one or two rental properties (houses) and do not plan on getting more, then to save money, go ahead and use your home address if you are not worried about your tenants knowing where you live and the kind of house you live in.

Corporation, LLC or DBA

We recommend you form an LLC or Corporation, S or C, get a Tax I.D. number which is not your Social Security number and open a corporate bank account in your new company name. There are various advantages and disadvantages of the different corporations and LLC. Ask your attorney what would be best for you.

You can also do it yourself. The process is easy. Forming a new corporation has many benefits, but it will also cost you a few hundred dollars and anywhere from $100 and more per year to maintain, depending on which state you incorporate in. You do not need an attorney to incorporate for you. Check online for "incorporation services"; they will save you hundreds of dollars.

Have your tenants make rental checks out to the corporation name.

Holding Property

We recommend that when you start buying property, whether for flipping or long term renal income, you do not put the property in your own name. There are two ways that we recommend, (1) form an LLC for each property and use the property address as the name; or (2) a Land Trust, where you would also use the property address as the name. The reason you do it this way is because it keeps things simple. We use Land Trust Agreements for almost all of our properties.

A Land Trust is free and all states that we know of, honor placing property in it. You should get a separate tax identification number for a Land Trust. The Land Trust is not a recordable document to be filed with the county recorder's office. A Land Trust has many benefits, but the most important for you is a shield of anonymity. For example, if you bought a property at 123 Main Street, your Land Trust could read "123 Main Street Land Trust." We have provided a copy of our Land Trust for you in the Appendix of this book. You can get a full copy of many of the best forms and agreements we use from the book *57 of The Best Real Estate Investors Forms & Agreements.*

Other forms of holding property include using your Individual Retirement Account (IRA), SEPP or other qualified plan that will give you tax deferment on your income or capital gain. Talk to an accountant or attorney who understands this and who can help set this up.

The idea starting out is to keep expenses low as possible, so you don't want to form a corporation or an LLC (Limited Liability Company) that will cost you more money when you haven't yet proven to yourself that this is the business you want to be in for the long-term.

You can run your venture as a DBA (Doing Business As) until the time comes and you are ready for growth.

Bank Account

Once you have your corporation or LLC set up, you should open your business checking account. Now you are in business.

All income (rents, ancillary income from coin-op washers and dryers, etc.) should be deposited into a new business account. Do not comingle funds with your other businesses or your salaried job, if you have one. This is easier for accounting reasons. In many states deposits such as security deposits or key deposits should also be in a separate account. Legally these funds are not yours—not yet. Check with your state regarding the proper holding of rental security deposits. The last month rent deposit is yours because it is a prepaid amount for rent. You can keep deposits in a savings or money market account.

Equipment and a Few other Things you'll Need to Be a Professional, Proactive Investor

Some of the items here you may already have.

- *Computer.* A desk top, lap top, Ipad, tablet—it doesn't matter as long it works well and you are comfortable with it.

- *Printer.* A monochrome printer is your best bet for cost efficiency. I have three HP monochrome printers that are used predominantly for printed order sheets, invoices, postage labels, and thank you and introduction letters to customers. I buy generic refurbished black ink cartridges that produce about 2500 sheets before ink runs dry. Don't forget copy paper.

- *Phone.* If it does not cut too much into your wallet starting out, you should get another phone or phone number for your business. Most people don't pay much more for long distance calling so it is not necessary that you get a toll free or an 800 number. Set your message to your phone to say something like: "Thank you for calling Red Rose Properties, our normal business hours are from

9 to 6. We are unable to take your call at this time. If you're calling about seeing a property we have listed for rent, please leave your name and phone number. We will get back to you shortly. Thank you."

Tenant's Welcome Package

A welcome package for new tenants shows that you are professional and that your landlording business of property management will represent a business relationship between you and your new tenant.

Here are a few things you will need for your Welcome Package (also called the Move-in Package):

- *Folder*: Two pocket folders printed professionally

- *Copy of lease and other attachments*: (Pet Agreement, disclosures…)

- *Return Mailing Envelopes*: Twelve envelopes to cover lease term. Monthly check with payment voucher.

- *Monthly Payment vouchers*: Included with monthly rental payment check

- *Important Phone Numbers*: Emergency numbers (911, Fire, Police, Poison Hotline)

- *Local government and city services phone numbers and websites*

- *Your Website and Phone numbers*

- *Places of interest brochures*: Brochures, flyers on locate attractions and events (you can get a number of brochures and discount coupons for local motel and hotel displays near check-in desk)

The Paperwork

In the Appendix of this book are the necessary forms you will need. This includes the full "Rental Package" as mentioned in Chapter 1:

- Rental Application (English / Spanish)
- Lease Agreement
- Pet Agreement
- Disclosures on Lead Based Paint, Asbestos, Mold and Radon
- Payment Policy
- Affidavit of Military Status
- Move-out Charges
- Welcome Letter
- Smoke Detector, Fire Extinguisher and Plunger Instruction
- Key Receipt with Deposit Form

- The "Rental Package" presentation explaining the tenant's obligations

We have written two other books on forms which you might what to add to your real estate investment library:

- **47 of The Best Landlording Forms & Agreements**
- **57 of The Best Real Estate Investor's Forms & Agreements**

We have used in our day-to-day real estate business and they have saved us and made us thousands of dollars in legal fees and from unreasonable tenants. They have been personalized and tweaked to be favorable for all landlords and real estate investors and fair for all tenants.

Business Cards

As a real estate investor it is important that people in your community know who you are. It is also important that you create a professional image of yourself and your rental business. One of the easiest ways to do this is by designing a business card. A professional has a business card to share with the world what they do. Your card will tell people that you are in the real estate business of investing and that you fix up properties and improve neighborhoods and also manage real estate. You can get cards printed and delivered to you by vistaprint.com or overnightprints.com for under $20.

Who do you give cards to?

- Give them to tenants
- Prospects
- Hand them out at Investment club meetings and Meetup Groups
- Chamber of Commerce meetings
- Appliance stores and hardware stores
- Special community functions
- Church picnics
- Post on bulletin boards

What should be on your card? Keep it simple. Here is an example:

123 Main St. Anytown, Fl U.S.A Phone: 561.555.5555	Email: CozyCottage@Prop.com Website: CozyCotProp.com

COZY COTTAGE PROPERTIES
PROFESSIONAL PROPERTY MANAGEMENT
M. Mitch Freeland
Property Manager
1 ♦ 2 ♦ 3 and 4 Bedrooms Available

The card shows your full address with phone number, email and website. The name of your enterprise is big and easy to read, as is your name. Your title is stated and what you offer is also stated. Even if you have your units rented it is always a good idea to mention on your card size of the units you have. You want to build a data base of people calling. You need to find out when they are ready to move in and what their budget is. You also want to screen them over the phone. For example: a prospect calls and says he is looking for a three bedroom house. You do not have anything available, but you still ask a few questions: When are you looking to move? How much is in his budget for lease? What is his or household income? How long has he been with his present employer? If he says he has been employed for ten years with the same company then you a good idea of his stability. If he has a wife and children this is another indication of a solid family man. This is a tenant you want. Keep him in your data base to call on. You also want to ask the reason he is moving from his current location. Now, if you have your real estate agent license, you can pick up a new client and show him other properties and make your commission.

---

123 Main St.
Anytown, Fl U.S.A
Phone: 561.555.5555

Email: Mitch@BigCountry.com
Website: BigCountryRE.com

BIG COUNTRY REAL ESTATE, INC.

I'LL BUY YOUR HOUSE FOR CASH—ANY CONDITION

M. Mitch Freeland

PRESIDENT

---

123 Main St.
Anytown, Fl U.S.A
Phone: 561.555.5555

Email: IBuyDumpyHouse@gmail.com
Website: BigCountryRE.com

I BUY TRASHY, DUMPY HOUSES

I'LL BUY YOUR HOUSE FOR **CASH**—ANY CONDITION

M. Mitch Freeland

CALL NOW 555-555-5555

FAST & EASY CLOSING

The card shows your full address with phone number, email and website. The name of your enterprise is big and easy to read, as is your name. Your title is stated and what you offer is also stated. Let people know that you are buying houses and you will buy el dumpos.

Using the Internet Effectively

As with most businesses, the internet has transformed the way real estate investors conduct business. Because of the internet, proactive investors save much needed time to get the information they need. The internet allows us to:

- Finding properties to buy—Realtor.com and the dozens of other real estate site.
- Check current rent rates in our area
- Check housing trends
- Learn about design and color trends
- Shop cost savings for supplies, fixtures and parts
- Compare prices on all products
- Have your own website explaining the benefits of living at your rentals
- Advertise your rentals available
- Learn from Real Estate forums and websites
- Learn of new laws and regulations regarding landlording and real estate transactions
- Use Facebook, Twitter, Youtube, Instagram and other social media sites to find and promote your properties.

Journaling and Keeping Records

In the old day's one kept records in a simple journal, writing down payments, tenant problems and noting maintenance repairs. A lot, if not all of this can be done on your smart phone or computer. You could even use websites like Evernote.com to organize your material: payments, tenant info, invoices and so on. Since landlording is a money generating enterprise, you want to keep good records. Do what is most comfortable for you. If you like using a journal book to write in, use it. If you are comfortable with software or online journaling or organizational websites like Evernote.com, then use them. You can also record your info in a spreadsheet. Note: with Evernote you will have to pay for certain services.

ACTION HIGHLIGHTS FOR
THE BUSINESS SIDE

1) Real Estate investing is a business – form a corporation or LLC.

2) Do not hold real estate in your own name; use LLC or Land Trust?

3) Get Business Cards and let people know what you are doing.

4) The internet and social media can be very helpful in finding properties to buy and tenants to lease.

5) Keep excellent records by journaling. Try Evernote.com for your recording and organizing records.

6

Tax Deferred Exchange
And Other Tax Advantages

The excitement of learning separates youth from old age. As long as you're learning, you're not old.
—Rosalyn Yalow

Whether you are a professional or part-time real estate investor, there is a strategy you should use--a 1031 Tax Deferred Exchange. The advantages of implementing this strategy into your real estate investment plan will prove to be one of the best moves you make. And over the long-term, this strategy will enable you to defer the taxes owed on capital gains when you sell your investment properties.

Like most investments, there are certain advantages of holding property for the long-term. However, when you are up a significant amount in your investment and the cycle change is imminent, you may want to sell your investment property at a high and then use the proceeds to buy one or more fixer-uppers at bargain prices. And the best way to do this and not pay taxes on your profit, is to use the funds from the sale in a 1031 Tax Deferred Exchange and buy other investment property.

What is a 1031 Tax Deferred Exchange?

When you sell your investment property, you will be taxed on the capital gain. To defer that tax you can invest the proceeds from your sale into another investment property which IRS rule 1031 states. This will allow you to buy and sell property continually over many years without paying current taxes on the capital gains incurred. This becomes an excellent way to build long-term wealth, provided you do not need the cash from the sale of your investment property.

There Are a Few Rules You Must Follow

1. **Qualified Intermediary.** When you sell your property, you can not physically take possession of the cash; you must use a "Qualified Intermediary." This is similar to an escrow account with an agency that is registered as a qualified intermediary to hold funds for a 1031 Exchange. Funds must move directly from es-

crow account to the account of the intermediary. To find a qualified intermediary near you, you can ask your escrow agent or real estate agent if they would recommend one, or you could Google and type in 1031 Exchange and pick one near you. We have used First American Exchange Company for several transactions and all transactions went smoothly. They have many offices across the U.S. and they did a good job for us. There website is: www.firstexchange.com.

2. **Time Frame to Identify.** You have 45 days from the sale date of your property to identify the property you will buy with the funds from the sale. You could list one or several properties you are interested in buying through an exchange.

3. **Time Frame to Buy.** You have up to 180 days or about 6 months to complete a transaction. In this time frame your money will be in an interest bearing escrow account with the "qualified intermediary."

4. **Type of Property of "Like Kind."** The property must be "like kind." This means it must be an investment property not a personal residence.

5. **One or More Properties.** You can exchange one property, the one you sell, for one or many other properties. If you are selling an investment property that has large equity and has increased in value substantially, instead of purchasing one large building, you could purchase many smaller properties with the exchanged funds.

What Does the "Qualified Intermediary" Charge?

The "qualified intermediary" will typically charge between $700 and $1,500 for the exchange. There are three documents that the intermediary and you will handle: The first would be a general agreement between you and the intermediary; the second, an assignment agreement, in which the intermediary becomes the seller of the property; and third, a notice to the buyer and other parties involved that you are completing an exchange.

What is the Actual Process?

One last word, make sure the intermediary in bonded and insured. Ask about the number of transactions they do annually and make sure they have sufficient experience in completing an exchange.

Also, contact your accountant or tax attorney for guidance on the transaction. You will realize after the first exchange you complete, that it is really a simple process. The difficulty may present itself when you are selling a property and you cannot find a suitable investment property to move the funds into. This is when you really must hustle and locate the right property.

The process is as easy as signing the documents as stated in the previous section. This is an escrow account in which funds from the sale of one property move in and then move-out for the purchase of one or numerous properties.

Other Tax Advantages

Make It Your Residence

Did you know you can make $500,000 tax-free. That's right, when you find a rehab, fix it up and decide to live in it for at least two years as your primary residence you do not have to pay any capital gains tax on the first $500,000 of profit. Of course, this is for you and your spouse. If you are single you are exempt of any taxes up to a $250,000 profit. If you are not married, you might want to think about the extra $250,000 you can make. How does this law sit with an apartment building? For example: You purchase a 16 unit fixer-upper. You spend $100,000 fixing it. You and your wife move into one of the units and live there for two years. After two years, you sell the building for $1,500,000. Your cost for the building and fix up is $1,100,000 leaving you with a $400,000 profit. Since you lived on the property, is the $500,000 exemption possible? Only if the other units were not rented and you did not receive income from them. This is something you might what to run by your accountant.

If you have owned a property for a long time, you must have made it your residence for at least two of the past five years upon its sale.

Here is example some investors might find themselves in: You are unable to find a house for you and your spouse that suites your needs. You are searching for a fixer-upper. However, you do find a triplex at a bargain basement price. It is vacant. Each unit is a 2 bedroom, 2 baths and each unit needs a lot of work. You purchase the property for $100,000. You know after rehab it should be worth about $380,000. You are short of fix-up cash and decide to move into one unit after you have fixed it up and gradually work on the other two units when you have the time and at your leisure. After two years of living in one unit and not renting out the other units you decide to move and rent-out all three units for one year and then sell the property. You end up selling the property for $410,000. After everything is finished, you make a profit of $250,000. Does this example qualify for the $500,000 exemption? Here are the facts: (1) You lived at the property as your primary residence for two of the past three years; (2) you did not use the property as income property when you lived there; and (3) you did not take standard income property deductions, such as depreciation and others on your taxes for the first two years as it was your residence. Now does this qualify? We have not done a transaction like this, but we believe it falls into the realm at your personal residence. Have your accountant or a tax expert figure this out for you.

Capital Gains

When you purchase property and sell it in less than 366 days (one year and one day) you are taxed on a short-term capital gain (the tax is like that of your ordinary income. If you are in the 35 percent tax rate, you will pay that amount on your short-term capital gain). If you sold it on the 366th day from the day you purchased the property, you would incur a long-term capital gain of 15 percent on your profits as of this writing. One year and one day can make an enormous difference in the taxes you pay. If you do not need to sell your flip immediately, you might want to think about holding it for a few more months. If it is a rental property, simply rent it out and put it up for sale in October. With some luck, you could have it sold and delay the closing until January. The difference in the tax you pay on your capital gains could be as high as 20 percent. For example, if you profit on the rehab is $60,000, a short-term gain in the 35 percent bracket would give you a tax liability of $21,000. If you waited a few months and held the property for 366 days, you would fall under the long-term capital gains rate of 15 percent, and your tax liability would be $9,000. By waiting to sell, you will incur more mortgage payments, insurance, property taxes and other maintenance repairs that could eat up your cash. But if the property is rented, most or all of those expenses could be paid for. When you are selling the property to another investor whose need for a rental property with a renter already in the property, then this works out great the you and the buyer/investor.

Here is another situation: Let's assume you bought a house in September, rehabbed it, and had it under contract on October 30 with a closing date of November 30. If you closed on November 30, your flip would be short-term flip and taxes on profit paid in April—only 4 months away. Now, if you are able to extend the closing to January 2, you will have over fifteen months to pay the taxes on your profit—and if you file an extension—20 months. Of course you will have to pay penalties for the extension when you do not pay anything on the 15th of April.

Waiting for the New Year

Timing your sale to close in January is smart, even if you haven't held the property for 366 days. Unless you have many "write-offs," try to postpone your closing to January when you can. If you get a property under contract in November, and you believe the buyers will close, try to extend the closing to January. By postponing the closing, you will not be liable for any capital gains taxes for another year if you decide not to do a 1031 Exchange. It will also give you time to work on deductions for the next year.

The Retired Class

If you are retired and wish to invest in income producing real estate, a major concern you might have, would be if you needed to sell stocks or liquidate your pension plan, 401K or IRA to raise cash to buy property. Of course, you will be taxed heavily on the proceeds, especially if you have been invested for many years and have accumulated a large sum. One way of cashing-out, in a sense, and not being taxed, is to refinance the home you live in. Instead of selling stock, bonds and other investments that may be performing well, you should think seriously about refinancing the home you live in, or other properties you own to raise cash. This is beneficial in three ways: (1) with the proceeds you can buy income producing property you want; (2) you won't have to pay the capital gains taxes on the profits from the sale of securities in your IRA, other pension plans, or investment account when investments are sold or funds withdrawn; and (3) the interest on the loan you obtain will be tax deductible. This is a great way to raise cash without costly yourself a lot of money in taxes--the best plan is always to defer or eliminate taxes when you can.

You should also keep in mind that this is for those of you with a lot of equity in your homes. Do not over extend yourself by getting a loan to value of 80 percent of your home. Keep 40 to 50 percent equity in the home you live in. This is for those of you who have owned your home for a longtime and have built-up a large amount of equity. If you have the inclination to invest, you might as well do it the right way when it comes to raising cash for an investment in real estate. With research and a thorough understanding of your target market, you will have a opportunity to make a lot more money with the cash taken out of your house. Rather than having cash equity simply parked in one property, why not have it income producing. And if you invest the funds correctly, you will be in a position to enjoy better than inflation rate appreciation.

Here is a situation you might see today, provided you are in an area or close to one that has had a real estate correction.

You are 65 years old and have lived in your home for the last 32 years. Your home is worth $350,000, free and clear. You have $450,000 in stocks and other investments including corporate bonds, and some U.S. savings bonds in your IRA. You have held your investments for many years and you are an investor not a trader. You have been following the real estate market in your area and in an area that has gotten hit hard with the credit crisis. Many homes that once sold for $175,000 are now selling the around $60,000 to $55,000. You conclude, these homes would make great rentals and with valuable upside potential and a lower than normal downside risk, you believe you could make some money. The homes are mostly selling for under $50 per square foot, and that is well under current building costs. There is more good news. You discover the single family homes in the area are renting for $850 for a three bedroom, two bath, 1,400 square foot family house. Everything appears to make sense. So, you proceed with your plan.

You find three investment houses and purchase them for $55,000 each. You pay cash for the houses from the $200,000 loan you got, using the home you live in as collateral. You got a $200,000 loan at 6.5 percent for 30 years. This leaves you with payments of $1,264 monthly. You use $165,000 to close on the homes and invest another $5,000 making minor repairs. Your total cash invested is $170,000. You keep the remaining funds of $30,000 in a money-market account paying 4% interest--this will cover for any emergencies. You are still receiving $1,400 per month from Social Security and your pension.

You now rent each of your three rental houses for $850 per month, which returns you a total of $2,550 per month gross. Now, let's break it down your expenses: (1) property tax for all three rental houses comes to a total of $3,300 annually; (2) insurance is $2,400 annually; and (3) you've decided on projected expenses and a vacancy allowance of $1,500 annually for each house. This equals total expenses of $4,500 for all three investment houses. This is a liberal number, but you want to play it safe. Here's how it looks:

Annual gross rents	$30,600
Mortgage	- 1,264
Taxes	- 3,300
Insurance	- 2,400
Expenses	- 4,500
Positive cash flow	$19,136
Money-market	
($30,000 @ 4%)	1,200
Retirement income	
($1,400 per month)	16,800
Total income	$37,136

Don't forget, you can write off the depreciation of the rental properties and the interest paid on your loan and all the other expenses related to your investments, property taxes and everything else you spent on the properties.

One aspect we still need to include in your investment is the potential appreciation of the properties. Since the properties were purchased at reasonably good prices, the appreciation potential is very high for the next two to five years. If the properties reach a price of sixty percent of their pre-bust value in five years, each house could be worth $105,000. You would have nearly doubled your investment, using somewhat of a conservative approach. If you add the rental income into the scenario, you then will have had well over a 250 percent return of your $200,000, which you obtained by mortgaging the home you live in.

Real Estate for Your IRA

Did you know you can hold real estate in your IRA? That's right, and it's easy once you know how. Whether it is a Regular IRA, Roth IRA, or another qualified plan, you could use your retirement funds for real estate investing. First, talk to your accountant about this. He or she may know a third party administrator near you who handles self-directed IRA's. There are several qualified companies that administer self directed retirement plans and handle real estate transactions with retirement funds. We list these companies later in this chapter.

Benefits of Buying Real Estate in Your IRA

The benefits of buying real estate in your IRA are the tax-free advantage on all profits. With your Roth IRA your profits are tax-free. Having a Roth IRA is the way to go. With a traditional IRA your profits are deferred until you take a distribution.

What Types of Real Estate Investments Can you Participate In?

All real estate can be purchased in your IRA, including transactions that deal in real estate, such as making loans and investing in trust deeds. The following list describes all the ways you can invest with funds from your IRA.

- You can buy rental property, houses, condos, co-ops, and multi-family buildings.
- You can buy commercial property and raw land.
- You can develop property.
- You can buy foreclosures and tax lien certificates.
- You can buy options on property.
- You can buy "Subject To" property, where the seller is liable to the lender and where you are not liable to the seller.
- You can be a partner, without guaranteeing a loan.
- You can buy fixer-uppers for the long-term or make short-term flips of them.
- All types of rental properties with income.
- A retirement home you rent and when you are ready to move in, that is when you take your Ira distribution.
- Simply, you can buy all types of investment properties.

Some Requirements of the Plan

You may not buy the property from any family member (children and spouse and parents). And you cannot have had any interest in the property prior to placing it in the plane. However, you can buy property from a sibling and place it in the plan.

1. You may not use the property as a rental to family members or have them live their. You may, however, rent it to your siblings.

2. You may not use the property personally. And you can not use the property for your business in anyway.

3. You may not use the funds or the property as collateral for a loan, otherwise the tax-free or tax-deferred status would be disqualified. Moreover, you cannot guarantee a loan.

4. You must use a qualified intermediary.

We've listed just a few of the requirements here. For more information, we've listed a few companies and their websites who specialize in completing transactions with your self-directed IRA and other retirement plans by investing in real estate. You can also go online to your favorite search engine for information.

- The Entrust Group: www.theentrustgroup.com
- Equity Trust: www.trustetc.com
- Guidant Financial: www.guidantfinancial.com
- Sterling Trust: www.sterlingtrustcompany.com
- Pensco Trust Company: www.penscotrust.com

Depreciation Deduction

You will need a top notch accountant to take advantage of all your deductions. Our tax laws are ridiculous and change all the time, so you should use an accountant, unless you enjoy this type of work. What can you depreciate?

- The building on the property.
- Machinery and Equipment (Clothes washer, dryer, lawn mower, and other equipment).
- Motor Vehicles

Property is depreciated over 27.5 years. This is the structure on the land, not the land itself. With motor vehicles you can use a straight-line depreciation of 3 years. Computers and similar equipment can be expensed the same year or on a straight-line 3 year basis. Tax laws change all the time, so talk to your accountant regarding deductions and depreciation.

Interest Deduction

The interest you pay on the mortgage for your investment property is deductible. If you already own a home with a mortgage you may also deduct the paid interest as well. Most fees on your loan settlement statement are deductible. Again, you should consult a professional tax specialist to determine all your deductions.

Other Deductions

As a real estate investor, you will have a lot of deductions. When in doubt, deduct it. Here are a few more things you can deduct:

- Legal
- Accounting
- Property taxes
- Utilities
- Supplies, including all office related supplies.
- Equipment
- Maintenance
- Gardening
- Leased Vehicles

Always consult with your accountant with every possible deduction. With some luck, he will be able to save you a lot more money when it comes tax time.

ACTION HIGHLIGHTS FOR
TAX DEFERRED EXCHANGE AND
OTHER TAX ADVANTAGES

1) Complete a 1031 Exchange when every possible.

2) Learn how to defer capital gains taxes.

3) Buy as much real estate in you IRA as you can.

4) Take all the deductions you can on your taxes.

> *"Using a 1031 Exchange is the second best possible way to pyramiding and growing your wealth. Investing in property through your IRA is the best, especially a Roth IRA."*

7

Real Estate Clubs and Associations: Benefits of Membership and Why you Should Join

"No matter what you're trying to accomplish, you can do it better with shared thinking."
—John C. Maxwell

Nearly all communities in the United States have some form of real estate investors club or association. Some large cities and metropolitan areas have several clubs that cater to a specific region, city or community. Some may cater to investors with specific types of investment property—multifamily or commercial—most cater to both. But most real estate clubs and associations are for all investors—investors with single-family homes, apartment buildings, or commercial strip centers.

Small clubs might have 20 to 50 active members and larger, regional associations range from 500 to over 1,000 members. During hot markets, memberships in clubs rise quickly and consequently during busted markets or corrections memberships drop sharply. Sometimes the decrease of active members is the fault of organizers not offering the members a significant amount of benefits to join. Clubs like any organization or corporate business have to prove they are a valuable resource. They have to present value at every stage of the investor's developmental life.

Most real estate clubs do not make a lot of money. The overall objective of clubs is to bring investors together, to share ideas, resources, and to offer the opportunity for investors to network with other investrs. In addition, clubs offer eduction and learning by having regional and national successful investors speak at their events. Members of investment clubs are there to expand their investment acumen and grow their business by the contacts they make at club meetings and events. Education is a big part of belonging to a real estate club or association. Buying and selling property among members is high on the activities list of the clubs and as an active investor it should be high on your list, too.

Each month new and novice investors turn out for the investor meetings. These pre-members (you may be one) are the back bone to real estate investment clubs. As with all organizations that deal with the needs of ongoing members, it is crucial for organizers to attract new members. To foster growth, clubs must encourage new and inexperienced investors to join. This is a necessary part of the organization and its overall existence depends on new members. To attract new members, meetings need to be exciting, informative and productive for all participants. If the meetings are not exiciting and informative, clubs will loose members, enrollment of new membership becomes stagnate or nonexistent and sometimes clubs close for good.

Structure and Format of Club Meetings

Most real estate investment clubs follow a similar format. The following is a common structure many meetings adhere to:

- Networking time before meeting begins.

- Introduction of meeting to new attendees and the evening program agenda including the guest speakers.

- Introduction of corporate members. Corporate members have a chance to talk to the group for 30 seconds to a minute. Sometimes there could be 20 or more corporate members. Corporate members join clubs to network and drum up business. Title companies, insurance agents, mortgage brokers, accountants, contractors, plumbers, tile setters, and others who have a interest in real estate and working with investors become corporate members.

- Introduction of a member or two completing a successful deal.

- Host presents deals (properties) available for investors.

- Introduction of secondary speaker (learning products or services available for sale).

- Introduction of key note speaker (learning products or services available for sale).

- Meeting concludes.

Procedure: What to Expect

Many investment clubs meet once per month for about two to three hours. Meetings are typically held in hotel conference rooms that accommodate on average thirty to three hundred people. This depends on the size of membership and attendees. Seating is usually arranged auditorium style. Some clubs provide tables for the guest to write. This makes it easier for members to take notes or use a laptop. And when you need to get connected to research information at the meeting, you can go wire-less comfortably.

Most meetings begin at 6 pm or 7 pm and are generally scheduled for two hours. Many meetings can run about three hours when several speakers are scheduled. Most meetings provide coffee, tea and simple snacks - cookies or other bakery items. Most clubs have websites where you can join online or at the meeting. There are also great online clubs that we recommend you join. One online organization is www.BiggerPockets.com. We will discuss more about the online clubs toward the end of this chapter.

When you are *serious* about investing, join a club and get active. Getting the right knowledge and meeting the right people is crucial. We highly recommend you get involved with an organization were you are exposed to new ideas that can make you the money you want. We all know that to get a great education it costs money—it costs something. When you purchased this book, you made an investment. Your investment and the knowledge you'll gain throughout your years is not free. One great idea from one book, one course, one web-site, or a membership fee from an investment club can make you thousands. What did this book cost you? $22.95. Is that a good tradeoff for something worth thousands of dollars? It's a great investment to me. And because you bought this book, it shows that it was a great investment to you as well. The lesson here is to not skimp on your education. We all know it costs a lot more to go to Harvard than to your Community College. That is because the knowledge you receive at Harvard is worth an amount that cannot possibly be measured or compared to that of your Community College. It is time to step up to the big leagues. Join a couple of investors clubs and take in all they have offer. And the more engaged you get, the more you'll learn. As the saying goes, "The more you learn, the more you earn."

What's Being Presented? What's Being Offered?

Many guest speakers at investment clubs speak for free. Some speakers sell back-room items; courses on Cds, DVDs, and books. Some also sell coaching programs that can last over several months or years. Typically, all sales proceeds are split 50/50 with the club. The membership fees don't keep the club in business. The club's participation in splitting sales proceeds keeps the club in business.

As a new investor, investment club speakers can give you the necessary information you might need to go forward in the direction of your goals. You will have to make an investment sooner or later, and later might be too late. So, seriously think about what you want to accomplish in your investing and look for courses or books that can help you reach your goals. Sometimes a $22.95 book will have the same pertinent information than a $300 or $400, or even a $1,000 course. So, check www.Amazon.com and other bookstores first, before you invest heavily into multi-thousand dollar courses and boot camps.

If you believe the information offered for sale at the meetings is useful toward the progression of your goal, then by all means purchase the material. The only way you are ever going to learn is to take action. Ask as many questions as possible and if you feel comfortable with the price, the authors, and the content of the material for sale, then purchase it. This is an investment in your education—your future as a real estate investor. You'll have to set aside money for investing in your future. There is no such thing as a free education. If you purchase a course, take action immediately. Do not place the course on your bookshelf and avoid it, take action and make it happen.

What Are the Rules?

Like any social event, there are a few rules you should follow:

1) Be polite and courteous to all.
2) Don't be late for meetings. It's disruptive.
3) Shut your phone off. It's disruptive.

4) Sit up close when you can. The closer you are to the speakers the more attentive you'll be and you will absorb information better.

5) Do not talk during a presentation. It is disruptive.

6) Do not move in and out of your seat or meeting room. It is disruptive.

7) Do not distribute your flyers without permission from the club leaders.

8) Wear your name tag or badge so everyone can read your name and the company you're with.

9) Handout your business card to everyone. You have to let everyone know who you are and why you are there – that's the whole point.

10) Write and take notes. Studies have shown, you retain things better when you write them down.

Getting the Most Out of the Club

Whatever your objective is in joining a real estate club, it should be your plan to get as much out of it as possible: you paid the fee and now you are a member. Many people join investment clubs and associations to learn about investing and opportunities available in their area. Others join clubs to meet and network with other investors and landlords. And others might join because of the many special events, programs and up-to-date information available in their target area.

Getting the most out of your club depends on what your main objective is. If it is to locate and invest in fixer-uppers then ask club members and organization leaders what you are looking for and ask often. Let everyone know what you do, including; all members and club vendors. You can even volunteer your time to the organization. The more people know what you do and what your intentions are, the closer you will get to fulfilling your goals.

Be as active as possible in the club. And spend the time to meet members and probe for the information that is most important to you. Be specific in your objective and be clear of what you want to accomplish by being a club member. If you are looking for money to invest with or partners—let it be known. If you are interested in small multifamily properties, talk to as many members as possible regarding your interest. If you are looking to sell property, buy property, rent property or option property—let is be known. Get out there and let the word out. The larger the net you cast, the greater the number of fish you'll catch.

Be a Social Animal

You've got to be out there as stressed earlier. You have to be introducing yourself to other members, investors, old-timers and new members. Below are seven tips for utilizing your time at an investors club meeting.

○

- *Be open to new ideas.* Listen carefully to all speakers, guests and questions from other members. You are there to learn and absorb as such information in the two to three yours the clubs meets for.

- *Take notes.* Studies show, you learn faster and retain information better when you take notes. So, take a notebook wit you and prepare yourself for writing.

- *Ask a lot of questions.* Any concern, any question, any suggestion you have—ask it. The club is for you to learn, so make the most of it by having all of your questions answered.

- *Keep all negative thoughts to yourself.* A good attitude is crucial. Don't criticize speakers, guests or other members—you're above that. And if you plan to be happy and successful in real estate invest-

128

ing turn any negative attitude into a positive one, or you'll find your self alone in a room full of enthusiastic, hopeful investors.

- *Don't be a loner.* You belong to an association to meet people. Like-minded, investor's who are goal driven and possess a positive attitude is what belonging to an investment club is all about. Get out there and introduce yourself to as many people as possible—this includes vendors, the club president and members like you, new members and experienced investors. You will be surprised at the business contacts you'll make.

- *Look for the positive.* It was noted above that when you attend an investor meeting you should drop any negative thoughts about the association immediately. Your intent is to network and meet people who can help you, educate you, motivate you, and inspire you to achieve your investing goals. To do all this you'll need to have a positive attitude. Remember to keep an open mind. You are there to learn, grow, and prosper. You joined up to learn how to make money, or make more money while investing in real estate. Do not forget this objective.

- *Study what is going on around you.* Pay attention and study all that is going on around you. Many deals come from members of investment clubs and associations. Members are selling or buying property, managing property, or brokering property. Vendors are also offering services which you may need. Vendros include hard money lenders, commercial lenders, Realtors® and mortgage brokers who can service your needs when you are ready. So, know who is in the room and at the tables. Study what is going on around you.

Networking with investors during one of out meetings. An investors association
meeting is a great venue to share your ideas with other investors.

129

We always offered food during a break between speakers

Why You Should Join?

As with any type of investment, the number one reason to join any business related organization is a financial one— learn, so you can make more money than you are currently making. Deciding to take-up membership in a real estate investment club/association no different: You want to make money—more money, faster money and when you time it right—easy-money. The only way to do this is by attracting more people (investors, or people associated with investors) into your circle of influence.

The business world revolves effectively by relationships. All successful individuals in all forms of business have reached world class status by forming top-notch relationships with others in their industry and with customers. And real estate investing is no different. When you are ready to explode as an investor, then it is time to join and actively participate in an investment club.

As noted earlier, people join investment clubs for many reasons, the most widely employed reason is to make more money; and this is accomplished by applying what they learn and the contacts they make at investment club meetings and being privy to special information provided by other members. This is a plain and simple way of networking.

All investors should belong to at least one club and if possible two. However, not all investment clubs are the same. And there are definitely large differences between the really great ones and the ones that are manages poorly. So check around your area and go with the one or two with the more dynamic, aggressive, value-driven, motivational, and educational format. Also, pay close attention to the leaders of the club and the members. Here are a few questions to ask:

1) Are the leaders of the club interesting? Are they sincere, are they highly engaged in the development of the club for the long-term?

2) Are the leaders really interested in the development of the club by creating passionate, conscientious and helpful members?

3) Does the club vision go hand in hand to your wants, desires and goals?

4) Do you feel comfortable with the format, the speakers and the subjects presented or is it the same humdrum meeting month after month with little helpful information?

5) Are the meetings educational?

6) Are you inspired, motivated when you leave the meeting?

7) Is membership increasing or is it contracting?

8) Is membership a good value? Are you receiving what you want? Are you receiving more than what you've expected?

Cost of Membership: A Small Price to Pay

Typically, the costs of individual membership ranges from $179 to $249 annual. And the price at the door is typically $20 to $30 for non members each month. But whatever you pay, $249, $199 or $179 for a year membership in an investment club, it is a small price to pay for all the resources available to you once you become a member. One contact, just one person that you meet at a meeting will make or save you many times more than the membership price. Becoming an active member of a real estate investors association is the least costly and the most productive way for an investor to increase his or her business:

There are other types of membership programs available for corporate members or sponsors of meetings. Corporate memberships are typically offered for different benefits and therefore are prices according to the services offered.

To learn more about investment clubs and associations refer to Appendix B, in the back of this book. There is information in Appendix B about Realty Advisors International Investor's Association, both individual membership and corporate membership is covered in detail. The material there should allow you gather enough knowledge from our investment club and how many of the top clubs operate.

John was the Master of Ceremony and organizer of the monthly meetings

Online Investment Websites, Blogs and Clubs

We recommend everybody to join an online real estate investment website, blog or club. From our new website **www.MitchFreeland.com**, we will be introducing new blog and current real estate news and articles. One of the best and well organized online websites is www.BiggerPockets.com. You can join for free or upgrade your membership to a paid level. The site has many podcast and audios that an investors can learn from. Another feature is that the site allows you to find other investors and members in your geographic area. You can start your own Meetup group from the people you find on the site. Go to www.Meetup.com to set this up. There are many real estate investor Meetup groups online. Some of these groups are large and some are small. These groups act as mini investment clubs and can be very helpful for an investor.

8

Staying the Course

"All my life I've been surrounded by people who are smarter than I am, but I found I could always keep up by working hard."
—Glenn Seaborg

Nothing worthwhile is easy. This is especially true with real estate investing and landlording. There are many obstacles to overcome, as in all new business endeavors. To be a success in real estate you must stay the course—you're the captain now and you are in charge.

If you are persistent and have an overwhelming desire to make real estate investing work for you, then real estate investing over the long-term can be an extremely lucrative and exciting business whether practiced full or part-time. Landlording, as we know, is a great wealth builder over the long-term.

While it might be hard to locate good deals in rapidly appreciating markets, it will also be easy to locate great deals in deflating or stagnated markets. Landlords have to keep a vigilant eye on value when looking for rental property that will cash flow. At times, you may also find yourself in a position to do several deals in a single month. Some projects will be easy and others might drive you crazy. Nothing is ever the same. And when you are dealing with labor and the personalities involved, your work ethic may not be exercised by those whom you employ. Trust in them anyway; however, always keep your eyes opened and focused on the big picture, the grand plan, the big payoff, the big enchilada, payday, or whatever else you call it. People are unique, as all properties are unique. And it is this uniqueness that makes each property a special opportunity to make money.

Your Coming Out Party

If you have not purchased any real estate before, then this book alone will not give you enough information to jump start your new real estate enterprise. To move you forward into serious investing or flipping and renovations, we suggest that you get a copy of <u>The Millionaire Real Estate Flippers</u>. We have written many books on real estate that cover specific subjects. These books are listed in the back of this book, and they are available on Amazon and **www.FlippingBrothers.com** and other fine websites and stores.

Most people talk a lot about the real estate investments they should have made. Don't introduce yourself as "Mr. and Mrs. Should Have" at your next Christmas party. Take the initiative and make your first investment

133

now. Keep a copy of this book next to you when you are driving. It will remind you, each time you look over to the passenger seat to focus on investing and finding the right properties. Read this book when you are waiting in your car and always make it a habit to have it with you when you are driving to look for investment properties.

Accountability

You are in charge. You are inevitably accountable for every decision, whether it's result is a positive outcome or a negative one. And the decisions you make will affect your bottom line and may even destroy your investment return if your decisions are based consistently on false information, poor judgment and an ill-conceived plan. On the positive side, the decisions you make regarding your real estate investing may bring you considerable wealth and life-time financial security. And that is the purpose of this book--to help you do just that. What you accomplish in your real estate investing is based on the effort you put into it. Recognizing you as person who is accountable shows integrity. You are accountable; standup, can you hear the applause.

Building Long-term Value

When you think about building long-term value in real estate investing, you must think about it on a daily bases. Real estate investing is a business, and therefore you must see it for what it is. The more times you invest on creating value, the more value you will eventually create.

Over the long-term most real estate investments will do well. Inflation will drive prices up and the improvements you make to your properties will force appreciation even higher. For many investors building long-term value is a solid plan to wealth and many landlords postpone instant gratification by investing and reinvesting a large percentage of any extra funds. Discipline yourself now to invest. You will thank yourself later.

Focus and a Clear Plan

To "stay the course" you must be focused and have a clear plan. Focus is what measures the successful investor from the person who does one deal and stops because the profit wasn't what he or she thought it would be.

Mistakes will be made and they will be made often. As long as they are small mistakes, it's no big deal. Having a clear plan and following through with your plan by focusing on the process and then the end result, will motivate you to complete the tasks necessary to fulfill your plan. It is consistent, positive, daily activity that will produce the results you want. And if you focus on the daily tasks at hand, you will achieve what you planned to achieve and you will be a better person for it. Your motivation begins when you complete hard tasks. Therefore, complete the tasks that are difficult first, and stick to your plan.

Establishing Your Goals

Goals are very important and very necessary. Writing out your real estate investment goals is the first step to personally identifying what you want and how you plan to accomplish want you want.

If you have never written your goals out before or are not sure of how to begin, try the book *Mini Goals Huge Results*. The book instructs you to define your goals that will help you clarify your dreams and long-term plans.

You should have short-term goals and long-term goals. They will keep you on track and help clarify your wants. Follow these simple rules when setting your goals:

1) Write down what you want

2) Write down why you want it

3) Write down the date you want it and the date in which you want it completed.

4) Write down how you plan to achieve your goals. What must you do?

5) You must read your goals daily; have them ingrained in your mind.

6) Your goals must be realistic. You should be able to achieve them by hard work and consistent effort. If you are four feet tall and want to play in the NBA, that isn't a realistic goal. However, if you are four feet tall and want to be a jockey, then that may be a realistic goal.

When you need to motivate yourself, read your goals. Your goals will motivate you to reach out and give you direction and a target to shoot for. You should actually read your goals every day. This way you will always know the direction to go.

A Clear Vision and a Will to Succeed

You have to see the future and how you see yourself in it. The future becomes a picture of what you are thinking about: Can you see it? You must have a clear vision. Your vision will motivate you to reach your goals.

You must have the will to do it--a will to follow through. A passionate desire and persistence are the focal points. Success is attained when vision creates the will to succeed.

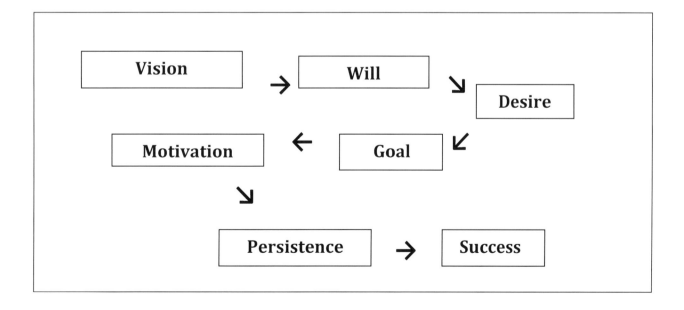

135

Your vision must be shared within your organization. Your organization can be your contractors, administrative assistant, friends and family, accountant, attorney and others in your life. If you have a company and employ many, then they are your organization. When everyone in the organization shares the same vision, then a great and inspiring transformation begins. However, when more people are introduced to the vision, it is likely, one will have a different vision which may affect your vision and the rest of the organization. To counter this, keep the vision of the organization alive by talking about it all the time. Let people in your organization know what your plans are and what you are striving to achieve. Share milestones and unique achievements among the group; for example, show members of the group the progress of the rehabs you are doing or offer contracts that have been accepted. A shared commitment of the vision will grow your business and your organization. Remember, what you think about most, you become. Moreover, developing a shared vision among the members of your organization will enhance growth both professionally and personally.

Who is In Your Organization?

Accountant	Attorney	Contractor
Inspectors Investor	Manager	Handyman
Property Manager	Personal Assistant	

Where there is no vision, the people perish.
—Proverbs 29:18 (KJV)

In the book and subsequent movie, *The Treasure of the Sierra Madre,* staring Humphrey Bogart, Walter Huston and Tim Holt, writer B. Traven creates a story powered by the vision of three down-and-outers searching for riches. The visions of the three men are the same: to find a rich gold-strike in the mountains of Mexico. Although, only one of the fortune seekers is an experienced miner, Howard, played by the older Walter Huston, the other two have big dreams, but absolutely no experience in mining for gold.

The vision is cast in a flop-house where a discussion is formed on the allure of gold:

Howard: Say answer me this one, will you? Why is gold worth some twenty bucks an ounce?

Flophouse Bum: I don't know. Because it's scarce.

Howard: A thousand men, say, go searchin' for gold. After six months, one of them's lucky: one out of a thousand. His find represents not only his own labor, but that of nine hundred and ninety-nine others to boot. That's six thousand months, five hundred years, scrambling' over a mountain, goin' hungry and thirsty. An ounce of gold, mister, is worth what it is because of the human labor that went into the findin' and the getting' of it.

As Howard speaks about the value of gold, Dobbs (Humphrey Bogart) and Curtin (Tim Holt) listen intently on nearby cots.

Dobbs: I think I'll go to sleep and dream about piles of gold getting bigger and bigger and bigger.

A day or two later Dobbs and Curtin question the old man, Howard about searching for gold and making a strike. They do not have enough money amongst themselves to buy equipment and supplies for the venture. Suddenly, Dobbs wins a few hundred dollars from a lottery and offers to stake Curtin with his portion. Dobbs' vision of riches is strong enough to encourage him to stake Curtin--and Howard, Dobbs and Curtin are now in the business of gold mining.

After trekking many days through harsh conditions, they locate a good spot and begin mining. The vision of riches among the three keeps them going day after day. When they finally find gold, it is in small sand-like form imbedded into the mountain. A lot of hard physical labor is needed to extract the gold.

Finding gold, motivates them more and they work diligently as a team to recover as much as possible. Their productivity is strong because they share the same vision--they want to achieve the same results. However, each has different plans with their share of the gold and the money they'll get for it.

After several months and recovery of many sacks of gold, Dobbs' vision changes to fear. He becomes fearful that Howard and Curtin are out to get him and his sacks of gold. As the vision of the venture has changed the output has also changed. Dobbs becomes obsessed with fear.

In the end, Dobbs' fears became reality. His gold is stolen by banditos and he is killed. What he obsessed about happening happens.

In the beginning, all three men had a vision of common interest, and that commonality bound them together to work productively as a team. And as a team, with the same vision, the three men working together accomplished more than they ever could have individually. Once one of the three's vision changed, so did the eventual outcome of the entire venture.

When you are building your organization, remain consistent with your vision. Share your plans and vision with all the members of your organization. Everyone must believe in the same vision. To accomplish what you want in real estate or in any endeavor, you must form a team that follows the same beliefs as you. When the entire team is working to achieve the same dream, the results will be clear. A target is met and clarity is defined by a consistent group vision.

When objectives are met, reward your team with bonuses and praise and when the time is right, with pay raises and your continued support for future projects and the prospects for long-term employment.

Five Principles to Investor Longevity

Investor longevity is a rarely achieved goal for many investors. The reason behind investor failure or disenchantment is the result of many factors; and two many to mention in this space. However, there are five powerful reasons for Investor longevity: (1) Research and diligence; (2) know why you are doing it; (3) don't over spend; (4) take risks; and (5) managing assets consistently.

1. *Research and Diligence*. To make prudent investments you must do the appropriate research on the property, its location and the costs associated with fix-up and the price you will sell it for after it has been rehabbed. You must know the local economy and in what price points properties are selling quickly.

Much of your research can be completed online and the county assessors site and other real estate websites such as www.Realtor.com can be very useful. These sites will give you the necessary information as to prices and comparables, and the properties legal description.

Conducting due diligence on the full package; for example, local growth, business development, rental rates, city incentives and many other informative measures should be researched if you are new to an area and unfamiliar with investment property.

2. *Know why you are doing it*. Follow your plan. Your plan has a great deal to do with your goals. Do you ever ask yourself, why are you doing this or that? And how do you reply to yourself? "I have to get it done, or, do you stop, think for a moment and reply: "Why am I doing this?" Then stop doing it and concentrate on doing something more worthwhile with your time and energy.

The purpose for what you are doing should be in the foundation of your goals. It must be a means to an end. And if it isn't, then stop doing it and focus on activities that will move you toward the achievement of your goals.

3. *Don't over spend*. Always look for ways to reduce your operating costs and keep close watch over your expenses. When you are rehabbing, set a firm budget and find ways to narrow the budget as you progress; it will not be easy, but keep this in mind. Your rental properties do not need the best fixtures and items--they need clean and functional items.

4. *Take Risks.* Have you asked yourself: What is the indirect costs of not taking risks? Everything worthwhile has a risk to it, and real estate investing can certainly be risky if simple rules are not followed.

Typically, the larger the risk, the higher the return, is a saying that is not always correct with real estate investing. A great deal of successful real estate investing is knowing more than the other fellow who is bidding on the same property or not bidding. Your knowledge of costs associated with repairs and current market conditions, your relationships with contractors, inspectors and mortgage brokers, and your money management skills are the advantages you possess over others in the real estate investment game.

Every investment is unique and the risks associated with each property you purchase will be more or less risky than the previous one, but may present a higher profit return with more or less equity at risk. Be courageous. Risk is necessary for your personal growth and the growth of your wallet. Always evaluate the risks involved with any transaction first. How much can you lose on the investment and can you handle the loss, psychologically and financially. You must also know what the upside is before you buy.

The indirect cost of not taking risks is future security. For, there is no security in poverty or mediocrity. And there is no security in any action or non-action you take. Don't let fear hold you back; take advantage of the opportunities presented to you today, for they may not be there tomorrow. Poker great Doyle Brunson said: "Feed your courage and your fears will starve to death." We couldn't agree more.

5. *Managing Assets Consistently*. When you are in a position to buy two or more properties in a short period of time and each property is in need of renovation before it can be rented or sold, evaluate the properties and budget your funds and your time equally among the properties. There would be only a few occasions, outside of adequate funding, that you wouldn't begin renovating the properties around the same time. Don't make the mistake of buying properties and have them sitting around for months before you begin work. Your carrying costs will soon eat away at your bankroll, this is the money you'll need for renovation. Your time will be limited, so make sure you have honest and capable contractors. You could use one general contractor to manage construction crews at each property.

When you begin on the acquisition trail, manage your rentals consistently. When it comes to managing rentals, many investors neglect less valuable and troublesome properties and spend more time with properties that are closer to where they live and have better tenants--that is the wrong approach, and it should be the exact opposite. You should spend more time at your troubled properties and get them up to par or simply put them up for sale and exchange them for better and more profitable investments.

Surviving the Dreadfully Ugly

Believe it or not, the dreadfully ugly houses and multi-family properties will usually make you the most money, particularly on flips. This concept is simple to understand and anyone who has renovated a truly dreadful property and sold it, would agree. But this property type will also cost the most to fix and will take longer to complete. However, once you have completed the fix-up, your profit margin will be high enough to have made it worth the trouble.

One concept you should remember, has to do with the ugliest house on the street strategy. Money will be made by using your creativity and imagination in transforming the ugliest house on the street into the pretties house on the street. Not only do you increase the value of your house, but you will inadvertently increase the value of all the other homes on the block; and the neighbors should love you. And some will come to you with great appreciation.

ACTION HIGHLIGHTS FOR
STAYING THE COURSE

1) Realize you are accountable for the investments and decisions you make.

2) Realize the long-term value of investing properly.

3) Focus on a clear plan.

4) Establish clear goals on what you want to achieve in your real estate investing.

5) What is your vision? Form a clear vision with members of your team.

6) Follow the five principles of investor longevity.

"Persistence is nothing more than believing in yourself. And group vision can transform a dilapidated mess into a stunning home."

9

Winning Principles of a Real Estate Investor

"I studied the lives of great men and famous women; and I found that the men and women who got to the top were those who did the jobs they had in hand, with everything they had of energy and enthusiasm and hard work."
—Harry S. Truman

There are fifteen principles professional real estate investors adhere to. Following these simple principles will not only guide you to a path of unlimited wealth, but also help clarify your desires and create within you a person of integrity and character, the embodiment of a winning real estate investor.

Many organizations today neglect to stress the importance of business ethics--business ethics and principals devoted to the development of quality personal traits of the successful real estate investor are necessary. When you follow these principles and incorporate them into your daily life, you will take the first step to become a highly successful real estate investor.

Remember to be respectful to all, pleasant, open-minded and reasonable when dealing with others. Let's begin now with the fifteen principles of a winning investor.

1. *Concentrate on Your Goals.* Your goals will give you a target to shoot for. They will enable you to stay focused on your wants. Your goals are more than just a wish list, they enable you to think clearly about your life, plans and dreams. By concentrating and thinking about your goals often, you are creating a powerful message for your subconscious mind. Look beyond your present situation. Your goals should be defined clearly and you should be able to see them being achieved in your own minds eye. Can you see what you can achieve? You can achieve everything you can see.

2. *Focus on the Process Not the Result.* Once you find a successful way to invest you should always focus on the process and not the result. Your business should be approached systematically. Although the money you invest and the money you make is important, it can also distract you from focusing on the process. You must repeat the process of correct investing over and over again, deal after deal. After a few transactions, you will realize what you can expect regarding results. Therefore, focus on the process; the end result will

come soon enough.

    3. *Work Diligently and Consistently.* It takes intelligent effort, hard work, and consistency to succeed in any business endeavor. Intelligent effort means doing your homework. Hard work means hustling; aggressively completely what must get done. And consistency means to keep going and going and going. Be consistent deal after deal and keep going. Do not waver; do not sit on your hands; keep moving forward. Be known as the person who is always out there; the person who others can depend on.

    4. *Take Risks Backed by Your Skills.* The only way to really succeed is to take risks; there is no other way. Once you have developed certain skills necessary and developed an understanding of real estate investment, as outlined in this book, you will realize the risks you take are not really that risky. Measuring the downside first in any investment is the starting point. Once, you have calculated the downside, measure the upside, your grand return. The upside should far exceed the downside. Now you are ready to invest. Here is an example of measuring risks:

You are interested in a house and present an offer to the seller for $90,000. You measure your risk at $15,000. This means, the ultimate downside is a house valued at $75,000, should the market for the property completely fall apart. Lot value alone is worth $60,000. You estimate about $25,000 in repairs and carrying costs for five months. Your total investment is $115,000. Once the house is rehabbed it will be worth $250,000. You list the house for $225,000 for a quick sale. Your return is $110,000. Your upside is 7.33 to 1 compared to the downside (estimated profit $110,000 over estimated loss $15,000). This is a good investment and a good risk to take.

---

    5. *There is No Competition—You are Your Competition.* Believe it or not, there is no competition, there is only you. There are people who invest correctly and there are those that do not. There are people who will constantly say "There is a lot of competition in this business"; that is completely false. You are competing with yourself. Great investors make money in up markets, down markets, sideways markets, booming markets, busted markets, at peaks, at bottoms, during stagnation, depression, recession, and times of confusion.

Great real estate investors believe in hard work and hustle. They eliminate the thought of competition with hard work, creativity and imagination; and so will you. Don't you know that a body in motion will stay in motion?

    6. *It Is Always You, Never the Economy or Market.* There are no excuses. It is always you. No one or thing or economy is responsible for your success. The desire to make a success as a real estate investor is within you. Focus and concentrate on your dreams and wishes. You are accountable for your success. No market, good or bad, has the ability to determine your success. Great investors make money in good and bad markets. They understand there really is no such thing as a bad market. It is always good for those who maintain a winners attitude and hustle to get business done.

    7. *Love Thy Neighbor.* Your neighbors are not only the people who live next to you or on your street--they are everyone you come in contact with. On any given day, when you are out and about searching for

property, you will come in contact with many people; and many of these people are sources of finding good deals. Here is an example:

After speaking to our neighbor about investing in real estate, she introduced us to a friend of hers who was getting older and owns a five unit building. We contacted her friend and after the initial meeting, we learned that the lady wanted to spend more time with her children who reside in Germany. The building was not for sale. She finally made up her mind to sell after we explained, she would not have to pay any sales commissions and we could close at her convenience, giving her time to collect and make arrangements for personal items. We met with her three times and went over a sales contract. She even carried paper for 40% of the purchase price at a good interest rate. We got a good price and terms and she got the price she wanted and she is getting almost double the interest the banks are paying now on the 40% she self financed; a win- win situation.

---

8. *Continue to Study and Learn about Your Market.* Knowledge is a great tool if applied correctly. You should continue to study and learn everything you can about your real estate business. Start by forming a library of books on the subjects you are interested in. Set aside a certain about of money to use on your education. Invest in books, tapes, courses and continue to learn throughout your life. You will be surprised from the outcome. Apply what you have learned and exercise your new found knowledge regularly. With some luck, you will become addicted to learning.

9. *Plan for the Long-Term.* Planning for the long-term is something most people just do not do. The long-term seems so far away; but the trouble is, we catch-up to it rather quickly when we are not being attentive to it. You must have long-term plans. And these plans should be apart of your long-term goals.
Look into the future. Can you answer the following questions?

- Where do you see yourself five years from now?
- Ten years from now?
- Twenty years from now?
- How many investment properties do you own?
- What is your net worth?
- What kind of a lifestyle do you see yourself having?

As you can realize, it is very important to plan for the long-term. The long-term catches-up with us quickly, so plan today so you can reap all the benefits tomorrow.

10. *Organization.* There are two types of organization; first, building relationships; second, personal organization. All successful real estate investors have learned to build long lasting relationships. Relationships with lenders, insurance agents, real estate agents and brokers, contractors and handymen, attorneys and accountants, and of course other investors. To grow your business, you need an organization of qualified individuals; people who think along the same lines as you do. Those individuals who understand your plans and who are motivated by the energy you possess to accomplish your goals; these are the people you want in your organization. Strong relationships will build your organization.

The second type of organization is of a personal nature. To succeed in any endeavor you must be organized. Time becomes your most important enemy and also your most important allei. Without organizing your time each day, you will soon be loosing more than just time. From the moment you awake in the morning, you should know exactly what you will be doing the rest of the day. Draft a list each day you leave the office or each night before you turn-in of the tasks and activities you will be doing the next day. Make a list of your priorities for each day. You should program yourself to a very regimented schedule. All extremely successful investors work all the time when they are at work. Do not waste time by doing activities that are unproductive and counteractive to your priorities for the day. Staying focused on the task that need to be completed first and then follow immediately with the second most important task without a break is the best way to get things done fast and on time. Be time conscious of every minute of your day.

11. *Be Fair and Honest with Everyone.* This should go without saying. We want to make it absolutely clear that honesty is now and will always be the best policy. True wealth is build by true and honest effort. Treat everyone fairly. Even though their will be those who will try to take advantage of your fairness, be fair anyway. Honesty is a great long-term wealth builder. Do not do business with anyone you suspect of being dishonest or untrustworthy, no matter how high the projected return on investment.

12. *Physical Conditioning.* To do all the things you need to do, you have to be in top physical condition. It takes a lot of energy to work productively and with all kinds of people, including tenants. You will be dealing with different and unique personalities, city employees, contractors and many others. To deal effectively with these types of people you will need a lot of energy. Some people will become an energy drain; avoid those who suck the energy right out of you. These are people who generally want to hang around you and talk about anything, mostly their sad and sorry circumstances. The energy zappers will be able to explain a thousand and one ways how to handle their one problem. They are huge time wasters. Cut your conversations with people quickly: Get to the point. Unless, you are negotiating a transaction, keep your conversations brief.

You should exercise regularly and maintain a comfortable weight. Stop smoking immediately and limit your alcohol consumption. And if you are doing other types of drugs, it's time to grow up and be accountable. It is proven that cigarette smokers and heavy alcohol consuming individuals clock-out more sick days than people who don't smoke or drink heavily, they also clock-out from life a lot faster. You can't afford to get sick; you've got to make your millions.

One last word, and that has to do with balance. Maintain a balanced lifestyle. Get plenty of sleep; you need your rest. There is no need to work all the time. Take time off; take vacations and have fun with your family. You will realize nothing really changes in your business when you take time away from it. Most of the time, when you do come back, you are reenergized and ready to work hard for your next vacation..

13. *Professionalism.* Always conduct yourself with a high level of professionalism. Those involved in the real estate industry, as a whole, do not exude a professional image when described by the public. By being professional, you can help change that image in your community. Be polite, courteous, respectful, civil, understanding, punctual, and kind. Dress appropriately. Possess the values you wish others to possess; and be that person of high integrity: It is already locked within you, all you have to do is use the key already have to unlock it.

14. *Charity.* Give when you can and give when you must, just give. Nothing says more without a utter word, than a charitable heart. Help people when they need help; help before they ask. Many people during the year do charitable work during the months of November and December, the holiday season; be a giver

year round. It's very true, the more you give the more you do receive; just ask all those givers.

15. *Discipline.* Lastly, the value of discipline is a principle all great leaders possess. And to be a successful real estate investor, you have to condition yourself to become a great leader. Discipline yourself to do the hard tasks first, each day. Discipline yourself today by sacrificing instant gratification for a stronger, better tomorrow. Plan for your future. Winning investors always look into the future. Discipline can take you into the future with a grander outcome than you ever imagined possible. And contrary to a popular proverb, you "should" count your chickens before they hatch, otherwise, you won't be able to plan your other investments. Learn to count your chickens correctly and don't over count them. A chicken can go a long way if it knows where to get its feed.

Following these fifteen principles daily and reviewing them often will keep you on track. There will be days when you are not very motivated, depressed or simply tired. The leader within you knows that motivation comes from completing the tasks--the really tough tasks first. Once you've completed something you've set out to do—that's when you become motivated. Doing your work well makes you more motivated. Doesn't it?

ACTION HIGHLIGHTS FOR
WINNING PRINCIPLES OF A
REAL ESTATE INVESTOR

1) Concentrate on your goals.

2) Focus on the process not the result.

3) Work diligently and consistently in everything you do.

4) Take risks backed by your skills.

5) There is no competition--you are your competition.

6) It is always you, never the economy or market.

7) Love thy neighbor.

8) Continue to study and learn about your market.

9) Plan for the long-term.

10) Organize yourself and your team.

11) Be fair and honest with everyone.

12) Enjoy the benefits of being physically fit.

13) Be a professional.

14) Develop a charitable heart.

15) It takes discipline to do the things you know you must do to succeed.

"The only difference between winners and losers, is that, the winners give that extra push—that extra 1%. They stick with it just a little bit longer.

Appendixes

Appendix I: Applications, Agreements, Forms, Letters and
               Advertisements

Appendix II: Real Estate Investment and Landlording Terms

Appendix I

Applications, Agreements, Forms, Letters and Advertisements

Land Trust Agreement
Assignment of Beneficial Interest in Trust
Certificate Of Resignation Of Trustee
Certificate of Appointment of Successor Trustee
Inspection Checklist for Rental Property
Rental Property Move-In Inspection Checklist with Tenant
Asbestos Disclosure Form
Mold Disclosure Form
Radon Gas Disclosure Form
Three Day Notice to Pay or Quit
Deposit to Reserve Apartment
Lease Agreement
Security Deposit Policy
Disclosure of Information on Lead-Based Paint and Lead-Based Paint Hazards
Payment Policy
Rules and Regulations
Affidavit of Military Status
Notice of Lease Violation
Monthly Rental Voucher
Rental Property Details
Tenant Estoppel Certificate
Tenant Welcome Letter
Pet Rent Agreement
Move-Out Charges
Move-Out Charges (CARGOS DE MUDANZA) (Spanish)
CONTRATO DE ARRENDAMIENTO (Lease Agreement—Spanish)
Late Rent Letter (English and Spanish)
Renters Insurance Letter to Tenant
Rental Application
Notice of Rent Increase English / Spanish
Key Receipt and Key Deposit
Rental Referral Flyer ($50 Referral Bonus)

LAND TRUST AGREEMENT

THIS LAND TRUST AGREEMENT is made this ___ day of _____, 20___, by and between
_____, Grantors and Beneficiaries, (hereinafter collectively referred to as the
"Beneficiaries"), and _____, Trustee of the _____ **LAND TRUST**,
(Hereinafter referred to as the "Trustee", which designation shall include all successor trustees).

WHEREAS, the beneficiaries are about to convey or cause to be conveyed certain real property to the
Trustee, and

WHEREAS, the Trustee has agreed to accept such conveyance and hold the real property in trust under
the terms and conditions set forth below.

NOW, THEREFORE, the parties, intending to be legally bound hereby, agree as follows:

1. TITLE. The trust created by this instrument shall be known as _____.

2. OBJECTS AND PURPOSES OF TRUST. The purpose of this trust is for the Trustee to take and hold
title to the property conveyed to the Trustee and to preserve the same until its sale or other disposition.

The Trustee shall not undertake any activity which is not strictly necessary to attainment of the foregoing
objects and purposes, nor shall the Trustee transact business within the same meaning of applicable state
law, or any other law, nor shall this Land Trust Agreement be deemed to be, or create or evidence the existence of a corporation, de facto or de jure, or a Massachusetts Trust, or any other type of business trust,
or an association in the nature of a corporation, or a co-partnership or joint venture by or between the
Trustee and the Beneficiaries, or by or between the Beneficiaries.

3. TRUST PROPERTY. The Beneficiaries are about to convey or cause to be conveyed to the Trustee in
trust certain real property as described more particularly in Schedule "A" attached hereto and made a part
hereof. This property, together with any property later added to the trust, shall be designated as the "Trust
Property". The Trustee will hold the Trust Property according to the terms and conditions of this Land
Trust Agreement for the purposes, terms and conditions contained herein until such time as all of the
Trust Property has been sold or otherwise conveyed, or until this rust has been terminated. The Trustee
shall maintain a list of the Trust Property, which shall be designated as Schedule "B" under this Agree-
ment.

4. POWERS AND DUTIES OF TRUSTEE. The Trustee shall have all of the powers allowed to him by
the provisions of the state law governing this Trust (see Paragraph 18). The Trustee shall specifically have
the power to make and execute contracts for the lease or sale of the Trust Property, mortgages otherwise
dispose of the Trust Property as the Trustee shall be directed by the majority in interest of the Beneficiaries. In addition, the Trustee shall have the power to perform any act that the majority-in-interest direct the

Trustee to perform. The Trustee shall exercise his powers only upon the written direction of a majority in interest of the Beneficiaries.

The Trustee shall have the duty to maintain an accurate record of the Beneficiaries of this Trust, which record shall include the names and addresses of the Beneficiaries and their respective interest in the Trust and be designated as Schedule "C". The Trustee shall only have such other duties as required in writing by a majority in interest of the Beneficiaries.

The Trustee shall not have the power to bind any of the Beneficiaries personally to any debt or obligation without the express written consent of the Beneficiary.

5. COMPENSATION OF TRUSTEE. The Trustee shall be compensated for his actions as Trustee according to the schedule of Compensation set forth in Schedule "D" attached hereto and made a part hereof. The Trustee shall be promptly reimbursed by the Beneficiaries for expense incurred by the Trustee in the administration of the Trust. The Trustee shall have a lien on the Trust Property for any unpaid compensation or un-reimbursed expenses.

The Trustee shall not be obligated to advance any money on account of the Trust. The Trustee shall not be obligated to commerce any legal action or to defend against any legal action unless the Trustee, in his sole discretion, is satisfied with the security provided by the Beneficiaries for the payment of the Trustee's costs and expenses in connection with the litigation.

If the Trustee shall pay or incur any liability to pay any money on account of this Trust, or incur any liability to any money on account of being made a party to any litigation as a result of holding title to the Trust Property or otherwise in connection with this Trust, without regard to the cause of action asserted or complaint filed, the Beneficiaries, jointly and severally, agree that on demand they will pay to the Trustee all such payments or liabilities, his expenses incurred in connection therewith, including reasonable attorney's fees, and any other sums advanced by the Trustee on behalf of the Trust for any reason whatsoever. These amounts, if not immediately paid to the Trustee, shall bear interest at the rate of ten (10%) percent per annum until paid in full. These amounts and any compensation due to the Trustee, until pain in full to the Trustee, shall constitute a lien on the Trust Property. Further, as long as these amounts or any compensation due to the Trustee remain unpaid, the Trustee shall not have any obligation to take any action with regard to the Trust Property.

6. LIABILITY OF Trustee. The Trustee shall not be personally liable for any obligation of the Trust. No Beneficiary shall be able to bind the Trustee nor contract on his behalf without the Trustee's express written consent. The Trustee and any successor Trustee shall not be required to give a bond. Each Trustee is liable only for his own actions and then as a result of his own gross negligence or bad faith.

7. REMOVAL OF TRUSTEE. A majority in interest of the Beneficiaries shall have the power to remove the Trustee from his office and appoint a successor to succeed him.

8. RESIGNATION AND SUCCESSOR. The Trustee may resign by giving written notice to each of the Beneficiaries of his intention to resign.

The majority in interest of the Beneficiaries shall have the power to elect a successor trustee. If the Beneficiaries have not elected a successor trustee within thirty (30) days of the date of the notice from the Trustee of his resignation, then the Trustee shall have the right to convey the Trust Property to the Beneficiaries in the same proportion as their interests in the Trust may appear at the time of said conveyance.

If the office of the Trustee shall become vacant for any reason, then the Beneficiaries shall proceed to elect a successor trustee. Said election shall occur with thirty (30) days of the occurrence of the vacancy. Upon election, the new Trustee shall cause to be prepared a certificate of his election containing a notice of election and his acceptance thereof in a form acceptable for recording in the office of the register of deed of all of the counties in which the Trust Property is located. The certificate of election shall be filed in the office of the register of deeds of all of the counties in which the Trust Property is located.

A successor Trustee shall have all of the rights, duties and powers of the original Trustee as if the successor Trustee was the original Trustee.

The removal, resignation or death of the Trustee shall not affect the lien of the Trustee upon the Trust Property for compensation or expense owed to the Trustee.

9. INCOME TAX RETURNS. The Trustee shall not be responsible for the preparation and/or filing of any tax returns, which may be due for the reporting of income and expenses of the Trust, although he will sign such returns upon request. The Beneficiaries shall each individually report receipt of their respective share of the profits, earnings, avails and proceeds.

10. INDEMNIFICATION OF THE TRUSTEE. The Beneficiaries agree to indemnify, hold harmless and defend the Trustee from any and all liability incurred in his capacity as Trustee. If the Trustee shall pay or incur any liability to pay any money on account of this Trust, or incur any liability to any money on account of being made a party to any litigation as a result to holding title to the Trust Property or otherwise in connection with the Trust, without regard to the cause of action asserted or complaint filed, the Beneficiaries jointly and severally, agree that on demand they will pay to the Trustee all such payments or liabilities, his expenses incurred in connection therewith, including reasonable attorney's fees, and any other sums advanced by the Trustee on behalf of the Trust for any reason whatsoever. These amounts, if not immediately paid to the Trustee, shall bear interest at the rate of ten (10%) percent per annum until paid in full. These amounts and any compensation due to the Trustee, until paid in full to the Trustee, shall constitute a lien on the Trust Property. Further, as long as these amounts or any compensation due to the Trustee remain unpaid, the Trustee shall not have any obligations to take any action with regard to the Trust Property.

11. DEALING WITH TRUSTEE. No party dealing with the Trustee, in relation to the Trust Property in any manner whatsoever, including, but not limited to, a party to whom the Trust Property or any part of it or any interest in it shall be conveyed, contracted to be sold, leased or mortgaged, by the Trustee, shall be obligated to see to the application of any purchase money, rent or money borrowed or otherwise advanced on the property; to see that the terms of this Trust Agreement have been complied with; to inquire into the authority, necessary or expediency of any act of the Trustee; or be privileged to inquire into any of the terms of this Trust Agreement. Every deed, mortgage, lease or other instrument executed by the Trustee in relation to the Trust Property shall be conclusive evidence in favor of every person this Agreement was in full force an effect; and that the instrument was executed in accordance with the terms and conditions of this Agreement and all its amendments, if any, and is binding upon all Beneficiaries under it; if a conveyance has been made to a successor or successors-in-trust, that the successor or successors have been appointed properly and are vested fully with all the title, estate, rights, powers, duties and obligations of its, his or their predecessor in Trust.

12. BENEFICIARIES. The Beneficiaries are the persons or legal entities identified, along with their respective interests, on schedule "C" which is attached hereto and made a part of thereof.

The Beneficiaries are entitled to all of the profits, earnings, avails, and proceeds of the Trust Property.

13. INTEREST OF BENEFICIARIES. The interest of the beneficiaries shall consist solely of (a) the right to lease, manage and control the Trust Property; and (c) the right to receive the profits, earnings, avails and proceeds from the rental, sale, mortgage or other disposition of the Trust Property.

The foregoing rights of the Beneficiaries are hereby declared to be personal property and may be assigned or otherwise transferred as such. The death of any Beneficiaries shall not affect the existence of the Trust nor in any way diminish or alter the powers of Trustee. No Beneficiaries shall have any right, title or interest, whether legal or equitable, in the real property, which is held as Trust Property. No Beneficiary shall have the right to require partition of the Trust Property.

The Beneficiaries shall not use the name of the Trustee for advertising or other publicity purposes without first obtaining the written consent of the Trustee.

The Beneficiaries shall be required to carry liability insurance in such forms and in such amounts as the Trustee, in his sole discretion, shall deem necessary to insure the Trust Property and the Trustee. If the Beneficiaries fail to obtain or maintain the required insurance policies, then the Trustee shall have the right, in his sole discretion, to advance the money necessary to pay for said insurance policies. The Beneficiaries will reimburse the Trustee for the insurance as set forth above in Paragraph 5.

No Beneficiaries shall have right to bind or otherwise contract for any other Beneficiaries except as provided for elsewhere under this Agreement.

14. ASSIGNMENT OF BENEFICIAL INTEREST. The Beneficiaries have the right to assign any part or all of their interests under this Trust. No assignment shall be valid or affect the interest of a Beneficiary hereunder until the original of the assignment shall be delivered to the Trustee and the Trustee's acceptance acknowledged thereon. The Trustee shall revise and update Schedule "C" as necessary. Any assignment of the right to direct the Trustee by a person who is not a beneficiary hereunder shall not be valid unless all of the Beneficiaries consent in writing to said assignment.

15. DISCLOSURE OF BENEFICIARIES. The Trustee and the Beneficiaries shall not disclose the identity of any Beneficiary without the written consent of said Beneficiary except as may be required by law or at the direction of an order of court issued by a court of competent jurisdiction. Any party who discloses the identity of a Beneficiary shall be personally liable for any and all losses and damages incurred by the Beneficiary as a result of the disclosure.

16. SPEND THRIFT PROVISION.
A. No beneficiary in anticipation of receiving benefits from this trust shall have the right to transfer all or any part of his or her interest in the trust assets either with or without the consent of the Trustee.
B. No person having a claim or demand of any sort including claims for alimony or support against a beneficiary shall have a right while the Trustee is in possession of any trust asset to reach the interest of any beneficiary by judicial process.

C. In the event a beneficiary attempts to encumber, assign or sell his or her rights as a beneficiary of the trust or any part thereof, or in event a creditor of the beneficiary attempts to reach a beneficiary's interest or for the duration of the attempts to reach such beneficiary's interest by judicial process as if the beneficiary had no interest in such trust whatsoever. The trustee shall vigorously defend against all claims.

Upon termination of the attempted assignment, sale or encumbering or the attempt to reach trust assets by judicial process, the beneficiary's interest in the trust shall be reinstated, however, the Trustee shall charge the cost of defending against any attempted encumbering, sale, assignment or judicial process to that beneficiary's share that is attempted to be reached.

17. RECORDING OF AGREEMENT. This Land Trust Agreement shall not be placed of record in any jurisdiction. If this agreement is placed of record, then it shall not be notice of any interest, which may affect the title or the powers of the Trustee.

18. ENTIRE AGREEMENT. This Land Trust Agreement contains the entire understanding between the parties hereto and may be amended, revoked or terminated only be written agreement signed by the Trustee and all of the Beneficiaries at the time of the amendment, revocation or termination.

19. GOVERNING LAW. This Agreement shall be governed by, construed and enforced in accordance with the laws of the **State of** _____. In the event that litigation shall arise between parties to this Agreement, then it is agreed that the losing partied shall reimburse the prevailing parties for all of

those parties' reasonable attorneys' fees, costs and expenses in addition to any other relief to which the prevailing parties may be entitled.

20. BINDING EFFECT. This Agreement shall be binding upon and inure to the benefit of the Trustee, any successor trustee, the Beneficiaries, and the Beneficiaries, and the Beneficiaries' successors, heirs, executors, administrators and assigns.

21. ANNUAL STATEMENTS. The Trustee shall be required to furnish annual statements to the Beneficiaries of the income and expenses of the Trust for each calendar year. The statements shall be provided to the Beneficiaries no later than March 1st of the following year.

22. PERPETUITIES. If any portion of the Trust Property is in any manner or time period capable of being held in this Land Trust for longer period of time than is permitted under laws of the state law governing this Land Trust Agreement (See Paragraph 18), or the vesting of any interest under this Land Trust could possibly occur after the end of such permitted time period, then upon the occurrence of the foregoing, the Trustee is directed to immediately terminate in Trust and to distribute the Trust Property to the Beneficiaries as their respective interests may appear at the time of the termination of the Trust. As much as possible, the Trustee will maintain the Trust Property intact and not liquidate it, but, rather, distribute the Trust Property in kind.

24. NOTICE. Any notice that is given in connection with this Land Trust Agreement shall be given (a) to the Beneficiaries at the address set forth in Schedule "C" as shall be changed from time to time upon notice to the Trustee from the Beneficiaries; and (b) to the Trustee at such address as he may hereafter specify. The notice shall be deemed to be validly given if personally delivered or mailed to a person by first class mail, postage prepaid, at the above specified address.

25. IN WITNESS WHEREOF, we have executed this Land Trust Agreement on the day and year first above written.

WITNESS: BENEFICIARIES:

_____   _____
Print Name: Print Name:

_____   _____

                                                               Trustee_____

                                                               _____
                                                               Print Name:

_____
Print Name

ACKNOWLEDGEMENTS

STATE OF   }
COUNTY   }

Before me, the undersigned officer in and for said county and state, personally appeared _____,, known to me (or satisfactorily proven) to be the person(s) whose name(s) (is) (are) subscribed to the foregoing instrument and acknowledged that (he) (she) (they) executed the same for the purposes contained therein.

IN WITNESS WHEREOF,   I have hereunto set my hand and official seal this _____ day of _____, 20___.

My Commission expires: _____
                                Notary Public

STATE OF   }
COUNTY OF   }

Before me, the undersigned officer in and for said county and state, personally appeared _____, known to me (or satisfactorily proven) to be the person(s) whose name(s) (is) (are) subscribed to the foregoing instrument and acknowledged that (he) (she) (they) executed the same for the purposes contained therein.

IN WITNESS WHEREOF,   I have hereunto set my hand and official seal this _____ day of _____, 20____.

My Commission expires: _____
                                Notary Public

SCHEDULE "A"

The following is the legal description of the Trust Property contained in the forgoing Land Trust:

Legal Description:

SCHEDULE "B"

The following are the addresses of the real estate, which is Trust Property:

SCHEDULE "C"

The following are all of the Beneficiaries who own the beneficial interest in the foregoing Land Trust:

Name _____ Address _____

_____ Percentage of Interest _____

SCHEDULE "D"

The Trustee will be compensated in the following manner:

$10.00 per annum plus expenses.

Assignment of Beneficial Interest in Trust

THIS ASSIGNMENT is made this____ day of _____,20____,
by _____ whose address is _____,
hereinafter referred to as "Assigner"), to _____, whose
address is _____, (hereinafter referred to as "Assignee").

WITNESSETH:

   WHEREAS, the Assignor is a beneficiary of a Trust created by _____,
by instrument dated _____, naming _____as Trustee; and

   WHEREAS, the Assignor desires to assign to the Assignee all of Assignor's beneficial interest in the trust; and

   WHEREAS, the trust instrument does not prohibit such assignment;

NOW, THEREFORE, for valuable consideration, the receipt of which is hereby acknowledged, the Assignor hereby assigns to the Assignee all Assignor's interest as a beneficiary of the Trust, including all moneys due or to become due to the Assignor thereunder; and

   The Assignor authorizes the Trustee of the Trust to pay directly to the Assignee all moneys or other benefits representing, or arising from, the interest assigned hereby.

IN WITNESS WHEREOF, the Assignor has executed this assignment the day and year first above written.

Signed, sealed and delivered in the presence of:

_____ _____
Witness   Assignor

_____
Witness

STATE OF _____
COUNTY OF _____

The foregoing instrument was executed and acknowledged before me this _____ day
of_____ , 20____ , by_____ .

              _____
              Notary Public
(SEAL)   State of _____
              My Commission Expires:

              _____

THIS DOCUMENT SHALL NOT BE RECORDED
IN THE PUBLIC RECORDS OF ANY COUNTY

Certificate Of Resignation Of Trustee

I, the undersigned, do hereby certify that I have duly tendered my resignation as Trustee under that certain Agreement and Declaration of Trust, dated _____ , by, between and among the undersigned, as Trustee, and the beneficiaries thereunder, whose names are as follows:

_____.

I further certify that said resignation shall take effect immediately upon the execution of the following Certificate of Election of Successor Trustee, Certificate of Acceptance of the office by the newly elected Trustee, and proper conveyance of all the properties of the trust to the successor trustee.

IN WITNESS WHEREOF, I have hereunto set my hand and seal this _____day of _____ , 20   .

Signed, sealed and delivered in the presence of:

_____   _____
Witness #1   Trustee

_____
Witness #2

STATE OF _____
COUNTY OF _____

The foregoing instrument was executed and acknowledged before me this day _____ of _____ , 20 _____ , by_____ .

_____
Notary Public
(SEAL)   State of _____
My Commission Expires:

_____

THIS DOCUMENT <u>SHALL NOT</u> BE RECORDED
IN THE PUBIC RECORDS OF ANY COUNTY

Certificate of Appointment of Successor Trustee

We, the undersigned, being all of the beneficiaries under that certain Agreement and Declaration of Trust dated _____ , by and between the undersigned and _____ , as the original Trustee, do hereby certify that we have this day duly elected _____ , to succeed to the office of Trustee under said Agreement and Declaration of Trust, and to the title of all the properties of the Trust, with all the powers and subject to all the restrictions upon the original Trustee, with the same powers, rights and interests regarding the Trust property and subject to the same restrictions and duties as the original Trustee, except as the same shall have been heretofore modified by amendment.

IN WITNESS WHEREOF we have hereunto set our hands and seals this _____ day of _____ 20 ____ .

Signed, sealed and delivered in the presence of:

"BENEFICIARIES"

_____

Witness #1

_____

Witness #2

_____

Witness #1

_____

Witness #2

_____

Witness #1

_____

Witness #2

STATE OF _____
COUNTY OF _____

The foregoing instrument was acknowledged before me this____day of _____ 20 ____ .

_____

Notary Public

(SEAL)   State of _____

My Commission Expires: _____

THIS DOCUMENT SHALL NOT BE RECORDED IN THE PUBLIC RECORDS OF THE COUNTY

Inspection Checklist for Rental Property

Date of Inspection: _____ **Inspector:** _____

Property Address: _____

Kitchen

Y/N
_____ All appliances cleaned and sanitized, including trays, shelves and handles
_____ Stove: Is it clean and does it work?
_____ Oven: Is it clean and does it work?
_____ Refrigerator: Is it clean and does it work?
_____ Disposal: Is it clean and does it work?
_____ Microwave: Is it clean and does it work?
_____ Dishwasher: Is it clean and does it work?
_____ Countertops: Cleaned and good condition?
_____ Sink and Faucet: Cleaned and in working condition?
_____ Plumbing under sink: In working condition without leaks?
_____ Cabinets/handles and knobs: Cleaned inside and out and in working condition?
_____ Floor: Is it clean and in good condition?

Utility Room

_____ Clothes washer: Is it clean and does it work?
_____ Clothes dryer: Is it clean and does it work?
_____ Cabinets cleaned inside and out and in working condition?
_____ Water heater: Is it in working condition?

Bathroom(s)

Indicate which bathroom.

_____ Floor: Is it clean and in good condition?
_____ Sink/base and faucet: Are they clean and working?
_____ Plumbing under sink and shower: Working and leak free?
_____ Tub or Shower: Clean and in working condition?
_____ Tile on walls: Clean and in good condition?
_____ Vanity Mirror: Clean and in good condition?
_____ Cabinets and knobs: Clean and in good condition?
_____ Towel and paper holders: Clean and in good condition?
_____ Toilet/tank and seat: Clean and in good condition?
_____ Caulking: Is their any caulking needed around tub or shower?
_____ Fan/Vent: Is it in good working condition?

Living Areas

_____ Painting: Are the walls clean?
_____ Wood Molding: Is it clean or does it need painting?
_____ Doors: Are all doors clean and in good working condition?

_____Door knobs and hinges: Are all door knobs and hinges in clean and in good working condition?
_____Windows: Are all windows clean and in good working condition?
_____Air conditioning and heater: Are all A/C and heating units clean and in good operating condition?
_____Lighting fixtures: Are all lighting fixtures clean and in good working condition?
_____Ceiling Fans: Are all ceiling fans clean and in good working condition?
_____Blinds and window coverings: Are the blinds or other window coverings in good, clean working condition?
_____Lighting fixtures should have 60 watt bulbs.
_____Fan/Lights should have 40 to 60 watt bulbs.
_____If landlord pays for electricity, all bulbs are 60 watt florescent.
_____Floors must be cleaned, mopped or vacuumed.
_____Baseboards and all woodwork (door framing and linen closets) must be clean, and free of any marks
_____Electrical outlets: All electrical switches and outlets and covers must be in clean working order.
_____Garbage: All garbage to be removed to outside cans.
_____ Holes in walls: Holes in walls must be puttied and painted.
_____ Smoke and Fire Alarm: Is it working? Does it need a battery? Is the fire extinguisher in good condition?

When Showing Property

_____Is A/C set at 75 degrees in hot weather?

_____Did you spray air freshener or plug in deodorizer?

Rental Property
Move-In Inspection Checklist with Tenant

Move-in Condition (MI) Move-out Condition (MO)
Good (G) Damaged (D)

Exterior

(MI)	(MO)
G Lawn & Landscaping G	
Trees, Shrubs	
Sprinkler System	
Water Valves	
Fences & Gates	
Driveway	
Walking Paths	
Roof	
Gutters	
Awning & Shutters	
Screens	
Mailbox	
Porch Light & Bulb	
Paint	
Siding	
Front Door	
Window Pain	
Door Bell	
Knob & Lock	
Weather tight	
Back Door	
Paint	
Bell	
Knob & Lock	
Weather tight	
Porch Light & Bulb	
Patio Doors	
Screens	

Garage
Roof	
Paint	
Floor	
Windows	
Walls & Ceiling	
Entrance Door	
Paint	
Knob & Lock	
Car Entry Door	
Paint	
Locks	

Shed	
Other Explain	

House Interior

Living Area	
Paint	
Doors	
Knobs & Lock	
Flooring	
Light Fixtures	
Fans	
Windows	
Electrical Outlets	
& Switches	
Shelving & Cabinets	
Closets	
Wood Trim	
& Molding	
Other Explain	

Dining Room	

Kitchen
Pantry	
Refrigerator	
Shelves	
Drawers	
Light Bulbs	
Range	
Oven	
Racks	
Knobs	
Broiler	
Vent Hood	
Light	
Fan	
Filter	
Dishwasher	
Basket	
Racks	

Family Room	

Other Explain	
Master Bedroom Explain	
Master Bath	
Bedroom 1	
Bedroom 2	
Bedroom 3	
Bedroom 4	
Bathroom 1	
Bathroom 2	

Utility Room
Paint	
Door	
Knob	
Floor	
Cabinets/Shelving	
Light Fixture/Bulb	
Washer	
Dryer	
Water Valves	
Window/Blinds	

Systems
Central A/C	
& Heating	
Thermostat	
Filter	
Window Unit(s)	
Gas Wall or Floor	
Heater	
Hot Water Heater	
Smoke Detectors	
Security System	
Other Explain	

The undersigned agree to the condition of the property as assessed above.

_____   _____
Landlord/Property Manager Date   Tenant   Date

                                          _____
                                          Tenant   Date

                                          _____
                                          Tenant   Date

                                          _____
                                          Tenant   Date

ASBESTOS DISCLOSURE FORM

Asbestos is a common building material that may be present in many buildings constructed prior to 1981.

The United States Environmental Protection Agency (EPA has determined the mere presence of asbestos materials does not post a health risk to residents and that such materials are safe as long as they are not disturbed or dislodged in a manner that causes the asbestos fibers to be released. Sanding, scraping, pounding and other remodeling techniques that release dust may cause asbestos articles to become airborne.

EPA rules do not require the material to be removed. Federal law requires that reasonable precautions are taken to minimize the chance of damage or disturbance of asbestos containing materials.

Tenant(s) acknowledge that this is a WARNING that the Leased Premises may contain asbestos and may expose him/her to a chemical know to cause cancer.

Tenant(s) agree that no improvements, alterations, modifications, or repairs to the premises shall be made without the express approval of the Landlord. This approval will depend upon acceptance of a written plan of protection from the release of or exposure to asbestos.

Tenant(s) may hang only pictures and other wall ornaments with hangers that are less than a quarter inch in diameter. Tenant(s) will notify the Landlord immediately where there exists a hole larger than a quarter inch in diameter, evidence of a water leak, and/or any appearance of crumbling or peeling in the wallboard or ceilings.

_____ Landlord discloses any know information concerning asbestos hazards located in or around the following areas of the Leased Premises.

_____

_____

_____ Landlord has no knowledge of asbestos and/or asbestos hazards located in or around the Leased Premises.

Tenant's Signature: _____ Date _____

Landlord's Signature_____ Date _____

MOLD DISCLOSURE FORM

This MOLD DISCLOSURE is incorporated into and made part of the Lease executed by the Landlord and Tenant referring to and incorporating the Leased Premises.

Potential health effects and symptoms associated with mold exposures include allergic reaction, asthma, and other respiratory ailments. Mold can be found almost anywhere and can grow on virtually any substance, providing moisture is present. There is no practical ay to eliminate all mold and mold spores in an indoor environment. The best way to control indoor mold growth is by controlling moisture.

Tenant acknowledges that the Landlord has provided direction to the Tenant on how to obtain mold informational pamphlets that are made available to the public through the United States Environmental Protection Agency (EPA). These pamphlets can be accessed by any on the methods listed below.

Mail: Protection U. S. EPA/Office of Radiation and Indoor Air
        Indoor Environments Division
        1200 Pennsylvania Avenue, NW
        Mail Code 6609J
        Washington, DC 20460

Phone: 212-343-9370

Website:www.epa.gov/mold/publications.html

_____ Landlord discloses any known information concerning mold located in or around the following areas of the Leased Premises.

_____

_____

_____ It is not known by the Landlord whether or whether not mold is located in or around the Leased Premises.

Tenant's Signature: _____   Date: _____

Tenant's Signature: _____   Date: _____

Landlord's Signature: _____   Date: _____

RADON GAS DISCLOSURE FORM

This RADON GAS DISCLOSURE is incorporated into and made part of the Lease executed by the Tenant and Landlord.

The Tenant of the Leased property is notified that the property may present exposure to dangerous levels of indoor radon gas that may place the occupants at risk of developing radon-induced lung cancer. Radon is a Class-A human carcinogen. It is a leading cause of lung cancer in non-smokers and the second leading cause overall. The Landlord is required to provide the Tenant with any information on radon test of the rental unit showing elevated levels of radon in the Landlord's possession.

Landlord's Disclosure (mark each that apply)

_____ Elevated radon concentrations that are above the EPA's recommended Radon Action Level are known to be present in the Tenants unit. Explain. _____

_____

_____ Landlord has provided the purchaser with all available records and reports pertaining to radon concentrations within the rental unit.

_____ Landlord has no knowledge of elevated radon concentrations in the unit.

_____ Landlord has no records or reports pertaining to elevated radon concentrations within the unit.

Tenant's Acknowledgment

_____ Tenant has received copies of all information listed above.

Tenant's Signature: _____ Date: _____

Tenant's Signature: _____ Date: _____

Landlord's Signature: _____ Date: _____

THREE DAY NOTICE TO PAY OR QUIT (Sample)

December 11, 2017

Mr. Joe Deadbeat
1313 Broadway, Apt. 7
Anytown, Florida 38373

Dear Mr. Deadbeat:

You are hereby notified that in accordance with Florida Statues, you are indebted to Landlord in the sum of **$650 for rent and $65** for additional rent, for a **total of $715** for use of the premises at 1313 Broadway, Apt. 7, Anytown County, Anytown, Florida 33401, now occupied by you, and that Landlord demands payment of the rent or possession of the premises within Three (3) days (not including Saturday, Sunday, and legal holidays) from the date of the delivery of this Notice: to wit, December 11, 20017.

Payment should be made by cashier's check or money order made payable to:
ACME Avenue Property Management. Payment should be mailed or hand delivered to:

> ACME Avenue Property Management
> 1234 First St.
> Anytown, Fl 33879

You may call us between the hours of 8 am to 6 pm at 561-555-5555.

AFFIDAVIT OF SERVICE

I certify that I served a copy of the foregoing Notice to the above-named Tenant,

on the _____, _____, 20____.

- ☐   By handing of a copy thereof to the above named tenant.
- ☐   By delivering of a copy thereof to _____ a person above the age of 18 residing at the above premises.
- ☐   By posting a copy thereof in a conspicuous place on the above premises, no one being in actual possession thereof.
- ☐   By sending a copy thereof by certified mail to the tenant at his place of residence.

John Goodguy
Property Manager
ACME Avenue Property Management

CASE NO:

Management Group, Inc.
A _____Corporation,

        Plaintiff,

Vs.
Joe Deadbeat

        Defendant,
_____/

COMPLAINT

COUNT I-Possession of Real Property

Comes now Plaintiff(s), Worth Avenue Property Management Group, Inc., and sues Defendant, Joe Deadbeat and alleges:

1.   This is an action to evict a tenant from real property in _____ County, _____.

2.   Plaintiff Worth Avenue Property Management Group, Inc. is Manager, under a property management agreement, of said real

    Property located at_____, _____ is said county.

3.   Defendant has possession of the property under a lease written

    agreement to pay rent of, $_____, payable monthly. A copy of the

    lease agreement is attached hereto as Plaintiff's Exhibit A.

4.   Defendant failed to pay the rent due on, _____ 20_____.

5.   Plaintiff, Worth Avenue Property Management Group, Inc., served

Defendant with a 3 day notice on _____ to pay rent or
deliver possession, but the Defendant has refused to do either. A copy of
the Notice is attached hereto as Plaintiff's Exhibit B.

WHEREFORE, Plaintiff(s) demands judgment for possession of the property against the Defendant.

COUNT II-Money Damages

Plaintiff, Worth Avenue Property Management Group, Inc. sues Defendant, Joe Deadbeat and alleges:

6.   This is an action for damages that exceed the sum of $_____ but do not

    exceed the sum of $_____.

7.   Defendant owes Plaintiff the sum of $_____ that is due and owing since

    _____, 20_____; and Plaintiff is entitled to pre-judgment interest

    since that date.

8. There is no justiciable issue of fact or law.

9. Plaintiff, Worth Avenue Property Management Group, Inc. moves

the court under _____(State) Rules of Civil Procedure 1.440 (a), to allow

Defendant 20 days from date of service to answer Count II.

WHEREFORE, Plaintiff(s) demands judgment against the Defendant for damages, costs, interest, and other just relief.

_____
Plaintiffs Name

_____
Registered Agen

DEPOSIT TO RESERVE APARTMENT

Name: _____

Phone: _____ Rental Address:_____

The undersigned has hereby given a deposit in the amount of _____
to reserve the dwelling located at the above address for possible owner consideration of acceptance for rental.

If prospective TENANT is declined residency for any reason whatsoever, deposit is fully refundable.

In the event prospective TENANT changes his/her mind about renting, deposit is NONREFUNDABLE.

I fully understand the above statements and agree to abide by them.

_____   _____

Tenant   Co-tenant

_____

Date

LEASE AGREEMENT

1. **PARTIES** – The parties to this agreement are _____ hereinafter referred to as "Landlord," and _____, and _____ hereinafter referred to as "Tenant(s)." All adult occupants of the subject premises must sign this Lease Agreement and each will be jointly and severally liable under the terms and conditions of said Agreement. Additional occupants of the premises will be _____ (Age _____); _____ (Age _____); and _____ (Age _____) only.

    Telephone Numbers:

    Home: _____   Work: _____

    Cell: _____   Emergency Contact: _____

2. **PROPERTY** – Landlord hereby lets the following property to Tenant for the term of this agreement; the property located at and known as: _____

3. **TERM** – The term of the Agreement shall be for <u>one year</u>, beginning on _____ and ending on _____.

4. **RENT** – The **monthly**/weekly rental for said property shall be $_____ **per month**/week. One full month's/week's rent shall be paid upon execution of this Agreement. Rent for the second month/week is the prorated amount of $ _____, and is due and payable on the _1st___ day of _____ 200__. The remaining payments are to be paid consecutively on the first day of each month/week (Saturday) at such place, as the Landlord shall direct. NOTICE OF TERMINATION OF TENANCY UNDER LEASE AGREEMENT FOR NONPAYMENT OF RENT IS HEREBY SPECIFICALLY WAIVED.

5. **LATE CHARGES** – Any rent installment that is paid more than five (5) days after its due date shall include a late charge of 10% (ten percent) of the rent installment. Said late charges shall become a separate portion of rent due under the Terms and Conditions of this Lease. Any rent installment that is paid more than ten (10) days after its due date shall include a late charge of 10% (ten percent) of the rent installment plus $25 per day as liquidated damages.

6. **RETURNED CHECK CHARGES** – A charge of $30.00 shall be paid by Tenant for any check that is returned unpaid. Upon return or dishonor of any check tendered as payment of rent, late charges will be assessed as if no rental payment was attempted.

7. **UTILITIES, APPLIANCES, AND OTHER ITEMS FURNISHED BY LANDLORD -**
    Utilities shall be paid by the party indicated on the following chart:

    Electricity
    Gas
    Water
    Garbage
    Other

    Appliances furnished to Tenant by Landlord:

    Refrigerator
    Stove
    Air conditioner
    Microwave Oven
    Washer/Dryer

    Yard care shall be the responsibility of the Tenant. Tenant shall keep the yard up by cutting grass and watering grass and other plants on the property.

174

When electricity, gas, or water is to be furnished by Landlord, Tenant agrees not to use any supplemental heating or air-conditioning units, clothes or dishwashing machines, or clothes dryers, other than those furnished by Landlord and above listed. Due to high utility costs involving use of such units or appliances, tenant agrees to obtain prior written approval before using or connecting such supplemental units or appliances.

Tenant agrees that any unauthorized use of supplemental heating or air-conditioning units, clothes or dishwashing machines, or clothes dryers, other than those furnished by Landlord and above listed, shall increase the monthly/weekly rental for subject property at the rate of $75.00 per month. Said increase shall be automatic upon discovery of any of the above mentioned units or appliances, without any notice required, and shall continue for the full term of this Lease. Said increase shall become a portion of rent due under the Terms and Conditions of this Agreement.

8. **USE OF PROPERTY, OCCUPANTS, AND GUESTS** – Tenant shall use the subject property for residential purposes only. The property shall be occupied only by those Tenants listed in item one (1): PARTIES, of this Lease.

9. **TENANT'S DUTY TO MAINTAIN PREMISES** – Tenant shall keep the dwelling unit in a clean and sanitary condition and shall otherwise comply with all state and local laws requiring tenants to maintain rented premises. If damage to the dwelling unit other than normal wear and tear is caused by acts of negligence of Tenant or others occupying the premises under his/her control, Landlord may cause such repairs to be made, and Tenant shall be liable to Landlord for any reasonable expense thereby incurred by Landlord.

10. **ALTERATIONS** – No alteration, addition, or improvements shall be made by Tenant in or to the dwelling unit without the prior written consent of Landlord. Such consent shall be totally at Landlord's option.

11. **NOISE** – Tenant agrees not to allow on the premises any excessive noise, or other activity, which disturbs the peace and quiet of others.

12. **INSPECTION BY LANDLORD** – The Tenant agrees to allow Landlord to enter the subject premises in order to inspect the premises, make necessary or agreed-upon repairs, decorations, alterations, or improvements, supply necessary or agreed-upon services, or exhibit the dwelling unit to prospective or actual purchasers, mortgages, tenants, workmen, or contractors. The Landlord may enter the dwelling unit without consent of Tenant in case of emergency.

13. **SECURITY DEPOSIT** – Tenant agrees to deposit with Landlord, upon execution of the Lease contract, receipt of which is hereby acknowledged, the sum of $_____ as security deposit against rent or damages. This deposit is held as security against any damage to the entire property, including but not limited to furniture, appliances, fixtures, and carpet; and against Tenant vacating the entire premises prior to the termination date of this Lease, of failing to perform any and all the covenants herein. Said deposit is neither an advance rental payment nor a bonus to the Landlord, and Landlord agrees that if all the covenants imposed up-on Tenant have been fulfilled, Landlord shall refund said deposit by mail to the address furnished by the Tenant, after the premises have been vacated by Tenant and inspected by Landlord as provided by statute or within 45 days of vacating, whichever is greater. In the event Resident/Tenant vacates the premises without giving proper notice, or before the expiration of this lease, said amounts are nonrefundable as a charge for Landlord's trouble in securing a new tenant, but Landlord/Owner reserves the right to seek additional payment for any damages to the premises. Failure to give forwarding address to Landlord after fifteen days of move-out date constitutes forfeit of security deposit.

    REDECORATING FEE: In addition to the rent and the Security Deposit provided for herein, Resident/Tenant agrees to pay in advance a one-time non-refundable fee in the amount of $**250.00** as a charge for redecorating the premises being vacated by the Resident/Tenant. This fee is to cover Landlord/Owner's costs for redecorating the apartment to compensate for normal wear and tear, which includes, but is not limited to the following: Touch-up painting, steam cleaning of carpets, disinfecting appliances and bathrooms, changing air filters, batteries, light bulbs where applicable, dusting hard to reach areas, etc.

14. **KEY DEPOSITS** – The following shall be deposits for keys:

A.	Apartment or Dwelling Key: $15 per key	_____
B.	Security Gate Key: $15 per key	_____
C.	Mail Box Key:$15 per key	_____
D.	Automatic Gate Opener$100 per opener	_____

15. **LIEN** – The Tenant hereby gives Landlord a lien upon all his personal property situated upon said premises, including all furniture and household furnishings. This lien is for the rent agreed to be paid hereunder, for any damage caused by Tenant beyond normal wear and tear, and for court costs and attorneys' fees incurred under the Terms and Conditions of this Agreement.

16. **SUBLEASING** – Tenant shall not assign this Agreement or sublet the dwelling unit without prior written consent of Landlord. Such consent shall be totally at Landlord's option.

17. **PERSONAL INJURY AND PROPERTY DAMAGE** – Subject to standards required by law, neither landlord nor its principal shall be liable to Tenant, his family, employees, or guests, for any damage to person or property caused by the acts or omissions of other Tenants or other persons, whether such persons be off the property of Landlord or on the property with or without permission of Landlord; nor shall Landlord be liable for losses or damages from theft, fire, water, rain, storm, explosion, sonic boom, or other causes whatsoever, nor shall Landlord be liable for loss or damages resulting from failure, interruption, or malfunctions in the utilities provided to Tenant under this Lease Agreement; nor shall Landlord be liable for injuries elsewhere on the premises.

LANDLORD IS NOT RESPONSIBLE FOR, AND WILL NOT PROVIDE, FIRE OR CASUALTY INSURANCE FOR THE TENANT'S PERSONAL PROPERTY.

In further consideration of this Agreement, Tenant agrees that, subject to standards required by law, Landlord does not warrant the condition of the premises by his or their invitation, shall be limited to injuries arising from such defects that are unknown by claimant and are known to Landlord or are willfully concealed by him. Additionally, Tenant has inspected the premises and binds himself to hold Landlord harmless against any and all claims for damages arising from those who sustain injuries upon the above leased premises, during the term of this Lease, or any extension thereof.

18. **IN CASE OF MALFUNCTION OF EQUIPMENT, DAMAGE BY FIRE, WATER, OR ACT OF GOD** – Tenant shall notify Landlord immediately of malfunction of equipment, damage by fire, water, or act of God and Landlord shall repair the damage with reasonable promptness, or if the premises are deemed by the Landlord to be damaged so much as to be unfit for occupancy, or if the Landlord decides not to repair or restore the building, this Lease shall terminate. If the Lease is terminated, rent will be prorated on a daily basis so that Tenant will pay only to the date of the damage, and the remainder of the month will be refunded.

19. **PETS** – Tenant shall not permit a pet to live on the premises with out signing and complying with the provisions of a separately negotiated Pet Agreement. All pets are subject to visual inspection and approval of Landlord at such times as Landlord may direct during normal working hours.

20. **TERMINATION – ALL TENANTS PLEASE TAKE NOTICE!** – At least forty-five (45) days prior to the termination date of this Lease Agreement, Tenant must give Landlord written notice of his intent to vacate the subject premises. Failure of Tenant to give Landlord said notice of intent to vacate the subject premises will cause Landlord to treat tenant as a holdover in accordance with item (20), **HOLDOVER**, of this Lease Agreement, no matter if Tenant continues to occupy the premises or not.

Upon proper termination or expiration of this Agreement, Tenant shall vacate the premises, remove all personal property belonging to him, and leave the premises as clean as he found them.

21. **HOLDOVER** – If Tenant holds over upon termination or expiration of this Agreement and/or Landlord accepts Tenant's tender of the monthly rent provided by this Agreement, this Agreement shall continue to be binding on the parties as a **month-to-month** agreement under the same Terms and Conditions as herein contained.

22. **ATTORNEYS' FEES** – Violation of any of the conditions of this Agreement shall be sufficient cause for eviction from said premises. Tenants agree to pay all costs of such action or cost of collection of damages as a result of Tenant's breach of this Agreement, including reasonable attorneys' fees.

23. **NOTICES** – All notices provided for by this Agreement shall be in writing and shall be given to the other party as follows: to Tenant, at the premises; Worth Avenue Property Management., at 222 Lakeview Ave., Suite 160-365, West Palm Beach, Fl 33401.

24. **MAINTENANCE REQUESTS** – All requests for maintenance must be made in writing to Landlord, at the following address: Worth Avenue Property Management., at 222 Lakeview Ave., Suite 160-365, West Palm Beach, Fl 33401. Tenant shall be responsible for the first $50.00 of any maintenance work that is completed at the request of Tenant. Tenant shall be responsible for any broken windows and for replacing any broken windows, whether the window broke as an accident, as a result of criminal activity or an act of God or natural disaster. Should Tenant not repair the broken window, Landlord shall repair the window and Tenant shall pay for material and labor, not to be less than $100.00 per window.

25. **PEST CONTROL** – Tenant shall be responsible for all pest treatment and control, including termites and rodents. Should a problem arise where pest are out of control, Landlord, at Landlords discretion may hire professionals to treat the problem and Tenant agrees to pay for any and all pest treatment.

26. **ABSENCE OR ABANDONMENT** – The Tenant must notify the Landlord of any extended absence from the premises in excess of seven (7) days. Notice shall be given on or before the first day of any extended absence. The Tenant's unexplained and/or extended absence from the premises for (10) days or more without payment or rent as due shall be prima facie evidence of abandonment. The Landlord is then expressly authorized to enter, remove, and either store all personal items belonging to Tenant, or dispose of (Garbage all personal items). All personal property becomes the property of the Landlord, at which Landlord may sell or dispose of said personal property and apply the proceeds of said sale to the unpaid rents, damages, storage fees, sale costs, and attorneys' fees.

27. **TERMINATION FOR VIOLENT OR DANGEROUS BEHAVIOR** – Landlord shall terminate this Lease Agreement within three (3) days from the date written notice is delivered to the Tenant if the Tenant or any other persons on the premises with the Tenant's consent willfully or intentionally commit a violent act or behave in a manner that constitutes or threatens to be a real and present danger to the health, safety, or welfare of the life or property of others.

28. **BREACH OF LEASE** – If there is any other material noncompliance of the Lease Agreement by the Tenant, not previously specifically mentioned, or a noncompliance materially affecting health and safety, the Landlord may deliver a written notice to the Tenant specifying the acts and omissions constituting the breach, and that the Lease Agreement will terminate upon a date not less than thirty (30) days after receipt of the notice. If the breach is not remedied in fourteen (14) days, the Lease Agreement shall terminate as provided in the notice subject to the following: If the breach is remediable by repairs or the payment of damages or otherwise and the Tenant adequately remedies the breach prior to the date specified in the notice, the rental agreement will not terminate.

    If the same act or omission that constituted a prior noncompliance, of which notice was given, recurs within six (6) months, the Landlord may terminate the Lease Agreement upon at least (14) days' written notice specifying the breach and the date of termination of the Lease Agreement.

29. **RULES AND REGULATIONS** – Tenant has read and agrees to abide by all Rules and Regulations of the Landlord as they presently exist or as they may be amended at Landlord's sole discretion. Said Rules and Regulations are attached hereto and are herein incorporated by reference.

30. **ALTERATIONS OR CHANGE IN THIS AGREEMENT** – It is expressly understood by Landlord and Tenant that the Terms and conditions herein set out cannot be changed or modified, except in writing. Tenant understands that neither Tenant nor Landlord or any of Landlord's agents have the authority to modify this Lease Agreement except with a written instrument signed by all parties.

31. **APPLICATION** – Tenant's Application is an important part of this Lease, incorporated by reference and made a part hereof. Any misrepresentations, misleading or false statements made by Tenant and later discovered by the Landlord shall, at the option of the Landlord, void this Lease Agreement.

32. **SAVINGS CLAUSE** – If any provision of this Lease is determined to be in conflict with the law, thereby making said provision null and void, the nullity shall not affect the other provisions of this Lease, which can be given effect without the void provision, and to this end the provisions of the Lease are severable.

33. **TENANTS ARE RESPONSIBLE FOR THEIR OWN SECURITY** – Tenant hereby states that he has inspected the subject premises and has determined to his satisfaction that the smoke detectors, door locks and latches, window locks and latches, and any other security devices within the subject premises are adequate and in proper working order. Tenant acknowledges that Landlord is under no obligation or duty to inspect, test, or repair smoke detectors during Tenant's occupancy. Further, Tenant acknowledges that Landlord is under no obligation or duty to inspect, test, or repair any other security device unless and until Landlord has received written notice of disrepair of the device.

    Tenant further acknowledges that neither Landlord nor his agents or representatives guarantee, warrant, or assume the personal security of Tenant. Tenant further acknowledges and understands that Tenant's personal safety and security is primarily Tenant's responsibility. In particular, Tenant recognizes that Tenant is in the best position to determine and foresee risks of loss and to protect himself and his property against such losses. In this regard, Tenant recognizes that any of Landlord's efforts are voluntary and not obligatory.

34. **ACCELERATION UPON DEFAULT** – In the event that one or more "Events of Default" shall occur, Landlord may declare the entire unpaid balance lease and all other obligations of Tenant secured hereby immediately due and payable without further notice.

35. **ADDITIONAL TERMS AND CONDITIONS** – Additional paragraphs _____ through _____ are attached hereto and are part of this Lease Agreement

Wherefore, we the undersigned do hereby execute and agree to this Lease Agreement, this _____ day of _____, _____.

_____/_____

LANDLORD

TENANT SS# _____

DRIVER'S LICENSE # _____

_____/_____

LANDLORD / MANAGER

TENANT SS# _____

DRIVER'S LICENSE # _____

SECURITY DEPOSIT POLICY

Refund of the security deposit referred to in the attached Lease Agreement is subject to compliance with all six (6) of the following provisions:

1. That a <u>full term</u> of the lease has expired and;

2. That thirty (30) day written notice is given, prior to vacating the subject premises at the end of said **full** term and;

3. That there are no damages to Landlord's property, including but not limited to furniture, appliances, carpet, drapes, blinds, floor coverings and;

4. That the entire apartment, including range, refrigerator, bathrooms, closets and cupboards are clean and;

5. That no late charges, delinquent rents, or fees for the damages remain unpaid and;

6. That all keys, including mailbox keys, are returned to the Landlord.

The following questions and answers are for the purpose of eliminating misunderstandings concerning the security deposit:

1. Question: What charges will be deducted from the deposit if Tenant has failed to comply with all of the above listed six (6) conditions?
   Answer: The cost of all material and labor for cleaning the apartment and making repairs, all delinquent payments and fees, and all rental income lost as a result of Tenant vacating the premises prior to the termination date of his lease, or during any holdover period.

2. Question: What should Tenant be careful to avoid?

   Answer: (a) Damage to property, furniture, wars and wall coverings, appliances, carpet, drapes/blinds, and floor coverings. Departing Tenant will be held responsible for all damages beyond normal wear and tear, (b) Dirty appliances. Be sure to clean range and refrigerator.

3. Question: How is the Security Deposit returned?

Answer. If Tenant has complied with all the terms and conditions concerning the Security Deposit, the deposit will be returned by check mailed to a forwarding address furnished to Landlord by Tenant within the require time allotted by State law.

NOTE: The Security Deposit may not be applied to the last monthly rental, or any other rent payment!

TENANT	Date	TENANT	Date

TENANT	Date	TENANT	Date

Disclosure of Information on Lead-Based Paint
and Lead-Based Paint Hazards

Lead Warning Statement

Housing built before 1978 may contain lead-based paint. Lead from paint, paint chips, and dust can pose health hazards if not taken care of properly. Lead exposure is especially harmful to young children and pregnant women. Before renting pre-1978 housing, landlords must disclose the presence of known lead-based paint and lead-based paint hazards in the dwelling. Tenants must also receive a Federally approved pamphlet on lead poisoning prevention.

Lessor's Disclosure (initial)

_____ (a) Presence of lead-based paint or lead-based paint hazards (check one below):

❑ Known lead-based paint or lead-@ paint hazards are present in the housing (explain).

_____

_____

❑ Lessor has no knowledge of lead-based paint and/or lead-based paint hazards in the housing.

_____ (b) Records and reports available to the lessor (check one below):

❑ Lessor has provided the lessee with all available records and reports pertaining to lead-based paint and/or lead-based paint hazards in the housing (list documents below).

_____

_____

❑ Lessor has no reports or records pertaining to lead-based paint and/or lead paint hazards in the housing.

Lessee's Acknowledgment (initial)

_____ (c) Lessee has received copies of all information listed above.
_____ (d) Lessee has received the pamphlet *Protect Your Family from Lead in Your Home.*

Agent's Acknowledgment (initial)

_____ (e) Agent has **informed** the lessor of the lessor's obligations under 42 U.S.C. 4582
_____ (d) and is aware of his/her responsibility to ensure compliance.

Certification of Accuracy

The following parties have reviewed the information above and certify, to the best of their knowledge, that the information provided by the signatory is true and accurate.

_____   _____   _____   _____
Lessor   *Date*   *Lessor*   *Date*

_____   _____   _____   _____
Lessee   *Date*   *Lessee*   *Date*

_____   _____   _____   _____
Agent   Date   Agent   Date

PAYMENT POLICY

I, _____, understand that all rent is due on the 1st of the month.

❖ late on the 6th

❖ On the 7th day you will receive a 3 Day Notice to Pay or Quit.

❖ Eviction begins on the 11th of the month.

❖ No exceptions.

I understand and agree that my rent will be paid on time.

_____   _____

Tenant's Signature   Date

_____   _____

Tenant's Signature   Date

RULES AND REGULATIONS

(Referred to in and made a part of the Parties' Lease Agreement)

1. No signs, notices, or advertisements shall be attached to or displayed by Tenant on or about said premises. Additionally, no antenna or satellite dish shall be attached to or displayed on or about the premises.

2. Profane, obscene, loud, or boisterous language, or unseemly behavior and conduct is absolutely prohibited, and Tenant obligates himself and those under him not to do or permit to be done anything that will annoy, harass, embarrass, or inconvenience any of the other tenants or occupants in the subject or adjoining premises.

3. No motor vehicle shall be kept upon the property that is unlicensed, inoperable, or in damaged condition. Damaged condition includes but is not limited to flat tires. Any such vehicle that remains on the property for more than ten (10) days after notice to remove same has been placed on subject vehicle shall be towed by wrecker and stored with a wrecker service at the tenant's and/or the vehicle owner's expense.

4. In keeping with Fire Safety Standards, all motorized vehicles including motorcycles must be parked outside. No motorized vehicles shall be parked in any building structure on the property except authorized garage spaces.

5. In accordance with Fire Safety Standards and other safety regulations, no Tenant shall maintain or allow to be maintained, any auxiliary heating unit, air conditioning units, or air filtering units without prior inspection and written approval of Landlord.

6. The sound of musical instruments, radios, televisions, phonographs, and singing shall at all times be limited in volume to a point that is not objectionable to other tenants or occupants in the subject or adjoining premises.

7. Only persons employed by Landlord or his agent shall adjust or have anything to do with the heating or air conditioning plants or with the repair or adjustment of any plumbing, stove, refrigerator, dishwasher, or any other equipment that is furnished by Landlord or is part of the subject premises.

8. No awning, Venetian blinds, or window guards shall be installed, except where prior approval is given by the Landlord.

9. Tenant shall not alter, replace, or add locks or bolts or install any other attachments, such as doorknockers, upon any door, except where prior approval is given by the Landlord

10. No defacement of the interior or exterior of the buildings or the surrounding grounds will be tolerated

11. If furnished by Landlord, garbage disposal shall only be used in accordance with the disposal victims. All refuse shall be timely removed from the premises and placed outside in receptacles.

12. No spikes, hooks, or nails shall be driven into the walls, ceiling or woodwork of the leased premises without consent of Landlord. No crating of or boxing of furniture or other articles will be allowed within the leased premises.

13. It is specifically understood that Landlord reserves solely to itself the right to alter, amend, modify, and add rules to this Lease.

14. It is understood and agreed that Landlord shall not be responsible for items stored in storage areas.

15. Landlord has the right to immediately remove combustible material from the premises or any storage area.

16. Landlord will furnish one (1) key for each outside door of the premises. All keys must be returned to Landlord upon termination of the occupancy.

17. Lavatories, sinks, toilets and all water and plumbing apparatus shall be used only for the purpose for which they were constructed. Sweepings, rubbish, rags, ashes or other foreign substances shall not be thrown therein. Any damage to such apparatus and the cost of clearing plumbing resulting from misuse shall be the sole responsibility of and will be borne by Tenant.

TENANT	Date	TENANT	Date

T'ENANT	Date	TENANT	Date

AFFIDAVIT OF MILITARY STATUS

STATE OF FLORIDA

COUNTY OF PALM BEACH

I, _____, hereby certify that I have no affiliation with the United States Armed Services. And therefore, will not be forced to terminate this lease as a result of being called to Active Duty.

_____

Tenant's Signature

_____

Tenant's Signature

NOTICE OF LEASE VIOLATION

ADDRESS: _____

_____

Dear Tenant:

We conduct weekly inspections of the property you are renting in order to check with your lease compliance and further to make sure we are in compliance with all city and county code requirements.

In our last inspection on _____ it was found that you are in violation of your lease for the following matters:

Paragraph
1:_____Description:_____
_____
_____
_____

Paragraph
2:_____Description:_____
_____
_____
_____

All violations shall be cured within 7 days. Please notify us when you receive this letter and when the violations have been cured. Any violation that is not cured in 7 days is grounds for termination of Lease.

Please comply immediately. If you have any questions please call me at _____.

Sincerely,

Montlhy Rental Voucher

Name _____ Phone_____

Rental Address _____

Amount of Rent: $ _____Amount Enclosed: $ _____ Check# _____

Date _____ Other Payments _____

(*Please Make Checks Payable to*: _____Address _____)

(Submit this voucher with your Check--Thank You)

Montlhy Rental Voucher

Name _____ Phone_____

Rental Address _____

Amount of Rent: $ _____Amount Enclosed: $ _____ Check# _____

Date _____ Other Payments _____

(*Please Make Checks Payable to*: _____Address _____)

(Submit this voucher with your Check--Thank You)

Montlhy Rental Voucher

Name _____ Phone_____

Rental Address _____

Amount of Rent: $ _____Amount Enclosed: $ _____ Check# _____

Date _____ Other Payments _____

(*Please Make Checks Payable to*: _____Address _____)

(Submit this voucher with your Check--Thank You)

Rental Property Details

Property
Address: _____

Neighborhood/Community:

_____

Property Type: ___ Single Family Home
___ Apartment
___ Duplex/Fourplex
___ Townhome/Condo

Bedrooms: ____ Bathrooms: ____ Garage: _____ Square Footage: _____

Property Features: (Check All That Apply)

Kitchen: __Refrigerator __ Dishwasher __ Microwave
__ Stove __ Island __ Breakfast Nook
__ Pantry __ Disposal __ _____

Flooring: __ Hardwood __ Ceramic Tile __Carpet

Laundry: __ W/D Included __ W/D Hookups __ Laundry Facility

Rooms: __ Living Room __ Dining Room __ Den/Family Room
__ Rec. Room __ Wet Bar __ Bonus Room
__ Study/Office __ Finished Basement __ Unfinished Basement
__ Laundry/Utility Room __ Crawl Space __ _____

Amenities: __ Air Conditioning __ Walk-In Closets __ Fireplace
__ Heat __ Vaulted Ceilings __ Cable-Ready
__ Security System __ Ceiling Fan __ Built-In Bookshelves
__ 5-Piece Bath __ Jetted Tub __ Skylights
__ Waterfront __ Scenic View __ Window Blinds
__ Attic __Furnished __ _____

Outdoor: __ Balcony __ Deck __ Patio __ Fenced Yard __ Sprinkler System __
Private Pool __ Jacuzzi __ Outdoor Storage __ Porch

Parking: __ Parking Lot __ Attached Garage __ Detached Garage

Community __ Business Center __ Playground __ Clubhouse

Facilities: __ Fitness Center __ Community Pool __ Spa/Jacuzzi __ Tennis Courts
__ Billiards __ Library __ Storage __ Guard House __ Access Gate
__ Volleyball __ Golf Course __ Handicap Acces

TENANT ESTOPPEL CERTIFICATE

Tenant: _____

Owner: _____ Lease Date: _____

Address: _____

The undersigned Owner and Tenant do hereby certify and confirm as follows:

1.   Owner and Tenant are parties to the above-described lease (the "Lease"). True and correct copies of the Lease and all amendments to the Lease are attached hereto as Exhibit A.

2.   The Lease has not been modified in any respect, other than as set forth on <u>Exhibit A</u>, and there are no verbal or written agreements or understandings to modify the Lease at a future date. Tenant has no Lease renewal options, signage agreements, options, or first refusal rights other than as expressly stated in the Lease.

3.   The primary Lease term commenced on_____ and will expire on _____, with _____ year option to renew.

4.   Rent commenced to accrue on_____ and has been paid through _____. The current monthly rent payable under the Lease is $_____. The current monthly common area charges payable under the Lease is _____.

5.   There is no prepaid rent or CAM reserve other than _____. Owner holds a security deposit from Tenant in the amount of $_____.

6.   All obligations of Owner and Tenant with respect to construction or repairs of the leased premises and the project of which the leased premises is a part have been fully performed with the exception of the following: _____.

7.   Tenant has unconditionally accepted the leased premises with the exception of the following _____.

8.   All construction and move-in allowances owing by Owner to Tenant (if any) have been fully paid. There are no rental concessions or abatements other than as expressly stated in the Lease, and no agreements or understandings that would otherwise modify the rights and obligations of the parties as set forth in the Lease.

9.   No event has occurred that does presently, or would with the passage of time, the giving of notice, or the expiration of a period of grace, constitute a default by either party under the Lease, give rise to a right of termination of the Lease by either party, or give rise to any rights of offset against rent by Tenant.

Owner and Tenant acknowledge that Purchaser is relying upon the above assurances in connection with the purchase of the property.

189

DATED this _____ day of _____, 2008.

OWNER: By _____
                              Its

                          By _____
                              Its

TENANT: By _____

Print Name: _____

TENANT WELCOME LETTER

Date: _____

Tenant Names: _____

Address: _____

Dear _____:

Welcome to your new home at _____. We hope you will enjoy living here. This letter is to explain what you can expect from the management and what we'll be for from you.

1. **Rental Agreement**: Your signed copy is attached. There are a few things we'd like to highlight:

   • Your security deposit will be applied to costs of cleaning, damages, or unpaid rent after you move out. You may not apply any part of deposit toward any part of your rent in the last month of your tenancy.

2. **Telephone Number**: Please notify us if your home and work phone number changes, so we can reach you promptly in an emergency.

3. **Keys and Locks**: If, for any reason, you find it necessary to have any door locks replaced or re-keyed, you must notify us in writing and provide a key for emergency access.

4. **Rental Payments.** All Rent is due on the 1st of each month and is considered late if received after the 5th of each month. All Payments for rent shall be in the form of a check, cashiers check or money order. We will not take cash. If you insist on paying cash you will be charged an additional $50.

All checks for rent shall be paid and mailed to:

For convenience, below are the phone numbers for the utility hook-ups.

Utilities:

Water: (561) 822-1300
Gas: (561) 832-0872
FPL: (561) 697-8000
Bellsouth: (888) 757-6500
Adelphia: (888) 683-1000
Police: 911
 Please let us know if you have any questions.

Sincerely,
Property Manager

PET RENT AGREEMENT

PET AGREEMENT

If you wish to have a pet in your rental unit, you will need to provide the following information and agree to the terms outlined herein. This agreement is an addendum to your lease and a breach of this agreement is also a breach of your rental lease.

Address:_____

_____ Date:_____

_____ I **DO NOT** have a pet. But if I get one, I will let the Landlord or Property Manager know immediately.

_____ **YES**, I do have a pet.

Check the following:

Dog:_____ Name:_____   Weight:_____ Age:_____

      Breed:_____

Dog:_____ Name:_____   Weight:_____ Age:_____

      Breed:_____

Dog:_____ Name:_____   Weight:_____ Age:_____

      Breed:_____

Puppy:_____ Name:_____ Breed:_____

Cat:_____ Name:_____ How Many?_____

Other types of animals:

_____Bird(s)

_____Rats, Mice, Hamsters, Guinea pig, Gerbils, Ferret. (Circle all that apply)

_____Snake

_____Fish _____Size of tank (over 10 gallons)

DOGS THAT ARE NOT ALLOWED

- Pit Bulls • Rottweilers • Akitas
- Alaskan Malamutes • Chow Chows
- Doberman Pinschers • Siberian Huskies
- Perro de Presa Canarios • Boxers
- Wolf-hybrid
- Great Danes
- American Staffordshire Terriers
- Any dog that is a mix of any of the above breeds

OTHER PETS NOT ALLOWED

- *Farm animals*: Chickens, roosters, goats, pigs, cows, horses, ponies and so on.

- *Uncommon pets*: Monkeys, and/or other endangered or undomesticated animals are not allowed.

PET RENT

- **Dogs (Small):** $35 each per month. Three dog maximum.
- **Dogs (Large, over fifty pounds**): $50 each per month.
- **Cats:** $35 per month for one cat and $15 for each additional cat. Three cat maximum.
- **Birds:** Caged birds $15 per cage per month. Two cage maximum. Loose birds (Parrot) $20.
- **Rats, Mice, Hamsters, Guinea Pig and Gerbils:** $5 per cage per month.
- **Snake, Lizards, Turtles:** $5 per cage per month.
- **Fish**: $10 per month for a 10 to 55 gallon tank.
- **Ferret**: $25 per month per animal.

Deposits

- Dog: $250 per animal
- Cat: $100 per animal
- All other animals: $50

PETS THAT ARE FREE OF CHARGE

- Seeing eye dog
- Trained care-giving dog or other pet (training credentials required)
- Goldfish bowl

Animals that are not on the lease and are staying with Tenant represent a breach of Tenants contractual lease agreement and are grounds for eviction and costs associated to the pet type. Tenant also agrees to care for the animal with regular grooming and baths. If flea, tick or other infestation occur, Tenant is responsible for costs incurred for fumigation and extermination services. Tenant understands that Landlord/Property Manager will not tolerate cruelty or mistreatment of animals and will notify the proper authorities immediately (all costs related to the care and removal of a pet will be incurred by Tenant). Tenant further understands, any animal that management request to be removed from the premises, by written notice from Landlord/Property Manager, must be done so within 3 days.

Tenant has paid the sum of $_____ as a Pet Security Deposit for animals indicated in this agreement.

Tenant has agreed to pay a monthly sum of $_____ as pet rent; this will be added to the monthly rent due as stated on the lease.

All Security Deposits are turned-over in the same timeframe and manner as described in the Lease Agreement. And Pet Security Deposits follow the same conditions as other Security Deposits stated in the Lease Agreement.

It is understood and agreed that Tenant is solely responsible for pets and the Landlord/Property Manager and its agents are not liable for damages to property or bodily harm to individuals.

Tenant: _____ Date: _____
      Signature
Print Name: _____

Tenant: _____ Date: _____
      Signature

Print Name: _____

_____
Landlord/Property Manager   Date

MOVE-OUT CHARGES

The following are charges billed to tenants when tenants move out and leave their dwelling in need of cleaning and repairs. These charges are averages. Sometimes the actual charges are higher. We give allowances for normal wear and tear, and for the length of time something has been in use. Replacement charges include parts and labor.

CLEANING		PLUMBING	
Clean refrigerator	$25	Replace kitchen faucet	$85
Clean stove top	$25	Replace bathroom faucet	$85
Clean oven	$35	Replace faucet handle	$15
Clean stove hood	$25	Replace faucet aerator	$10
Clean kitchen cabinets	$30	Replace shower head	$25
Clean kitchen floor	$45	Replace toilet tank lid	$35
Clean tub/shower	$35	Replace toilet and tank	$160
Clean toilet and sink	$30	Replace garbage disposer	$150
Clean bathroom cabinets and floors $30		**LOCKS**	
Vacuum through dwelling	$50	Replace key (doors or mailbox)	$15
Clean oily parking space	$35	Replace cylindrical door lock $50	
FLOORING		Replace passage door lock	$30
Remove carpet stains	$90	Replace deadbolt lock	$50
Deodorize carpet	$90	Replace mailbox lock	$25
Repair carpet	$90	**WINDOWS**	
Repair hardwood floors	$120	Replace window pane (1)	$75
Refinish hardwood floor	$550	Replace blinds (1)	$75
Repair linoleum	$55	Replace window shade	$25
Replace kitchen or bath linoleum $375		Replace drapery rod	$45
Replace bathroom floor tile	$250	Replace drapes (2)	$150
Replace Floor tile (1 room)	$425	Repair or replace screens	$50
WALLS		**MISCELLANEOUS**	
Remove mildew and treat surface $25		Replace refrigerator shelf	$45
Cover crayon marks	$45	Paint refrigerator	$85
Repair hole in wall	$55	Replace stove or cabinet knob (1)	$10
Remove wallpaper	$225	Repair ceramic tile	$85
Repaint (per wall/ceiling)	$60	Replace ceramic tile counter top	$650
DOORS		Replace formic counter top	$280
Repair forced door damage	$65	Replace mirror	$55
Replace door (interior)	$150	Replace medicine cabinet	$75
Replace door (exterior)	$350	Replace towel bar	$30
Replace mirrored closet doors	$250	Replace toilet paper holder	$20

ELECTRICAL		Replace shower rod	$25
Replace light bulb	$5	Replace shower/tub enclosure	$350
Replace light fixture globe	$20	Replace thermostat	$95
Replace light fixture	$65	Recharge fire extinguisher	$35
Replace ceiling fan	$85	Replace fire extinguisher	$45
Replace electrical outlet/switch	$25	Fumigate for bugs	$150
Replace electrical cover plate	$5	Remove junk and debris	$75
FURNITURE AND APPLIANCES		Replace mailbox	$35
Remove furniture (each)	$50	Replace country mail box	$55
Replace refrigerator	$450	Replace kitchen sink	$125
Replace stove	$450		
Replace microwave	$100		
LANDSCAPING			
Replacing sod (Grass)	$50 to $2000		
(Tenants neglect)			
Replacing outdoor plants	$50 to $500		
(Tenants neglect)			
Replace/Fencing Repair	$50 to $1000		
Repair/Replace Sprinklers	$50 to $2000		
AIR CONDITIONERS			
WINDOW UNITS:			
Replace/Repair window box unit	$50 to $500		
(Tenant neglect)			
▪ Tenant responsible for cleaning,			
replacing filters, and maintaining			
air units in working order			
CENTRAL AIR UNITS:			
▪ Tenant responsible for cleaning	$50 to $3000		
&replacing filters, and for all cost			
to the use of the unit, including			
maintenance cost			

CARGOS DE MUDANZA (Spanish)

Los siguientes cargos seran aplicados a los inquilinos cuando se muden y dejen el apartamento con necesidad de limpieza o reparacion. Nosotros autorizamos el uso de todos los equipos en el apartamento por el tiempo que usted lo habite pero no por reparaciones por negligencia. Los cargos incluyen partes y labor.

LIMPIEZA:		Limpieza de refrigerador	$25
Limpieza de fogon	$25	Limpieza del horno	$35
Limpieza del interior/fogon	$25	Limpieza de gabinetes/cocina	$30
Limpieza del piso/ cocina	$45	Limpieza de la bañadera	$35
Limpieza de la taza/lavamano	$30	Limpieza piso/gabinetes/baño	$30
Aspirar las tuberias	$50	Limpieza de aceites/	$35
PISO:		Quitar manchas/alfombras	$90
Poner olores en la alfombra	$90	Reparar la alfombra	$90
Reparar pisos de madera	$120	Pulir piso de madera	$550
Reparar tablas/piso	$55	Gabinetes/cocina	$375
Lozas/baño	$250	Loza/por cuarto	$425
PAREDES:		Remover manchas	$25
Remover manchas/crayolas	$45	Reparar huecos/paredes	$55
Remover papeles/paredes	$225	Re-pintar/por pared/techo	$60
PUERTAS:		Reparar puertas/forzadas	$65
Cambiar puerta/interior	$150	Cambiar puerta/exterior	$350
Cambiar/puertas/closet	$250	**ELECTRICO:**	
Cambiar un foco	$5	Cambiar esfera/lampar	$20
Cambiar lampara/foco	$65	Cambiar ventilador/techo	$85
Cambiar electrico toma	$25	Cambiar tapas/toma	$5
MUEBLES Y EQUIPOS:		Remover muebles/cada uno	$50
Cambiar refrigerador	$450	Cambiar fogon	$450
Cambiar micro-ondas	$100	**PLOMERIA:** **GRAMA:**	
		Cambiar la tuberia/cocina Re-emplazar grama	$85 $50 to $2000
Cambiar la tuberia/baño (negligencia del inquilino)	$85	Cambiar la tuberia/mango Re-emplazar plantas/ext	$15 $20 to $500
Cambia la tuberia/otras piezas Re-emplazar/reparar cercas	$10 $50 to $1000	Cambiar ducha/parte arriba Reparar/cambiar sprinklers	$25 $20 to $2000
Cambiar solo tanque/taza	$35	Cambiar taza/tanque	$160

		AIRE ACONDICIONADO:	
Cambiar tuberia/abajo lavamano	$150	**LOQUES:**	
		UNIDADES DE PARED:	
Cambiar llaves(puertas/correo)	$15	Cambiar los loques/redondos	$50
		Re-emplazar/reparar $20 to $500	
Cambiar loques	$30	Cambiar pieza/puerta y loque	$50
(negligencia del inquilino)		▪ Inquilino responsable por	
Cambiar loque/correo	$25	**VENTANAS:**	
limpieza/re-emplazar los		filtros y mantener las unidades	
Cambiar ventana	$75	Cambiarventana/exterior	$75
en total funcionamiento			
Cambiar cobertura/ventana	$25	Cambiar cortinas/piezas $45	
AIRE CENTRAL:			
Cambiar cortinas/exterior (2)	$150	Reparar o cambiar screens	$50
▪ Inquilino responsable $50 to $3000		por limpieza/re-emplazar	
OTROS:		Cambiar refrigerador/bandeja	$45
filtros y todos los costos		incluyendo mantenimiento	
Refrigerador/pintar	$85	Cambiar fogon/gabinete agarradera	$10
Reparar lozas	$85	Cambiar meseta/cocina	$650
Cambiar meseta/formica	$280	Cambiar espejos	$55
Cambiar gabinete/medicina	$75	Cambiar toalleros	$30
Cambiar papel baño/pieza	$20	Cambiar ducha/pieza	$25
Cambiar ducha/bañadera	$350	Cambiar termostato	$95
Cargar extinguidor fuego	$35	Cambiar extinguidor fuego	$45
Fumigar	$150	Remover basura	$75
Cambiar caja de correo	$35	Cambiar caja de correo/estado	$55
Cambiar lavamano/cocina	$125		

CONTRATO DE ARRENDAMIENTO (Lease Agreement—Spanish)

1. **Miembros:** Los miembros de este contrato incluso en el futuro con Casa Partners son: como "Dueño," y
_____ , y _____ como " Inquilino(s)." Todos los inquilinos mayores de edad tienen la obligacion de firmar este contrato de arrendamiento y cada uno de ellos estaran bajo los terminos y condiciones dichas en este contrato. Inquilinos additional serian_____
(edad: _____); _____ (edad:____);
y_____ (edad:_____) solamente.

Numeros de telefono:

de la Casa: _____   # del Trabajo:_____

de Celular:_____   En Caso de Emergencia: _____

2. **Propiedad:** El dueño permite al inquilino(s) durante el termino de este contrato en la propiedad ubicada:
_____

3. **Terminos:** El termino de este contrato debe ser por un año, comenzando en
_____ y terminando_____ .

4. **Renta:** La renta semanal/mensual en dicha propiedad sera $_____ por semana/o mes. Un mes completo /o una semana tendra que ser pagada para que este contrato se ejecute. La renta del segundo mes/o semana es por la cantidad $_____, y debe ser pagada el ___ dia de _____, 200__. Los siguientes pagos deben ser efectuados consecutivamente el primer dia de cada mes/o semana incluyendo Sabados. En caso de que no se pague la renta establecida en este contrato de arrendamiento un anuncio de terminacion del mismo sera entregado.

5. **Cargos Por PagoTarde:** Cualquier pago que sea pagado despues de cinco(5) dias del dia acordado en este contrato incluira un cargo del 10%(diez porciento) del pago total de la renta por mes/o semana. Tambien cualquier pago que sea pagado despues de diez(10) dias del dia acordado en este contrato incluira un cargo del 10% (diez porciento) del pago total de la renta por mes/o semana mas $25.00 por dia.

6. **Cheques Devueltos**: Un cargo de $30.00 sera impuesto al inquilino(s) si al cheque es devuelto por falta de fondos. Hasta que no traigan otro cheque como pago de la renta, otros cargos por pago tarde sera aplicado.

7. **Utilidades, Equipos Electricos, y otros Objetos Incluidos por el Dueño:**

	Dueño	Inquilino
Electricidad	_____	_____
Gas	_____	_____
Agua	_____	_____
Basura	_____	_____
Otros	_____	_____

- **Equipos electricos includes por el dueño:**

Refrigerador	_____X_____	_____
Fogon	_____X_____	_____
Aire Acondicionado	_____X_____	_____
Microondas	_____	_____X_____
Lavadora/Secadora	_____	_____X_____

- El cuidado del patio es responsibilidad del inquilino. El inquilino debe mantener el patio con la hierba y otras plantas cortada en la propiedad.
- El inquilino esta de acuerdo a no colocar otros equipos electricos en la propiedad debido al alto costo de electricidad que esto implica, por ejemplos: otras unidad de aire acondicionado, lavadoras, lavadoras de platos, otros. Solamente puede usar los equipos electricos colocados por el dueño de la propiedad. Ademas el inquilino esta de acuerdo a pedir autorizacion por escrito al dueño antes de conectar cualquier equipo antes mencionado.
- El inquilino esta de acuerdo que la colocacion no authorized de cualquier equipo electrico antes mentioned: lavadora, lavadora de platos, otras unidades de aire conditionado, otros aumentara la renta mensual/o semial de $75.00 por mes. Esta cantidad sera automaticamente cargada como porcion de la renta durante el termino del contrato de arrendamiento.

8. **Uso de la Propiedad, Inquilinos, e Invitados:** El inquilino debe usar la propiedad para uso residential solamente. La propiedad debe ser ocupada por los inquilino(s) mencionados en (1): Inquilino(s), en este contrato.

9. **Responsibilidades Mantenidas por el Inquilino(s):** El inquilino debe mantener la unidad habitada limpia y en condiciones sanitarias de otra manera se aplicara las leyes estatales y locales para mantener la unidad en buenas condiciones. En caso de cualquier daño a la unidad por negligencia del inquilino(s), el dueño arreglara los daños a la unidad pero el inquilino(s) sera responsable por los gastos que seran determinado por el dueño.

10. **Alteraciones:** Ningun tipo de alteracion o de adicion es permitida sin previa autorizacion por escrito del dueño. Que estaria a total consideration del dueño.

11. **Ruidos:** El inquilino esta de acuerdo a no hacer ruido excesivo u otras activities que interrumpan la tranquilidad de otros.

12. **Inpeccion por el Dueño:** El inquilino esta de acuerdo en permitir que el dueño entre a la propiedad para inspectional, hacer reparaciones necessaries, decoraciones, alteraciones, or mejoras dentro de la propiedad. Tambien mostrar la unidad a futuros compradores, contratistas, trabajadores, inspectores, o inquilinos. El dueño puede entrar a la propiedad sin autorizacion del inquilino en caso de emergencia.

13. **Deposito de Seguridad:** El inquilino esta de acuerdo en pagar un deposito por la suma de $_____, este deposito sera usado para cualquier destruccion en la propiedad, incluyendo equipos electricos, alfombra; no sera entregado en caso que el inquilino(s) desocupe la propiedad antes de lo establecido en este contrato de arrendamiento o por desobedecer lo establecido en el mismo. Este deposito no puede ser usado como pago por la renta del mes/o semana. El dueño enviara el deposito por correo a la direccion indicada por el inquilino despues de ser inspeccionada en un periodo de 45 dias despues de ser desocupada. Una vez de desocupar la propiedad, $250.00 del deposito de seguridad sera usado automaticamente para cargos de limpieza.

14. **Deposito para llaves**: Los siguientes serian:

      A.   Llave del apartamento/o propiedad: $15.00 por llave_____

      B.   Llave de la puerta de seguridad: $15.00 por llave _____

      C.   Llave del correo: $ 15.00 por llave _____

      D.   Puerta automica: $ 100.00 por cada uno___

15. **Autorizacion**: El inquilino le da autorizacion al dueño por todos los objectos personales que se encuentran dentro de la propiedad, incluyendo los muebles. El inquilino esta de acuerdo en pagar la renta, y cualquier daño ocurrido dentro de la propiedad, incluyendo cargos de corte y abogados.

16. **Sub-Arrendamiento**: El inquilino no debe mostrar este acuerdo sobre la propiedad sin autorizacion previa o el consentimiento del dueño; la cual sera a total opcion del dueño.

17. **Daños Fisicos y a la Propiedad**: Debido a los estandas requeridos por la ley, el dueño no es responsable de ningun daño fisico ocurrido al inquilino(s), el/la familia, empleados, o invitados del mismo, ni de ningun daño causado a la propiedad por los mismos u otras personas que esten dentro o fuera de la propiedad con o sin la autorizacion del dueño; el dueño no es responsable por perdidas, o robos, fuego, lluvia, tormentas, hurricanes, explosion, bombas, u otras causas que dañe la propiedad personal del inquilino. Tampoco es responsable por daños causados por el mal uso o mal funcionamiento de las utilidades en la propiedad proveidas en este contrato de arrendamiento; ni es responsable por ningun daño fisico en cualquier parte de la propiedad.

- El dueño no es responsable por, y no provee ningun tipo de seguro por fuego u otras causas para la propiedad privada del inquilino(s).

- Como consideracion additional a este contrato, el inquilino esta de acuerdo que el dueño se limita a cualquier daño fisico ocurrido en la propiedad siguiendo los estandas legales. Ademas el inquilino asegura que inspecciono la propiedad y esta de acuerdo con ella; por lo tanto no puede levanter ningun tipo de demanda causada por la condicion de la propiedad durante el termino de este contrato u otra extension del mismo.

18. **En Caso de Equipo Descompuesto, Dañado por Fuego, Agua o Acto de Dios:** El inquilino debera de notificar al dueño immediatamente al dueño y el dueño debera arreglar los daños durante un tiempo rasonable. En caso de que el dueño decida no arreglar el problema ocurrido, el contrato queda terminado immediatamente. Y si el contrato queda terminado, el inquilino pagara solo renta hasta ese dia, y la cantidad restante del mes o/semana sera devuelta.

19. **Animales**: El inquilino no puede tener ningun tipo de animal sin la autorizacion del dueño y entonces tendra un contrato separado para el animal. Todos los animales tienen que ser inspeccionado por el dueño y aprobado durante horas laborables.

20. **Terminacion-Todos los Inquilinos Esten Atentos!** - Por lo menos cuarenta y cincos(45) dias antes de que este contrato de arrendamiento sea terminado, el inquilino tiene que darle una nota por escrito si el mismo va a dejar la propiedad una vez terminado el contrato o si va a renovarlo. Si el inquilino no le entrega esta nota por escrita en el tiempo acordado, entonces el mismo tendra que pagar la renta sin importar si la ocupa o no

Una vez terminado el contrato, el inquilino debe dejar la propiedad totalmente vacia y sacar todos los objetos personales y dejarla en las mismas condiciones que se le entrego.

21. **Renovar:** Una vez terminado este contrato el dueño/inquilino aceptan continuar los mismos terminos del contrato aunque la renta sea mes/a mes.

22. **Cargos de Abogado**: Cualquier violacion de cualquiera de las condiciones dichas en este contrato y ocurra sufficient causas para una eviccion, el inquilino acepta a pagar cualquier gasto de abogados que esta violacion traiga consigo, o costos por colleccion por otros daños o rompimiento de este contrato incluyendo cargos de abogados.

23. **Anuncios:** Todas los anuncios al igual que este contrato sera entregado por escrito a los otros miembros/el inquilino de la compañia: Casa Partners, Inc, 222 Lakeview Ave, suite 160-103, West Palm Beach, Fl 33401.

24. **Mantenimiento:** Excepto en caso de emergencia, todos los mantenimientos requerido por el inquilino debe hacerse por escrito a: Casa Partners, Inc, 222 Lakevie Ave, suite 160-103, West Palm Beach, Fl 33401. El inquilino es responsable por los primero $50.00. Este es responsable por cualquier ventana dañada incluyendo que se haya dañado por accidente, por actividad criminal, por obra de Dios, o por desastre natural. El inquilino no debera reparar la ventana, porque el dueño la arreglara pero el inquilino debera pagar por el material y la mano de obra, no menos de $100.00 por cada ventana.

25. **Control de Animales**: El inquilino es responsable por el control y el tratamiento del animal, incluyendo tramites y licencias. En caso de que haya algun problema con el animal, el dueño de la propiedad puede buscar ayuda profesional pero el inquilino esta de acuerdo a pagar cualquier cargo aplicado por el tratamiento del animal.

26. **Ausencia o Abandonamiento**: El inquilino esta obligado a notificar al dueño en caso de una ausencia extendida de mas de siete (7) dias de la propiedad. Una ausencia por mas de diez (10) dias sin notificacion de la propiedad sin pagar la renta, sera considerado abondamiento de la propiedad. El dueño esta autorizado a entrar a la misma y a sacar todos los objetos personales del inquilino y ademas echarlos(a la basura). Immediatamente el dueño esta autorizado a rentar o vender la propiedad, ademas se aplicaran procedimiento por rentas no pagada, daños causados, cargos de abogados.

27. **Terminacion por Violencia or Actitud Peligrosa:** El dueño puede terminar este contrato de arrendamiento dentro de un plazo de tres (3) dias una vez que una nota por escrito sea entregada al inquilino por cualquier conducta peligrosa, acto de violencia, u otra actitud que ponga en peligro la salud, seguridad, o la vida de otros.

28. **Violacion de Contrato:** Si algun otro acto de violacion ocurre de parte del inquilino que no sea detallado en este contrato de arrendamiento, y afecte la salud y la seguridad de otros. El dueño esta autorizado a entregar un anuncio por escrito que aclare los actos de violacion, y el contrato de arrendamiento sera terminado dentro de treinta (30) dias de haber recibido el anuncio de abandono de la propiedad. En un periodo de catorce (14) dias, la violacion puede ser remediada si es por reparaciones o pagos de renta, y si el inquilino resuelve la situation antes de la fecha acordada en el anuncio entregado el contrato no sera terminado.

- Si el mismo acto de violacion ocurre en el trascurso de seis (6) meses antes de terminar el contrato, el dueño puede terminar el contrato de arrendamiento una vez de haber entregado el anuncio de abandono de la propiedad /el cual especifica la causa de violacion y el dia que el contrato debera de ser terminado / en un plazo de catorce (14) dias de haber recibido el mismo.

29. **Reglas y Regulaciones**: El inquilino ha leido, entendido y esta de acuerdo con todas las reglas y regulaciones establecidas en este contrato.

30. **Alteraciones o Cambios en este Contrato**: El inquilino y el dueño entienden y estan de acuerdo que ningun cambio o modificacion podra ser realizada en este contrato, al no ser con una autorizacion por escrito firmada por ambos miembros del mismo : dueño/inquilino.

31. **Aplicacion:** La aplicacion del inquilino es una parte importante en este contrato, incluyendo referencias. Una vez descubierta cualquier informacion falsa en la aplicacion del inquilino; el dueño tendra como opcion la cancelacion de este contrato de arrendamiento.

32. **Clausulas**: Si cualquiera de las proviciones realizadas en este contrato no esta legalmente aprobada por la ley, la misma sera anulada pero sin afectar cualquier otra establecida en este contrato.

33. **El Inquilino(s) es/son Responsable(s) por su Propia Seguridad**: El inquilino ha inpeccionado la propiedad y esta satisfecho con los detectores de humo, seguro de puertas, seguros de ventanas, y otros equipos de seguridad ubicados en la propiedad. El inquilino esta conciente que el dueño no esta en la obligacion de inpeccionar, o reparar los detectores de humo una vez que el inquilino(s) ocupe la propiedad. El dueño no esta en la obligacion de reparar o inpeccionar cualquier otro equipo de seguridad sin antes haber recibido una nota por escrito que explique la situacion con el equipo.

- El inquilino esta conciente de que el dueño u otros representantes no garantizan la seguridad personal del inquilino y que la misma esta a total responsibilidad del inquilino(s).

34. **Aceleracion por Falta o Desobedencia**: En el evento de que una o mas faltas ocurran, el dueño puede declarar el balance total del contrato y otras obligaciones del inquilino con pago immediato sin ningun anuncio.

35. **Terminos Adicionales y Condiciones**: Parrafos adicionales_____ hasta _____son incorporados como parte de este Contrato de Arrendamiento.
Por lo tanto este Contrato de Arrendamiento sera ejecutado, el dia_____de_____,2006.

Casa Partners, Inc.

Dueño

_____/_____
Nombre del Inquilino/Firma

de Seguro Social/Inquilino:_____

de Licencia de Conduccion:_____

_____
Dueño/Gerente

_____/_____
Nombre del Inquilino/Firma

de Seguro Social/Inquilino:_____

de Licencia de Conduccion:_____

Date: _____

Late Rent Letter (English and Spanish)

Property Address

Dear Tenant:

This is a notice regarding the monthly payment (March) amount that you must pay immediately to Casa Partners, Inc (check or money order), and you will need to add 10% of your monthly payment (late fee) before we apply an eviction on your apartment. You can drop your payment at the office located at 139 N County Rd., Suite 18A, Palm Beach, Fl 33480 between 8:30a.m. to 4:30 p.m. today. Any questions, feel free to call at 561-255-3683. Sorry for the inconvenience.

Querido Inquilino:

Esta noticia es para recordarle que usted tiene que pagar su pago mensual (Marzo) a Casa Partners, Inc (cheque o money order solamente) immediatamente, y necesita agregar un 10% de su pago mensual a la renta (cargo por pago tarde) antes de que apliquemos una eviccion a su apartamento. Usted puede dejar su pago en nuestra oficina localizada en 139 N County Rd., Suite 18A, Palm Beach, Fl 33480 de 8:30 a.m. a 4:30p.m. hoy. Cualquier pregunta puede llamar al 561-255-3683. Disculpe la incoveniencia.

Thank you,
Yours truly,

Office Manager

Renters Insurance Letter to Tenant

Dear Valued Tenant:

Some tenants have asked us about coverage concerning renters Insurance.

What is renters Insurance? Are you protected?

Renters insurance is coverage for personal property for anyone who rents or leases space. The personal property is covered from theft and damage. Other insurance may cover the cost of repairing items inside the rental unit, such as doors, window, holes in walls, ect., caused by the renter.

If you are interested in obtaining renters insurance, or other insurance please call our offices at 561-255-3683

For a one time charge of only $49 we will:

1. Contact a licensed insurance company.
2. Handle all the paperwork
3. Negotiate for the lowest quote possible on your behalf
4. You will receive a stress-free transaction and maintain the security and piece of mind knowing all of your valued possessions are insured.

Let us know what kind of insurance coverage you would like.

Call us now.   555-55-5555

_____ **YES**, help me with my renters insurance. Enclosed is my $49 check.

Make check or money order to: Best Property Managers

Mail to: Big Boy City, Anywhere

Name _____   Address_____

Phone _____

Rental Application Form

PLEASE PRINT

Dr., Mr., Mrs., Ms, Mdm.: _____ _____ Date: _____

First Middle Last

SECTION 1: Rental Property For Which You Are Applying

Property address: _____ Apartment number if Applicable: _____

Rent per month: _____ Security: _____

Names of others to occupy unit:

_____

each Applicant must fill out a separate Application From and provide all required info

Dates of Occupancy: From: _____ To: _____

How did you find us? (circle and/ or fill in as applicable)

🕐 Internet Search Engine(s) Used

_____

🕐 Real Estate Broker _____ Agency _____ Which listing did you use?_____

🕐 Print Advertisement: NY Times / Village Voice / Other (name)

_____

🕐 Did you see a sign on one of our buildings? Which building?

_____

🕐 Referral: Friend / Relative / Current or former tenant

_____

🕐 School Housing Office: NYU / Parson's / FIT / New School / Other

(name)_____

SECTION 2: Applicant Information

Date of Birth: _____/_____/_____ Social Security Number: _____-_____-_____

Driver's license number: _____ State: _____

Passport number (if not a U.S. Citizen): _____ Issuing Country: _____Type: _____

Present home address: _____ City_____

State_____ Zip_____

Home phone: ( ) _____ Work phone: ( ) _____ Cell phone: ( ) _____

Email _____

How long at present address? _____ Leaseholder: _____ (If different from applicant)

Landlord or Property Manager: _____ Phone: ( )_____

Landlord address: _____ City_____

State_____ Zip_____

Applicant Previous Home address: _____ City_____

State_____ Zip_____

How long at previous address? _____ Leaseholder: _____ (If different from applicant)

206

Do you have any pets? _____ How many? _____ What kind?
_____ .

SECTION 3: Applicant Financial Information
Employer: _____ Address:

_____
City_____ State_____ Zip_____
Position/title: _____ Supervisor: _____
Phone: _____ Annual income: _____ How long with present employer? _____
OR if currently enrolled:
Name of School: _____ Year: _____ Expected Graduation: _____
Program: _____
Address: _____ City_____ State_____ Zip_____
Bank Information:
Name of Bank: _____
Address: _____ City_____ State_____ Zip_____
Checking Account Number: _____ Savings Account Number: _____
Other Accounts:
Name of Institution: _____ Account Number _____ Type of Account _____
Name of Institution: _____ Account Number _____ Type of Account _____

SECTION 4: Guarantor Information
Guarantor Name: Dr., Mr., Mrs., Ms, Mdm.: _____
                                        First Middle Last
Social Security Number: _____ - _____ - _____ Date of Birth: _____ / _____ / _____
Month Day Year
Relationship to applicant: _____ Years known: _____
Address: _____ City_____ State_____
Zip_____
Home Phone: ( ) _____ Cell phone: ( ) _____ Work phone: ( ) _____
Fax: ( ) _____ Email: _____
Employer: _____ Address:

_____
City_____ State_____ Zip_____
Position/title: _____ Supervisor: _____
Phone: _____ Annual income: _____ How long with present employer? _____ 3

SECTION 5: Personal References
(Applicant must provide at least 3 verifiable references, not relatives)
Ref. #1 Name: _____ Time known: _____
Address: _____ Phone: ( ) _____
Ref. #2 Name: _____ Time known: _____
Address: _____ Phone: ( ) _____
Ref. #3 Name: _____ Time known: _____
Address: _____ Phone: ( ) _____
I hereby certify to the best of my knowledge that the above information (from page 1 to page 3) is true and correct
and I hereby authorize _____ to obtain any credit, criminal check, job,
and school, past rental history or references at its discretion.

Applicant's Signature_____ **Date**_____

STEPS FOR SUBMITTING APPLICATION:
Each Applicant for the Apartment must bring a completed application directly to our office along with the following:

1. Photo ID (Driver's license or passport or other U.S. Government issued ID)

2. FOR STUDENTS: Enrollment certification is required FOR OTHERS: Employment letter and the 1st page of the latest 1040 tax return is required

3. A Guarantor is required for EACH applicant (The 1st page of the latest 1040 tax return is required)

4. $50.00 processing application charge per applicant. (Note: All human occupants over 18 must be named on the lease.)

5. $500.00 Deposit to hold property during application process. Additional deposit may be required for rentals greater than $3,000 per month.

♦ If applicant is accepted, deposit is applied to balance of rent and security due at signing

♦ If applicant is rejected by Worth Avenue Property Management any deposits will be refunded.

♦ Deposit is NOT refundable for ANY other reason.

♦ MOST applicants are notified within 24 hours.

♦ Application processing charges are non-refundable.

♦ All funds are payable in the form of **CASH, CERTIFIED CHECK**, or **MONEY ORDER**

♦ No **PERSONAL CHECKS** or **CREDIT CARDS** are accepted

One deposit is required per unit regardless of how many other prospective occupants are applying. If Applicant is accepted, this deposit is applied to balance. If Applicant is rejected for any reason, any deposit will be refunded immediately. All fees are due in cash, certified check, money order or cashier's check. No personal checks or credit cards are accepted. Most Applicants are notified within 48 hours. Application processing fees are non-refundable.

NOTICE OR RENT INCREASE

ENGLISH / SPANISH

Date:

Occupying Tenants

Dear Tenants:

Due to the increase costs for maintenance, taxes, repairs and of course inflation, the time has come where we must raise rents.

Effective on _____ **20_____**, the new rent will be **$_____ per month.** Enclosing is a new lease. Please execute and return to our offices. You are also required to increase your security deposit to **$_____** .

If you wish not to renew a lease, you must give us written notice on or before _____ , **20_____** in order to get your security deposit returned. If you should have any questions, please call our offices at _____ or mail us at the above address. Thank you for your understanding and for being a valued tenant.

Queridos Inquilinos:

Debido a los altos costos de mantenimiento, taxes, y reparaciones; entonces llega el momento en donde tenemos que aumentar las rentas.

Comenzando en _____ , **20___**; la nueva renta sera **$_____ por mes**. Junto a esta carta es un nuevo contrato de arrendamiento. Por favor firmelo y regreselo a la oficina. Tambien se require un aumento del deposito de seguridad a **$_____** .

En caso que no desee renovar el contrato de arrendamiento, usted debe enviarnos una nota por escrito antes de _____ , **20_____** para regresarle su deposito de seguridad . Si usted tiene alguna pregunta, por favor llame a la oficina al _____ o mandenos una nota por escrito a la direccion localizada en la parte superior de esta carta. Muchas gracias por su comprension y por ser un buen inquilino.

Very truly yours,

Key Receipt and Key Deposit

Tenant(s):_____

Address:_____

Tenant(s) have received the following number of keys:_____

Entrance door keys:

Other keys: _____ for the following:_____

There is a $15 for each key issued. The deposit is the _____ number of keys. The total key deposit is $_____. At the end of the lease if keys are not returned to property manager, deposits will be forfeited.

Tenant agrees not to add any additional locks or make any lock changes or additional keys without the manager's written consent.

The Tenant(s) acknowledges receipt of the copy of this statement.

Tenant(s): _____ Date: _____

Property Mananger _____Date _____

☺ $50 ☺

REWARD/RECOMPENSA

We Will Pay You for Referring Renters to Us

Who Do you Know?

- Family Members—Brothers or Sisters, Uncles or Aunts?
- Friends—Who do you do things with and talk to daily?
- Co-Workers? Neighbors?

Nice, Clean Houses and Charming Apartments

Address	Description
1000 Main St. Anytown, FL 30989	Studio & 1 bedroom Apartments Starting at $600 per month
11122 Georgia Ave. Anytown, FL 39095	Beautiful Studio, All Utilities Included - $700 per month

Call Now:

Acme Housing Corp Rental Office: (555) 535-0911 or

Ann Landlady (555) 255-5683 (Se Habla Espanol)

SPECIAL SIGN-UP BONUS

- *12 Month lease – get 10% discount on 13th month**
- *24 Month lease – get 25% discount on 25th month**
- *36 Month lease – get FREE RENT on 37th month**
  *Must have no late payments or lease violations.

Appendix II

Real Estate Investment & Landlording Terms

ABSORPTION RATE
The ratio of the number of properties in an area that have been sold against the number available. Used to show the volatility of a market.

ABSTRACTION METHOD
This method of estimating the value of property uses similar properties available in the same market to extract the value of a parcel of land.

ACCELERATION CLAUSE
A provision in a mortgage that gives the lender the right to demand immediate payment of the outstanding loan balance under certain circumstances. Usually when the borrower defaults on the loan.

ACCESSORY BUILDING
A building separate from the main structure on a property. Often used for a specific purpose, such as a workshop, storage shed or garage.

ACCRETION
The natural growth of a piece of land resulting from forces of nature

ACRE 43,560 square feet. A measurement of area.

ACTUAL AGE
The amount of time that has passed since a building or other structure was built. See also: EFFECTIVE AGE

ADJUSTMENT DATE
The date the interest rate changes on an adjustable rate mortgage.

AD VAL OREM TAX
Taxes assessed based on the value of the land and improvements.

ADDENDUM
A supplement to any document that contains additional information pertinent to the subject. Appraisers use an addendum to further explain items for which there was inadequate space on the standard appraisal form.

ADJUSTABLE-RATE MORTGAGE (ARM)
A type of mortgage where the interest rate varies based on a particular index, normally the prime lending rate.

ADJUSTED BASIS
The value of an asset (property or otherwise) that includes the original price plus the value of any improvement, and less any applicable depreciation.

ADJUSTED SALES PRICE
An opinion of a property's sales price, after adjustments have been made to account for differences between it and another comparable property.

AESTHETIC VALUE
The additional value a property enjoys based on subjective criteria such as look or appeal.

AFFIRMATION
A declaration that a certain set of facts are truthful.

AFFORDABILITY ANALYSIS
A calculation used to determine an individual's likelihood of being able to meet the obligations of a mortgage for a particular property. Takes into account the down payment, closing costs and on-going mortgage payments.

AGENT

A person who has been appointed to act on behalf of another for a particular transaction.

AMENITY

Any feature of a property that increases its value or desirability. These might include natural amenities such as location or proximity to mountains, or man-made amenities like swimming pools, parks or other recreation.

AMERICAN SOCIETY OF APPRAISERS

An organization of appraisal professionals and others interested in the appraisal profession.

AMORTIZATION

The repayment of a loan through regular periodic payment.

AMORTIZATION SCHEDULE

The breakdown of individual payments throughout the life of an amortized loan, showing both principal contribution and debt service (interest) fees.

AMORTIZATION TERM

The length of time over which an amortized loan is repaid. Mortgages are commonly amortized over 15 or 30 years.

AMPERAGE

A measure of electric current describing the magnitude.

ANNUAL PERCENTAGE RATE (APR)

The rate of annual interest charged on a loan.

ANNUITY

A sum of money paid at regular intervals, often annually.

APPLICATION

A form used to apply for a mortgage loan that details a potential borrower's income, debt, savings and other information used to determine credit worthiness.

APPRAISAL

A "defensible" and carefully documented opinion of value. Most commonly derived using recent sales of comparable properties by a licensed, professional appraiser.

APPRAISAL FOUNDATION

A not-for-profit educational organization established by the appraisal profession in the United States in 1987. It is dedicated to the advancement of professional valuation and responsible for establishing, improving, and promoting the Uniform Standards of Professional Appraisal Practice (USPAP).

APPRAISAL INSTITUTE

A world-wide organization dedicated to real estate appraisal education, publication and advocacy.

APPRAISAL PRINCIPLES

The basic building blocks of the property valuation process, including property inspection, market analysis and basic economics.

APPRAISAL REPORT

The end result of the appraisal process usually consists of one major standardized form such as, the Uniform Residential Appraisal Report form 1004, as well as all supporting documentation and additional detail information. The purpose of the report is to convey the opinion of value of the subject property and support that opinion with corroborating information.

APPRAISAL STANDARDS BOARD (ASB)

An independent board of the APPRAISAL FOUNDATION, which writes, amends, and interprets USPAP. The ASB is composed of up to seven appraisers appointed by the Foundation's Board of Trustees. The ASB holds public meetings throughout the year to interpret and amend USPAP.

APPRAISED VALUE

An opinion of the fair market value of a property as developed by a licensed, certified appraiser following accepted appraisal principals.

APPRAISER

An educated, certified professional with extensive knowledge of real estate markets, values and practices. The appraiser is often the only independent voice in any real estate transaction with no vested interest in the ultimate value or sales price of the property.

APPRECIATION

The natural rise in property value due to market forces.

ARMS LENGTH TRANSACTION

Any transaction in which the two parties are unconnected and have no overt common interests. Such a transaction most often reflects the true market value of a property.

ASSESSED VALUE

The value of a property according to jurisdictional tax assessment.

ASSESSMENT

The function of assigning a value to a property for the purpose of levying taxes.

ASSESSMENT RATIO

The comparative relationship of a property's assessed value to its market value.

ASSESSOR

The jurisdictional official who performs the assessment and assigns the value of a property.

ASSET

Any item of value which a person owns.

ASSIGNMENT

Transfer of ownership of a mortgage usually when the loan is sold to another company.

ASSUMABLE MORTGAGE

A mortgage that can be taken over by the buyer when a home is sold.

ASSUMPTION

When a buyer takes over, or "assumes" the sellers mortgage.

ATTACHED HOUSING

Any number of houses or other dwellings which are physically attached to one another, but are occupied by a number of different people. The individual houses may or may not be owned by separate people as well.

BACKFILL

The slope of the ground around a house.

BALL COCK VALVE

The valve inside a toilet tank that controls the filling of the tank.

BALLOON MORTGAGE

A mortgage loan in which the monthly payments are not large enough to repay the loan by the end of the term. So at the end of the term, the remaining balance comes due in a single large payment.

BALLOON PAYMENT

The final large payment at the end of a balloon mortgage term.

BANKRUPTCY

When a person or business is unable to pay their debts and seeks protection of the state against creditors. Bankruptcies remain on credit records for up to ten years and can prevent a person from being able to get a loan.

BEAM

A structural supporting member.

BILL OF SALE

A physical receipt indicating the sale of property.

BIWEEKLY MORTGAGE

A mortgage where you make "half payments" every two weeks, rather than one payment per month. This results in making the equivalent of 13 monthly payments per year, rather than 12, significantly reducing the time it takes to pay off a thirty year mortgage.

BLIGHTED AREA

Any region of a city or town that has fallen into disrepair or otherwise has become undesirable.

BONA FIDE

Any genuine offer, made without intent to defraud or deceive.

BRIDGE FINANCING

An interim loan made to facilitate the purchase of a new home before the buyer's current residence sells and its equity is available to fund the new purchase.

BRIDGING

Structural members used between beams to strengthen the structure.

BROKER

An individual who facilitates the purchase of property by bringing together a buyer and a seller.

BTU

British Thermal Unit. A unit of measurement used to describe heating or cooling capacity.

BUFFER ZONE

A segment of land between two disparate municipal zones which acts as a shield to keep one zone from encroaching upon the other. Often used to separate residential districts from commercial areas.

BUILDING CODE

Regulations that ensure the safety and material compliance of new construction within a municipality. Building codes are localized to ensure they are adequate to meet the risk of common hazards.

BUILDING LINE OR SETBACK

The statutory distance between buildings and the property line, imposed by municipalities, home associations, or other agreements.

BUILT-INS

Specific items of personal property which are installed in a real estate improvement such that they become part of the building. Built-in microwave ovens and dishwashers are common examples.

BUNGALOW

A one-story, home-style dating from the early twentieth century. Often characterized by a low-pitched roof.

BUY DOWN

Extra money paid in a lump sum to reduce the interest rate of a fixed rate mortgage for a period of time. The extra money may be paid by the borrower, in order to have a lower payment at the beginning of the mortgage. Or paid by the seller, or lender, as incentive to buy the property or take on the mortgage.

BX CABLE

Electrical cable shrouded in a galvanized steel outer cover.

CALL OPTION

A clause in a mortgage which allows the lender to demand payment of the outstanding balance at a specific time.

CAP

Associated with Adjustable Rate Mortgages. A limit on how high monthly payments or how much interest rates may change within a certain time period or the life of the mortgage.

CAPE COD COLONIAL

A single-story house style made popular in New England. Often characterized by a steep roof with gables.

CAPITAL

Accumulated goods and money which is most often used to generate additional income.

CAPITAL EXPENDITURE

An outlay of funds designed to improve the income-producing capabilities of an asset or to extend its economic life.

CASH-OUT REFINANCE

Refinancing a mortgage at a higher amount than the current balance in order to transform a portion of the equity into cash.

CAULKING

A pliable material used to seal cracks or openings such as around windows.

CAVEAT EMPTOR

Literally translated: "Let the buyer beware." A common business tenet whereby the buyer is responsible for verifying any and all claims by the seller of property.

CERTIFICATE OF DEPOSIT

A document showing that the bearer has a certain amount of money, at a particular amount interest, on deposit with a financial institution.

CERTIFICATE OF DEPOSIT INDEX

An index based on the interest rate of six month CD's. Used to set interest rates on some Adjustable Rate Mortgages.

CERTIFICATE OF ELIGIBILITY

A document issued by the Veterans Administration that certifies eligibility for a VA loan.

CERTIFICATE OF OCCUPANCY

Issued by an appropriate jurisdictional entity, this document certifies that a building complies with all building codes and is safe for use or habitation.

CERTIFICATE OF REASONABLE VALUE (CRV)

Usually based on an independent appraisal, a CRV for a particular property establishes the maximum amount which can be secured by a VA mortgage.

CERTIFICATE OF TITLE

A document designating the legal owner of a parcel of real estate. Usually provided by a title or abstract company.

CERTIFIED GENERAL APPRAISER

Generally, any professional who has met the local or state requirements, and passed the appropriate certification exam, and is capable of appraising any type of property.

CERTIFIED RESIDENTIAL APPRAISER
A sub-classification of appraiser who is only licensed to appraise residential property, usually up to four units.

CHAIN OF TITLE
The complete history of ownership of a piece of property.

CHATTEL
Any personal property which is not attached to or an integral part of a property. Chattel is not commonly taken into consideration when appraising the value of real property.

CIRCUIT BREAKERS
Electrical devices which automatically open electrical circuits if they are overloaded.

CLEAR TITLE
Ownership of property that is not encumbered by any counter-claim or lien.

CLOSING
The process whereby the sale of a property is consummated with the buyer completing all applicable documentation, including signing the mortgage obligation and paying all appropriate costs associated with the sale.

CLOSING COSTS
All appropriate costs generated by the sale of property which the parties must pay to complete the transaction. Costs may include appraisal fees, origination fees, title insurance, taxes and any points negotiated in the deal.

CLOSING STATEMENT
The document detailing the final financial arrangement between a buyer and seller and the costs paid by each.

CO-BORROWER
A second person sharing obligation on the loan and title on the property.

COLLATERAL
An asset which is placed at risk to secure the repayment of a loan.

COLLECTION
The process a lender takes to pursue a borrower who is delinquent on his payments in order to bring the mortgage current again. Includes documentation that may be used in foreclosure.

CO-MAKER
A second party who signs a loan, along with the borrower, and becomes liable for the debt should the borrower default.

COMMON LAW
As opposed to statute law. Laws that have been established by custom, usage and courts over many years.

COMMISSION
A percentage of the sales price or a fixed fee negotiated by an agent to compensate for the effort expended to sell or purchase property.

COMMON AREA ASSESSMENTS
Fees which are charged to the tenets or owners of properties to cover the costs of maintaining areas shared with other tenets or owners. Commonly found in condominium, PUD or office spaces.

COMMON AREAS
Any areas, such as entryways, foyers, pools, recreational facilities or the like, which are shared by the tenets or owners of property near by. Commonly found in condominium, PUD or office spaces.

COMMUNITY PROPERTY
In many jurisdictions, any property which has been acquired by a married couple. The ownership of the property is considered equal unless stipulated otherwise by both parties.

COMPARABLES
An abbreviated term used by appraisers to describe properties which are similar in size, condition, location and amenities to a subject property whose value is being determined. The Uniform Standards of Professional Appraisal Practice (USPAP) establish clear guidelines for determining a comparable property.

COMPOUND INTEREST
Interest paid on the principal amount, as well as any accumulated interest.

CONCESSIONS
Additional value granted by a buyer or seller to entice another party to complete a deal.

CONDEMNATION
The official process by which a property is deemed to be uninhabitable or unusable due to internal damage or other external conditions.

CONDENSATION

The transition of water vapor to liquid. Typically forms in areas of high humidity.

CONDOMINIUM

A development where individual units are owned, but common areas and amenities are shared equally by all owners.

CONDOMINIUM CONVERSION

Commonly, the conversion of a rental property such as an apartment complex into a CONDOMINIUM-style complex where each unit is owned rather than leased.

CONDUIT

The pipe through which electric wiring is run.

CONSTRUCTION LOAN

A loan made to a builder or home owner that finances the initial construction of a property, but is replaced by a traditional mortgage one the property is completed.

CONTIGUOUS

Connected to or touching along an unbroken boundary.

CONTINGENCY

Something that must occur before something else happens. Often used in real estate sales when a buyer must sell a current home before purchasing a new one. Or, when a buyer makes an offer that requires a complete home inspection before it becomes official.

CONTRACT

A legally binding agreement, oral or written, between two parties.

CONVENTIONAL MORTGAGE

A traditional, real estate financing mechanism that is not backed by any government or other agency (FHA, VA, etc.).

CONVERTIBLE ARM

A mortgage that begins as and adjustable, that allows the borrower to convert the loan to a fixed rate within a specific timeframe.

COOPERATIVE (CO-OP)

A form of ownership where each resident of a multiunit property owns a share in a cooperative corporation that owns the building. With each resident having rights to a specific unit within the building.

CORPORATE RELOCATION

A situation where a person's employer pays all or some of the expenses associated with moving from one location to another, usually over a substantial distance. Relocation expenses often include the amounts, such as brokerage fees, incurred in the selling and buying of the employee's primary residence.

COST OF FUNDS INDEX (COFI)

An index of financial institutions costs used to set interest rates for some Adjustable Rate Mortgages.

COVENANT

A stipulation in any mortgage that, if not met, can be cause for the lender to foreclose.

CREDIT

A loan of money for the purchase of property, real or personal. Credit is either secured by an asset, such as a home, or unsecured.

CREDIT HISTORY

A record of debt payments, past and present. Used by mortgage lenders in determining credit worthiness of individuals.

CREDITOR

A person to whom money is owed.

CREDIT REPORT

A detailed report of an individuals credit, employment and residence history prepared by a credit bureau. Used by lenders to determine credit worthiness of individuals.

CREDIT REPOSITORY

Large companies that gather and store financial and credit information about individuals who apply for credit.

CUL-DE-SAC

A dead-end street. One with only one entrance/exit.

DATE OF APPRAISAL

The specific point in time as of which an appraiser designates the value of a home. Often stipulated as the date of inspection

DEADBEAT

A tenant who does not pay rent.

DEBT
An obligation to repay some amount owed. This may or may not be monetary.

DEBT EQUITY RATIO
The ratio of the amount a mortgagor still owes on a property to the amount of equity they have in the home. Equity is calculated at the fair-market value of the home, less any outstanding mortgage debt.

DEED
A document indicating the ownership of a property.

DEED-IN-LIEU (OF FORECLOSURE)
A document given by a borrower to a lender, transferring title of the property. Often used to avoid credit-damaging foreclosure procedures.

DEED OF TRUST
A document which transfers title in a property to a trustee, whose obligations and powers are stipulated. Often used in mortgage transactions.

DEED OF RECONVEYANCE
A document which transfers ownership of a property from a Trustee back to a borrower who has fulfilled the obligations of a mortgage.

DEED OF RELEASE
A document which dismisses a lien or other claim on a property.

DEED OF SURRENDER
A document used to surrender any claim a person has to a property.

DEFAULT
The condition in which a borrower has failed to meet the obligations of a loan or mortgage.

DELINQUENCY
The state in which a borrow has failed to meet payment obligations on time.

DEPOSIT
Cash given along with an offer to purchase property, Also called EARNEST MONEY.

DEPRECIATION
The natural decline in property value due to market forces or depletion of resources.

DETACHED SINGLE-FAMILY HOME
A single building improvement intended to serve as a home for one family.

DISCOUNT POINTS
Points paid in addition to the loan origination fee to get a lower interest rate. One point is equal to one percent of the loan amount.

DISTRESSED PROPERTY
A mortgaged property which has been foreclosed on.

DOWNSPOUT
The pipe that water moves through to reach the ground from the rain gutter.

DUE-ON-SALE PROVISION
A clause in a mortgage giving the lender the right to demand payment of the full balance when the borrower sells the property.

DUPLEX
A single-building improvement which is divided and provides two units which serve as homes to two families.

DWELLING
A house or other building which serves as a home.

DOWN PAYMENT
An amount paid in cash for a property, with the intent to mortgage the remaining amount due.

EARNEST MONEY DEPOSIT
A cash deposit made to a home seller to secure an offer to buy the property. This amount is often forfeited if the buyer decides to withdraw his offer.

EASEMENT
The right of a non-owner of property to exert control over a portion or all of the property. For example, power companies often own an easement over residential properties for access to their power lines.

EAVE

The part of the roof that extends beyond the exterior wall.

ECONOMIC DEPRECIATION

The decline in property value caused by external forces, such as neighborhood blight or adverse development.

ECONOMIC LIFE

The amount of time which any income-producing property is able to provide benefits to its owner.

EFFECTIVE AGE

The subjective, estimated age of a property based on its condition, rather than the actual time since it was built. Excessive wear and tear can cause a property's effective age to be greater than its actual age.

EMINENT DOMAIN

The legal process whereby a government can take ownership of a piece of property in order to convert it to public use. Often, the property owner is paid fair-market value for the property.

ENCROACHMENT

A building or other improvement on one property which invades another property or restricts its usage.

ENCUMBRANCE

A claim against a property. Examples are mortgages, liens and easements.

ENERGY EFFICIENCY RATIO

An efficiency rating system for air conditioning units that corresponds to the number of BTU's output per watt of electricity used.

EQUAL CREDIT OPPORTUNITY ACT (ECOA)

U.S. federal law requiring that lenders afford people equal chance of getting credit without discrimination based on race, religion, age, sex etc

EQUITY

The difference between the fair market value of a property and that amount an owner owes on any mortgages or loans secured by the property.

EQUITY BUILDUP

The natural increase in the amount of equity an owner has in a property, accumulated through market appreciation and debt repayment.

ERRORS AND OMISSIONS INSURANCE

An insurance policy taken out by appraisers to cover their liability for any mistakes made during the appraisal process.

ESCROW

An amount retained by a third party in a trust to meet a future obligation. Often used in the payment of annual taxes or insurance for real property.

ESCROW ACCOUNT

An account setup by a mortgage servicing company to hold funds with which to pay expenses such as homeowners insurance and property taxes. An extra amount is paid with regular principal and interest payments that go into the escrow account each month.

ESCROW ANALYSIS

An analysis performed by the lender usually once each year to see that the amount of money going into the escrow account each month is correct for the forecasted expenses.

ESCROW DISBURSEMENTS

The payout of funds from an escrow account to pay property expenses such as taxes and insurance.

ESTATE

The total of all property and assets owned by an individual.

EXAMINATION OF TITLE

The report on the title of a property from the public records or an abstract of the title.

EXCLUSIVE LISTING

An agreement between the owner of a property and a real estate agent giving the agent exclusive right to sell the property.

EXECUTOR

The person named in a will to administer the estate.

FACADE

The front exposure of any building. Often used to describe an artificial or false front which is not consistent with the construction of the rest of the building.

FAIR CREDIT REPORTING ACT

A federal law regulating the way credit agencies disclose consumer credit reports and the remedies available to consumers for disputing and correcting mistakes on their credit history.

FAIR MARKET VALUE

The price at which two unrelated parties, under no duress, are willing to transact business.

FANNIE MAE

A private, shareholder-owned company that works to make sure mortgage money is available for people to purchase homes. Created by Congress in 1938, Fannie Mae is the nation's largest source of financing for home mortgages.

FASCIA

The boards that enclose the eaves.

FEDERAL DEPOSIT INSURANCE CORPORATION (FDIC)

The U.S. Government agency created in 1933 which maintains the stability of and public confidence in the nation's financial system by insuring deposits and promoting safe and sound banking practices.

FEDERAL HOUSING ADMINISTRATION (FHA)

A sub-agency of the U.S. Department of Housing and Urban Development created in the 1930's to facilitate the purchase of homes by low-income, first-time home buyers. It currently provides federally-subsidized mortgage insurance for private lenders.

FEE APPRAISER

A certified, professional appraiser who forms an opinion of the fair market value of property and receives a set fee in exchange.

FEE SIMPLE

A complete, unencumbered ownership right in a piece of property.

FEE SIMPLE ESTATE

A form or ownership, or holding title to real estate. It is the most complete form of title, having an unconditional and unlimited interest of perpetual duration.

FHA MORTGAGE

A mortgage that is insured by the Federal Housing Administration (FHA).

FINAL VALUE ESTIMATE

The opinion of value of a piece of property resulting from an appraisal following the USPAP guidelines.

FIRST MORTGAGE

The primary loan or mortgage secured by a piece of property.

FIXED-RATE MORTGAGE (FRM)

A mortgage which has a fixed rate of interest over the life of the loan.

FIXTURE

Any piece of personal property which becomes permanently affixed to a piece of real property.

FLASHING

The metal used around the base of roof mounted equipment, or at the junction of angles used to prevent leaking.

FLOOD INSURANCE

Supplemental insurance which covers a home owner for any loss due to water damage from a flood. Often required by lenders for homes located in FEMA-designated flood zones.

FLOOR PLAN

The representation of a building which shows the basic outline of the structure, as well as detailed information about the positioning of rooms, hallways, doors, stairs and other features. Often includes detailed information about other fixtures and amenities.

FLUE

The furnace exhaust pipe, usually going through the roof.

FLUSH VALVE

The valve between the toilet bowl and the tank.

FOOTING

The partially buried support for a vertical structural member such as a post.

FORECLOSURE

The process whereby a lender can claim the property used by a borrower to secure a mortgage and sell the property to meet the obligations of the loan.

FORFEITURE

The loss of property or money due to the failure to meet the obligations of a mortgage or loan secured by that property.

FOUNDATION

The solid structural element upon which a structure is built.

FRONTAGE

The segment of a property that runs along a point of access, such as a street or water front.

FUNCTIONAL OBSOLESCENCE

A decrease in the value of property due to a feature or lack thereof which renders the property undesirable. Functional obsolescence can also occur when the surrounding area changes, rendering the property unusable for its originally intended purpose.

GABLE ROOF

A steeply angled, triangular roof.

GALVANIZED PIPE

Iron pipe with a galvanized (zinc) coating.

GAMBREL ROOF

A "barn-like" roof, where the upper portion of the roof is less-steeply angled than the lower part.

GENERAL LIEN

A broad-based claim against several properties owned by a defaulting party.

GEORGIAN

A classic, English-style hose characterized by simple rectangular shape and multiple stories.

GFI

Ground Fault Interrupter. A type of circuit breaker required in areas where water is present.

GINNIE MAE

A wholly owned corporation created in 1968 within the U.S. Department of Housing and Urban Development to serve low-to moderate-income homebuyers.

GIRDER

A main supporting beam.

GOVERNMENT MORTGAGE

Any mortgage insured by a government agency, such as the FHA or VA.

GRADE

The slope of land around a building. Also ground level.

GRANTEE

Any person who is given ownership of a piece of property.

GRANTOR

Any person who gives away ownership of a piece of property.

GROSS AREA

The sum total of all floor space, including areas such as stairways and closet space. Often measured based on external wall lengths.

GROUTING

Material used around ceramic tile.

GUTTER

The trough around the edge of the roof that catches and diverts rain.

HALF-SECTION

320 acres.

HAZARD INSURANCE

Insurance covering damage to a property caused by hazards such as fire, wind and accident.

HEADER

The framing elements above an opening such as a window or door.

HEARTH

The floor of a fireplace or the area immediately in front of it.

HEIGHT ZONING

A municipal restriction on the maximum height of any building or other structure.

HIDDEN AMENITIES

Assets of a property which contribute to its value, but are not readily apparent. Examples might include upgraded or premium building materials.

HIGHEST AND BEST USE

The most profitable and likely use of a property. Selected from reasonably probable and legal alternative uses, which are found to be physically possible, appropriately supported and financially feasible to result in the highest possible land value.

HOME EQUITY CONVERSION MORTGAGE (HECM)

Also known as a reverse annuity mortgage. It allows home owners (usually older) to convert equity in the home into cash. Normally paid by the lender in monthly payments. HECM's typically do not have to be repaid until the borrower is no longer occupying the home.

HOME EQUITY LINE OF CREDIT

A type of mortgage loan that allows the borrower to draw cash against the equity in his home.

HOME INSPECTION

A complete examination of a building to determine its structural integrity and uncover any defects in materials or workmanship which may adversely affect the property or decrease its value.

HOME INSPECTOR

A person who performs professional home inspections. Usually, with an extensive knowledge of house construction methods, common house problems, how to identify those problems and how to correct them.

HOMEOWNER'S ASSOCIATION

An organization of home owners in a particular neighborhood or development formed to facilitate the maintenance of common areas and to enforce any building restrictions or covenants.

HOMEOWNER'S INSURANCE

A policy which covers a home owner for any loss of property due to accident, intrusion or hazard.

HOMEOWNER'S WARRANTY

An insurance policy covering the repair of systems and appliances within the home for the coverage period.

HUD MEDIAN INCOME

Median family income for a particular county or metropolitan statistical area (MSA), as estimated by the Department of Housing and Urban Development (HUD).

HUD-1 STATEMENT

A standardized, itemized list, published by the U.S. Department of Housing and Urban Development (HUD), of all anticipated CLOSING COSTS connected with a particular property purchase.

IMPROVED LAND

Any parcel of land which has been changed from its natural state through the creation of roads, buildings or other structures.

IMPROVEMENTS

Any item added to vacant land with the intent of increasing its value or usability.

IMPROVEMENT RATIO

The comparative value of an improved piece of land to its natural, unaltered state.

INCOME APPROACH

The process of estimating the value of property by considering the present value of a stream of income generated by the property.

INCOME PROPERTY

A piece of property whose highest and best use is the generation of income through rents or other sources.

INDEPENDENT APPRAISAL

An estimation of value created by a professional, certified appraiser with no vested interest in the value of the property.

INSPECTION

The examination of a piece of property, its buildings or other amenities.

INSURABLE TITLE

The title to property which has been sufficiently reviewed by a title insurance company, such that they are willing to insure it as free and clear.

INTEREST RATE

A percentage of a loan or mortgage value that is paid to the lender as compensation for loaning funds.

INVESTMENT PROPERTY

Any piece of property that is expected to generate a financial return. This may come as the result of periodic rents or through appreciation of the property value over time.

JAMB

The side of a door frame.

JOINT TENANCY

A situation where two or more parties own a piece of property together. Each of the owners has an equal share, and may not dispose of or alter that share without the consent of the other owners.

JOISTS

Horizontal beams laid on edge to support flooring or a ceiling.

JUDGMENT

An official court decision. If the judgment requires payment from one party to another, the court may put a lien against the payee's property as collateral.

JUDICIAL FORECLOSURE

A type of foreclosure conducted as a civil suit in a court of law.

JUMBO LOAN

A mortgage loan for an amount greater than the limits set by Fannie Mae and Freddie Mac. Often called non-conforming loans.

LALLY COLUMN

A concrete filled steel pipe used to support beams.

LATE CHARGE

An extra charge, or penalty added to a regular mortgage payment when the payment is made late by an amount of time specified in the original loan document.

LATENT DEFECTS

Any defect in a piece of property which is not readily apparent, but which has an impact of the value. Structural damage or termite infestation would be examples of latent defects.

LEASE

A contract between a property owner and a tenant specifying the payment amount, terms and conditions, as well as the length of time the contract will be in force.

LEASEHOLD ESTATE

A type of property "ownership" where the buyer actually has a long-term lease on the property.

LEASE OPTION

A lease agreement that gives the tenant an option to buy the property. Usually, a portion of the regular monthly rent payment will be applied towards the down payment.

LEGAL DESCRIPTION

The description of a piece of property, identifying its specific location in terms established by the municipality or other jurisdiction in which the property resides. Often related in specific distances from a known landmark or inter-section.

LENDER

The person or entity who loans funds to a buyer. In return, the lender will receive periodic payments, including principal and interest amounts.

LIABILITIES

A person's outstanding debt obligations.

LIABILITY INSURANCE

Insurance that covers against potential lawsuit brought against a property owner for alleged negligence resulting in damage to another party.

LIEN

Any claim against a piece of property resulting from a debt or other obligation.

LIFE CAP

A limit on how far the interest rate can move for an Adjustable Rate Mortgage.

LIKE-KIND PROPERTY

Any property which is substantially similar to another property.

LINE OF CREDIT

An extension of credit for a certain amount for a specific amount of time. To be used by the borrower at his discretion.

LIQUID ASSET

Any asset which can be quickly converted into cash at little or no cost, or cash itself.

LOAN

Money borrowed, to be repaid with interest, according to the specific terms and conditions of the loan.

LOAN OFFICER

A person that "sells" loans, representing the lender to the borrower, and the borrower to the lender.

LOAN ORIGINATION

How a lender refers to the process of writing new loans.

LOAN SERVICING

The processing of payments, mailing of monthly statements, management and disbursement of escrow funds etc. Typically carried out by the company you make payments to.

LOAN-TO-VALUE RATIO (LTV)

The comparison of the amount owed on a mortgaged property to its fair market value.

LOCK-IN

An agreement between a lender and a borrower, guaranteeing an interest rate for a loan if the loan is closed within a certain amount of time.

LOCK-IN PERIOD

The amount of time the lender has guaranteed an interest rate to a borrower.

MAJOR DEFICIENCY

A deficiency that strongly impacts the usability and habitability of a house. Or a deficiency that may be very expensive to repair.

MANUFACTURED HOUSING

Once known as "mobile homes," manufactured housing is any building which has been constructed off site, then moved onto a piece of real property.

MARGIN

The difference between the interest rate and the index on an adjustable rate mortgage.

MARGINAL LAND

Land whose value has been diminished due to some internal defect or external condition. In most cases, the cost to correct the flaw or condition is as much or more than the expected return from the property.

MASTER ASSOCIATION

An umbrella organization that is made up of multiple, smaller home owner's associations. Often found in very large developments or condominium projects.

MATURITY

The date on which the principal balance of a financial instrument becomes due and payable.

MERGED CREDIT REPORT

A credit report derived from data obtained from multiple credit agencies.

METES AND BOUNDS

A traditional way of describing property, generally expressed in terms of distance from a known landmark or intersection, and then following the boundaries of the property back to its origin.

METROPOLITAN AREA

The accumulated land in and around a city or other municipality which falls under the political and economic influence of that entity.

MINERAL RIGHTS

The legal right to exploit and enjoy the benefits of any minerals located below the surface of a parcel of land.

MISREPRESENTATION

A statement by one party in a transaction that is incorrect or misleading. Most misrepresentations are deemed to be intentional and thus may constitute fraud. Others, however, some are rendered through simple mistakes, oversights or negligence.

MORTGAGE

A financial arrangement wherein an individual borrows money to purchase real property and secures the loan with the property as collateral.

MORTGAGE BANKER

A financial institution that provides primary and secondary mortgages to home buyers.

MORTGAGE BROKER

A person or organization that serves as a middleman to facilitate the mortgage process. Brokers often represent multiple mortgage bankers and offer the most appropriate deal to each buyer.

MORTGAGEE

The entity that lends money in a real estate transaction.

MORTGAGE INSURANCE

A policy that fulfills those obligations of a mortgage when the policy holder defaults or is no longer able to make payments.

225

MORTGAGE INSURANCE PREMIUM (MIP)

A fee that is often included in mortgage payments that pays for mortgage insurance coverage.

MORTGAGE LIFE INSURANCE

A policy that fulfills the obligations of a mortgage when the policy holder dies.

MORTGAGOR

The entity that borrows money in a real estate transaction.

MULTI-FAMILY PROPERTIES

Any collection of buildings that are designed and built to support the habitation of more than four families.

NATIONAL ASSOCIATION OF MASTER APPRAISERS (NAMA)

A non profit professional association organized in 1982, dedicated to the advancement of professionalism in real estate appraisal.

NATIONAL SOCIETY OF REAL ESTATE APPRAISERS

An organization founded in 1956 which promotes standards of professionalism in its members.

NATURAL VACANCY RATE

The percentage of vacant properties in a given area that is the result of natural turnover and market forces.

NEGATIVE AMORTIZATION

When the balance of a loan increases instead of decreases. Usually due to a borrower making a minimum payment on an Adjustable Rate Mortgage during a period when the rate fluctuates to a high enough point that the minimum payment does not cover all of the interest.

NEIGHBORHOOD LIFE-CYCLE

The evolution of neighborhood use and demographics over time. Economic fluctuations, municipal zoning changes and population shifts can effect the life cycle.

NEIGHBORHOOD

A subsection of a municipality that has been designated by a developer, economic forces or physical formations.

NET LEASABLE AREA

The space in a development, outside of the common areas, that can be rented to tenants.

NEW ENGLAND COLONIAL

An architectural style dating from early American history typified by a two-story building with clapboard siding.

NO-COST LOAN

Many lenders offer loans that you can obtain at "no cost." You should inquire whether this means there are no "lender" costs associated with the loan, or if it also covers the other costs you would normally have in a purchase or refinance transactions, such as title insurance, escrow fees, settlement fees, appraisal, recording fees, notary fees, and others. These are fees and costs which may be associated with buying a home or obtaining a loan, but not charged directly by the lender. Keep in mind that, like a "no-point" loan, the interest rate will be higher than if you obtain a loan that has costs associated with it.

NO-POINT LOAN

A loan with no "points". The interest rate on such a loan will be higher than a loan with points paid. Also sometimes refers to a refinance loan where closing costs are included in the loan.

NON-CONFORMING USE

The use of land for purposes contrary to the applicable municipal zoning specifications. Often occurs when zoning changes after a property is in use.

NONLIQUID ASSET

Any asset which can not be quickly converted into cash at little or no cost.

NOTE

A legal document that obligates a borrower to repay a mortgage loan at a stated interest rate during a specified period of time.

NOTE RATE

The interest rate stated on a mortgage note.

NOTICE OF DEFAULT

Formal written notice from a lender to a borrower that default has occurred.

OBSOLESCENCE

The process of an assets value diminishing due to the development of more desirable alternatives or because of the degradation of its capabilities.

OCCUPANCY

A physical presence within and control of a property.

OCCUPANCY RATE
The percentage of properties in a given area that are occupied.
OCTOPUS RECEPTACLE
An outlet with too many devices plugged into it, using a power strip or other device to multiply the outlets.
OFF-SITE IMPROVEMENTS
Buildings, structures or other amenities which are not located on a piece of property, but are necessary to maximize the use of the property or in some way contribute to the value of the property.
OFF-STREET PARKING
Designated parking spaces associated with a particular building or other structure which are not located on public streets.
OLD TERMITE ACTIVITY
Where no termites are currently active, but indications of past activity can be seen.
ON-SITE IMPROVEMENTS
Buildings, structures or other amenities that are erected on a piece of property and contribute to its value.
OPEN SPACE
Any land which has not had any significant buildings or structures erected on it. Most often used to describe desirable neighborhood features like parks.
OPEN SPLICE
An uncovered electrical connection.
ORIGINAL EQUITY
The amount of cash a home buyer initially invests in the home.
ORIGINAL PRINCIPAL BALANCE
The total amount of principal owed on a mortgage loan at the time of closing.
ORIGINATION FEE
Refers to the total number of points paid by a borrower at closing.
OWNER FINANCING
A transaction where the property owner provides all or part of the financing.
OWNER OCCUPIED
The state of property wherein the owner occupies at least some portion of the property.
PARGING
The cement coat applied to block foundations.
PARTIAL INTEREST
A shared ownership in a piece of property. May be divided among two or more parties.
PARTIAL PAYMENT
A payment of less than the regular monthly amount. Usually, a lender will not accept partial payments.
PERIODIC PAYMENT CAP
The limit on how much regular monthly payments on an Adjustable Rate Mortgage can change during one adjustment period.
PERIODIC RATE CAP
The limit on how much the interest rate on an Adjustable Rate Mortgage can change during any one adjustment period.
PERSONAL PROPERTY
Owned items which are not permanently affixed to the land.
PERSONAL RESIDENCE
The primary domicile of a person or family.
PLANNED UNIT DEVELOPMENT (PUD)
A coordinated, real estate development where common areas are shared and maintained by an owner's association or other entity.
PLAT
A plan or chart of a piece of land which lays out existing or planned streets, lots or other improvements.
POINT
A percentage of a mortgage amount (one point = 1 percent).
PRE-APPROVAL
The process of applying for a mortgage loan and becoming approved for a certain amount at a certain interest rate before a property has been chosen. Pre-approval allows the borrower greater freedom in negotiations with sellers.

PREFABRICATED

Any building or portion thereof which is manufactured and assembled off site, then erected on a property.

PREPAYMENT

Payment made that reduces the principal balance of a loan before the due date and before the loan has become fully amortized.

PREPAYMENT PENALTY

A fee that may be charged to a borrower who pays off a loan before it is due.

PRE-QUALIFICATION

Less formal that pre-approval, pre-qualification usually means a written statement from a loan officer indicating his or her opinion that the borrower will be able to become approved for a mortgage loan.

PRIME RATE

The interest rate that banks and other lending institutions charge other banks or preferred customers.

PRINCIPAL

The amount owed on a mortgage which does not include interest or other fees.

PRINCIPAL BALANCE

The outstanding balance of principal on a mortgage. Does not included interest due.

PRINCIPAL, INTEREST, TAXES, AND INSURANCE (PITI)

The most common constituents of a monthly mortgage payment.

PRIVATE MORTGAGE INSURANCE (PMI)

A form of mortgage insurance provided by private, non-government entities. Normally required when the LOAN TO VALUE RATIO is less that 20%.

PROPERTY

Any item which is owned or possessed.

PURCHASE AGREEMENT

A written contract signed by the buyer and seller stating the terms and conditions under which a property will be sold.

QUADRAPLEX

Any building designed to accommodate four families.

QUALIFYING RATIOS

Two ratios used in determining credit worthiness for a mortgage loan. One is the ratio of a borrower's monthly housing costs to monthly income. The other is a ratio of all monthly debt to monthly income.

QUITCLAIM DEED

A legal document which transfers any ownership an individual has in a piece of property. Often used when the amount of ownership is not known or is unclear.

RAFTER

A structural element of the roof, sloping from the peak to the outer walls.

RANCH HOUSE

An architectural style typified by a single-story, low-roof construction. Popular in the western U.S.

RATE LOCK

A guarantee from a lender of a specific interest rate for a period of time.

RAW LAND

Any land which has not been developed.

REAL ESTATE

A piece of land and any improvements or fixtures located on that land.

REAL ESTATE AGENT

A licensed professional who facilitates the buying and selling of real estate.

REAL ESTATE SETTLEMENT PROCEDURES ACT (RESPA)

A federal law requiring lenders to give full disclosure of closing costs to borrowers.

REAL PROPERTY

Land, improvements and appurtenances, and the interest and benefits thereof.

REALTOR

A real estate agent or broker who is a member of the National Association of Realtors.

RECEPTACLE

An electrical outlet to plug into.

RECORDER

A local government employee whose role it is to keep records of all real estate transactions within the jurisdiction.

RECORDING

The filing of a real estate transaction with the appropriate government agent (normally the RECORDER). A real estate transaction is considered final when it is recorded.

REFINANCE TRANSACTION

A new loan to pay off an existing loan. Typically to gain a lower interest rate or convert equity into cash.

REGISTER

Where air from a furnace or air conditioning system enters the room.

RELOCATION SERVICE

Any company or agency that assists corporate employees in relocating from one place to another. Services may include hiring and coordinating real estate agents, moving companies, utilizes and the like.

REMAINING BALANCE

The amount of principal, interest and other costs that has not yet been repaid.

REMAINING TERM

The amount of time remaining on the original amortization schedule.

REMODEL

An activity designed to improve the value or desirability of a property through rebuilding, refurbishing, redecorating or adding on to it.

REPAYMENT PLAN

A plan to repay delinquent payments, agreed upon between a lender and borrower, in an effort to avoid foreclosure.

REPLACEMENT RESERVE FUND

An account, or fund, setup for the replacement of short life items, such as carpeting, in the common areas of a cooperative property.

RESIDENTIAL PROPERTY

A piece of property whose highest and best use is the maintenance of a residence.

REVOLVING DEBT

A type of credit that allows the borrower/customer to make charges against a predetermined line of credit. The customer then pays monthly installments on the amount borrowed, plus interest.

RIDGE BOARD

The structural member of a roof where the rafters join at the top.

RIGHT OF FIRST REFUSAL

An agreement giving a person the first opportunity to buy or lease a property before the owner offers it for sale to others.

ROOF PITCH

The degree of slope in a roof.

RURAL

An area outside of an established urban area or metropolitan district.

SALE PRICE

The actual price a property sells for, exclusive of any special financing concessions.

SALES COMPARISON APPROACH

An appraisal practice which estimates the value of a property by comparing it to comparable properties which have sold recently.

SCARCITY

An economic principal that dictates the price of a good or service through the interaction of supply and demand. When an item is scarce, its price tends to rise, given a constant demand. Real Estate is a classic example of scarcity.

SECOND MORTGAGE

A loan secured by the equity in a home, when a primary mortgage already exists.

SECONDARY MORTGAGE MARKET

An economic marketplace where mortgage bankers buy and sell existing mortgages.

SECURED LOAN

A loan that is backed by collateral. In the case of a mortgage loan, the collateral is the house.

SECURITY

The property used as collateral for a loan.

SEMIDETACHED HOUSING

Two residences which share a common wall.

SERVICER

A financial institution which collects mortgage payments from borrowers and applies the appropriate portions to principal, interest and any escrow accounts.

SERVICING

The processing of payments, mailing of monthly statements, management and disbursement of escrow funds etc Typically carried out by the company you make payments to.

SHEATHING

The covering on outside walls beneath the siding or exterior finish such as stucco.

SHEETROCK

Also called drywall, the gypsum board commonly used on interior walls.

SILL PLATE

The lumber used around the foundation to support exterior wall framing.

SILL COCK

Garden hose pipe connection.

SINGLE-FAMILY PROPERTY

A property designed and built to support the habitation of one family.

SOFFIT

The underside of a cornice at the eaves.

STUCCO

A textured plaster exterior (and occasionally interior) wall finish.

STUD

A vertical framing piece in a wall, generally 2x4 lumber in interior walls.

SUBDIVISION

A residential development that is created from a piece of land which has been subdivided into individual lots.

SUBJECT PROPERTY

A term which indicates a property which is being appraised.

SUMP

A basin into which water drains and from which the water is pumped out.

SURVEY

A specific map of a piece of property which includes the legal boundaries and any improvements or features of the land. Surveys also depict any rights-of-way, encroachments or easements.

SWEAT EQUITY

The method whereby a home owner develops equity in a property, either during the purchase or throughout its life, by personally constructing improvements rather than paying to have them built.

TAX-EXEMPT PROPERTY

Any property which is not taxed.

TENANCY

The right to occupy a building or unit.

TENANCY IN COMMON

A form of holding title, whereby there are two or more people on title to a property, ownership does not pass on to the others upon the death of one individual.

THIRD PARTY ORIGINATION

When a lender uses a third party to originate and package loans for sale to the secondary market (Fannie Mae, Freddie Mac).

TITLE

A specific document which serves as proof of ownership.

TITLE COMPANY

An organization which researches and certifies ownership of real estate before it is bought or sold. Title companies also act at the facilitator ensures all parties are paid during the real estate transaction.

TITLE INSURANCE

A policy which insures a property owner should a prior claim arise against the property after the purchase has been completed. This also covers a lender should a question of ownership arise.

TITLE SEARCH

The process whereby the TITLE COMPANY researches a properties title history and ensures that no outstanding claims exist.

TRANSFER OF OWNERSHIP

Any means by which the ownership of a property changes hands.

TRANSFER OF TAX

Taxes payable when title passes from one owner to another.

TRAP

A bend in water pipe.

TRUSTEE

A fiduciary that holds or controls property for the benefit of another.

TRUTH IN LENDING

A federal law requiring full disclosure by lenders to borrowers of all terms, conditions and costs of a mortgage.

TUDOR

A style of architecture typified by exposed stone, wood and brick construction. Similar in style to English manor homes.

UNDER IMPROVED LAND

A piece of land which has been improved, but not to the full extent of its potential.

UNENCUMBERED PROPERTY

Any property which has no outstanding claims or liens against it.

UNIFORM STANDARDS OF PROFESSIONAL APPRAISAL PRACTICE (USPAP)

Developed in 1986 by the Ad Hoc Committee on Uniform Standards and copyrighted in 1987 by The Appraisal Foundation, USPAP forms the guidelines followed by every licensed and certified real estate appraiser in the United States. The purpose of these Standards is to establish requirements for professional appraisal practice, which includes appraisal, appraisal review, and appraisal consulting. The intent of these Standards is to promote and maintain a high level of public trust in professional appraisal practice.

USEFUL LIFE

The span of time over which a property can be used or can provide benefits to its owner.

VACANCY RATE

The current percentage of vacant properties in a given area, regardless of why they are vacant.

VA MORTGAGE

A mortgage that is guaranteed by the Department of Veterans Affairs (VA).

VARIANCE

An exception to municipal zoning regulations granted for a specific time period to allow for non-conforming use of the land.

VENT PIPE

A pipe allowing gas to escape.

VESTED

Having the right to use a portion of a fund such as an IRA. Typically vesting occurs over time. If you are 100% vested, you have a right to 100% of the fund.

VETERANS AFFAIRS, DEPARTMENT OF (VA)

The successor to the Veteran's Administration, this government agency is responsible for ensuring the rights and welfare of our nation's veterans and their dependents. Among other duties, the VA insures home loans made to veterans.

VOLTAGE

An expression of electric force, or pressure. One volt being the force needed to move one amp against one ohm resistance.

WALK-THROUGH INSPECTION

A process whereby an appraiser examines a property in preparation for estimating its value. Also, the process of inspecting a property for any damage prior to that property being bought or sold.

WARRANTY

An affidavit given to stipulate the condition of a property. The person giving the warranty assumes liability if the condition turns out to be untrue.

WATT

An expression of amount of electrical power. Volt multiplied by amps equals watts.

WEAR AND TEAR

A term used to indicate the normal damage inflicted on a property through every-day use.

WEATHER STRIPPING

Material used around windows and doors to prevent drafts.
WEEP HOLE
Drainage hole that allows water to escape.
ZERO LOT LINE
A municipal zoning category wherein a building or other fixture may abut the property line.
ZONE
A specific area within a municipality or other jurisdiction which conforms to certain guidelines regarding the use of property in the zone. Typical zones include single-family, multi-family, industrial, commercial and mixed-use.

Would You Like to Know More?

You can learn a lot more about investing in real estate in our other eBooks books or paperbacks.

What else?

We frequently run special promotions where we offer free or discounted books (usually $0.99). One way to get instant notifications for these deals is to subscribe to our email list. By joining you receive updates on the latest offer, you'll also get a free copy of our "Special—FREE" book of the quarter from **www.MitchFreeland.com.**

Check out the link below to learn more.

> > > www.MitchFreeland.com < < <

Did You Like *The Millionaire Real Estate Landlords*

Before you go, we'd like to say "thank you" for buying our book. We know you could have picked from dozens of books on real estate investing and landlording, but you took a chance with us. So a big thanks for getting this book and reading all the way to the end. Now we would like to ask for a **small** favor.

Could you please take a minute and leave a review for this book on Amazon or the website you bought this book from. Your feedback will help us continue to write the kind of eBooks and paperback books that help you get results. If you found this book helpful, please let us know with a review.

Thank you.

M. Mitch Freeland

What's Next?

THE

MILLIONAIRE
REAL ESTATE FLIPPERS

Flipping Fixer-Uppers
How Anybody Can Buy, Fix and Flip Real Estate and
Earn a Six Figure Income

*"Prolific Investor, John Freeland...finds plenty of
properties to buy and sell"*
—The Palm Beach Post

M. MITCH FREELAND
JOHN FREELAND

Authors of *The Millionaire Real Estate Landlords*

The Millionaire Real Estate Flippers (New Edition) is an indispensable resource book that shows you "How to" *Force Appreciation* and Flip Fixer-uppers to capture phenomenal profits.

M. Mitch Freeland and John Freeland know how to flip properties. With *The Millionaire Real Estate Flippers* they show you how to do the same with any property, in any market, in any economy—good or bad.

Explained by professional flippers and long-time investors, this book takes you into the field and up the ladder of real estate investing—*flipping style*. It exposes the good, the bad, and the rightfully ugly, from mild fixer-uppers to the massive "el dumpos," and shows you what to look for and how to profit like the pros.

Let Mitch and John explain the nuts-and-bolts, strategies and methods used to secure a real estate profit plan. This book is the real "stuff" and it is destined to be among an investor's closest companion....Guaranteed!

In *The Millionaire Real Estate Flippers*, **you'll learn how to:**

- Choose the best type of property starting out
- Fix and renovate on the inexpensive side for maximum profit for small and large fixer-uppers
- What materials to use and how to use them
- Finance your properties quickly
- Hire and manage contractors and sub-contractors efficiently, saving you thousands of dollars
- Inspect property like a pro
- Flip properties profitably every time
- Make 50% + profit on every property you buy
- Locate great deals and turn opportunities into cash cows
- Substantially Increase value to property (what's needed and what isn't)
- Price, list and sell your properties for tremendous profits

Short-term or long-term, seasoned pro or just starting out, *The Millionaire Real Estate Flippers* are to the serious real estate investor as ammunition to a soldier or water to a farmer. This book is a required read for everybody seeking financial freedom and belongs in the library of every real estate investor. And it's on target to be a real estate classic! **GET STARTED TODAY!**

Format: Paperback and eBook available now
Size: 8.5 x 11
Pages: 310

<u>Buy now on www.MitchFreeland.com</u>
and at Fine Bookstores Everywhere

THE MILLIONAIRE REAL ESTATE FLIPPERS

M. MITCH FREELAND

Author of *The Millionaire Real Estate Flippers*

HOW TO RENT

YOUR HOUSE, DUPLEX, TRIPLEX & OTHER MULTI-FAMILY PROPERTY FAST!

The Concise Authoritative Owner's Manual for
Rental Property with a Special Section on
Airbnb Rentals

You will get 129 Simple Ways for Landlords to
Fill Vacancies and a Whole Lot More

In *How to Rent Your House....*, M. Mitch Freeland reveals 129 simple ways that landlords can fill vacancies fast and substantially increase cash flow. A special section is also included with money generating ideas for Airbnb rentals.

Owning and managing over 100 units for many years, Mitch has discovered that rental houses and multi-family rentals deserve a hands-on, proactive approach from landlords who want to get the most out of their investment. Passivity is not the way to riches—let service ring the bells to prosperity, and let Mitch Freeland show you how.

In *How to Rent Your House....*, you will learn:

- How to create the best signs and the best strategies used to attract renters
- Proven sales techniques that few if any landlords use to secure good renters
- How to attract the best tenants that stay for years
- Why you can't get your property rented
- For the first time, how to increase cash flow with new ancillary income opportunities
- The simple, yet effective, way to secure qualified tenants
- Creative copy writing using the best descriptive words and phrases to attract tenants
- How to advertise and where to advertise for free and 68 other ways to attract renters
- The 60 websites that you can use for advertising your rentals, including more than 10 sites that are Free and 20 websites specifically for vacation and short-term rentals like Airbnb, HomeAway, VRBO and others
- How to get started and make more with airbnb rentals
- How to answer the 12 most common renter objections with ease

DON'T LET VACANCIES RUIN YOUR CASH FLOW!

How to Rent Your House, Duplex, Triplex & Other Multi-Family Property Fast!

Available now at www.MitchFreeland.com
and at Fine Bookstores Everywhere

GET YOUR **FREE** BOOK

Did you know less than 10 percent of the population has goals? Even fewer, 3 percent, have written, specific and measurable goals.

Studies show people with goals succeed faster and with better results than people without goals. Did you know that nearly all high achievers set goals in some form or fashion? From athletes, business people, entrepreneurs, educators and world leaders, all have goals: big ones, small ones and *mini-goals*.

In *Mini Goals Huge Results*, you will discover how to:

- Set mini goals related to family, career, health and fitness, financial, religious and spirituality goals, and personal and physical wants goals.
- Create mini goals that lead to the achievement of large goals
- Visualize the process toward successful goal achievement
- Create specific affirmations that are tested to produce results
- Motivate yourself and articulate your vision and why having goals, written down, work toward life-long happiness
- Set Mini-Goals to combat non-clinical depression
- Create positive, long-lasting change
- Transform your life with Mini Goals using an easy 7 Step Process

www.MitchFreeland.com

More Books by
M. MITCH FREELAND

Writer, poker player, gambler, real estate investor, and businessman, M. Mitch Freeland has been called the *modern day polymath*. A prolific writer, he has authored over one hundred books and continues to write daily.

Casino Gaming Books

Winning Craps: How to Play and Win Like a Pro. Learn How I Beat the Craps Out of the Casinos for 30 Years

Tested Gambling Systems That Can Make You $100,000+ a Year: Craps, Horses, Poker, Blackjack

How to Play Craps and Win: The 3 Irrefutable Winning Plays and How to Profit from Them

How to Win at Casino Craps

Craps: Basic Strategy for Smart Players

How to Play Baccarat

Blackjack: Basic Strategy for Smart Beginners

How to Count Cards at Blackjack

How to Play Blackjack for Beginners and Win! Learn Basic and Advanced Strategies for Optimum Winning Play

Poker Books

The Small Stakes Poker Hustle: How I Make $3,500+ A Month Part-Time Playing $1-$2 & $1-$3 No-Limit Hold'em & How You Can Too!

Poker Tells and Body Language: How to Substantially Improve Your Income by Studying Your Opponents Mannerisms and Eccentricities

Cash Poker: How to Make $250,000 Over the Next 5 Years Playing Small Stakes Poker

The Poker System: How to Play No-Limit Texas Hold'em: A Primer for Smart New Players Who Want to Start with A Winning Edge in the World's Greatest Poker Game

Online Bookselling

How I Make $4,000 a Month Selling Used Books Online

How to Make $1,000+ Online as a Part-Time Book Scout

Mastering the Art of Sourcing for Online Booksellers and Collectors

How to Succeed as a Book Scout

How to Identify First Editions (Spring 2019)

Caring for Books: A Repair and Preservation Handbook for Booksellers, Collectors, Book Lovers and Librarians Interested in Improving the Condition of their Books

Real Estate Books by
M. MITCH FREELAND and JOHN FREELAND

The Millionaire Real Estate Flippers (New Edition)

High Engagement Landlording

How to Make Real Estate More Valuable

How to Rent you House, Duplex, Triplex & Other Multi-Family Property Fast!

The Real Estate Hustle

5 Day Flip: How to Get Offers Accepted Fast on Fixer-Uppers

NEW RELEASES FOR 2019

The Airbnb Hustle: How Ordinary People and Enterprising Landlords are Cashing-in and How you can Too!

The Cash Flow Book: The 10 Most Important Calculations for Smart Real Estate Investors

Cash Flow & Co.: A Super System for Real Estate Investors
Discover 64 Proven Ways That Show you How to Substantially Improve Cash Flow from Your Rental Properties

How to Maximize Profits with Coin-Operated Laundry & Vending Machines for Rental Property

57 of the Best Real Estate Investors Forms & Agreements

51 of the Best Landlording Forms & Real Estate Agreements

SPECIAL SALES

Books published by Las Vegas Book Company are available at special quantity discounts worldwide to be used for training or for use in corporate promotional programs. Quantity discounts are available to corporations, educational institutions and charitable organizations. Personalized front or back covers and endpapers can be produced in large numbers. If you are interested in exploring options for bulk purchases of twenty or more copies, send us an email for discounts.

We encourage you to share this book with others.

- Give this book to friends as a gift
- Present this book on your website or blog
- Link your site to www.MitchFreeland.com
- Write a book review for your local paper, your favorite magazine, school, or a website you spend time on. Place your review on Amazon or Goodreads.
- Introduce us on radio stations or pod casts—author guest
- Display this book at your shop or business on the counter for resale to customers. Email us at **MMitchFreeland@gmail.com** for wholesale rates on bulk orders and volume discounts
- Review a copy for your newsletters, schools papers and magazines, websites, and review journals
- Mention this book on your email lists
- Share this book with family members, friends, and co-workers who own rental property or interested in investing in real estate

For information, contact us at:
www.MitchFreeland.com or wwwMMitchFreeland@gmail.com

CASH POKER

How to Make $250,000 Over the Next 5 Years Playing Small Stakes Poker

"The book that will change your view of poker"

It's true "*Most People Are Too Busy Earning a Living to Make Any Money*"

Have you thought about playing winning cash game poker? How about making a living playing poker part-time or in your spare-time? With the vast expansion of casinos across the U.S. it is now possible for anybody to play poker for a living—even part-time.

I have been playing winning Poker for over 30 years and I've decided to write a book to show others how to play and win for life. Can you really become a winning cash game player in small stakes No-limit Hold'em? You better believe you can! How would you like an extra $25,000, $50,000 or even $100,000 next year? How would you like to have a nest egg of $500,000?

It all starts by taking action.

If you practice the principles I outline in my book and you put in the time to play, you will be on your way to a lifestyle that could give you the financial freedom that you have always dreamed about. This could be the greatest bargain of your life. Because I am going to tell you what took me over 15 years to master.

How would it make you feel to return from your Las Vegas trips with more money in your pocket than when you left? How would you like to crush your friendly home game week after week?

--There is no age requirement for winning
--You can be 18 or 80
--You don't need a lot of money to start
--You don't need experience
--You don't need talent
--You don't need a high school diploma
--You do not need luck
--And you do not have to be fluent in English

What do you need? You need belief. Enough to take a chance. Enough to absorb what I'll send you. Enough to put the principles into action. If you do just that—nothing more, nothing less—the results will be hard to believe. Remember—I guarantee it.

A wise man once said something I never forgot: "*Most people are too busy earning a living to make any money.*" Don't wait—life is short. Take action Today!

I know you're skeptical—that's human nature. What I am saying is probably different to what you've heard from friends, your family, teachers and everyone else you know. I can only ask you one question: **How many of them are millionaires?**

NOTES:

Made in the USA
Columbia, SC
19 June 2023

18051513R00135